KENNETH MORE

KENNETH MORE

The Making of a Movie Legend

NATHAN MORLEY

Quiller

Books by Nathan Morley and published by Amberley Publishing

Radio Hitler: Nazi Airwaves in the Second World War
Holidays with Hitler: State-sponsored Fun in Nazi Germany

Copyright © 2026 Nathan Morley

First published in the UK in 2026
by Quiller, an imprint of Amberley Publishing Ltd

British Library Cataloguing-in-Publication Data
A catalogue record for this book is available
from the British Library

ISBN 978-1-84689-420-6 (hardback)
ISBN 978-1-84689-421-3 (ebook)

The right of Nathan Morley to be identified as the Author of this work has been asserted in accordance with the Copyright, Design and Patent Act 1988. The information in this book is true and complete to the best of our knowledge. All recommendations are made without any guarantee on the part of the Publisher, who also disclaims any liability incurred in connection with the use of this data or specific details.

All rights reserved. No part of this book may be reproduced or transmitted in any form or by any means, electronic or mechanical including photocopying, recording or by any information storage and retrieval system, without permission from the Publisher in writing.

Typesetting by SJmagic DESIGN SERVICES, India.
Printed in the UK

Quiller

An imprint of Amberley Publishing Ltd
The Hill, Merrywalks, Stroud, GL5 4EP
Tel: 01453 847800
Email: info@quillerbooks.com
Website: www.quillerpublishing.com

Appointed GPSR EU Representative:
Easy Access System Europe Oü, 16879218
Address: Mustamäe tee 50, 10621, Tallinn, Estonia
Contact Details: gpsr.requests@easproject.com, +358 40 500 3575

CONTENTS

Acknowledgements 7

1. Overture 9
2. The Call of the Stage 37
3. Kenny Goes to War 46
4. Breakthrough 66
5. The Emerging Star 87
6. Celebrity Fulfilled 111
7. The Film Star 138
8. A New Reality 172
9. Cold Shoulder 194
10. Saved by the Saga 209
11. Ageing Juvenile 216
12. A New Decade 232
13. Final Years 251
14. Fade Out 264

Endnotes 278
Bibliography 285

ACKNOWLEDGEMENTS

First and foremost, thanks are owed to Connor Stait at Icon Books and Angeline Wilcox, my commissioning editor at Quiller, who both saw the potential of this project. From the outset, numerous folks have provided invaluable help and guidance. During the two years of research into the life of Kenneth More, many who knew, worked with, and had professional and personal connections with him kindly shared their memories, experiences, and impressions. While respecting the wishes of those who granted me off-the-record interviews, I am equally grateful to those that went on the record, including Martin Jarvis, Susan Penhaligon, Chris Sarandon, Jane Asher, Anneke Wills, Alvin Rakoff, Erin Geraghty, Francis White, Barry MacGregor, Peter Medak, David Wilkinson, Tony Hatch, Bob Wilson, Fiona Lewis, Raoul Björkenheim (Taina Elg's son), Lone Faerch, and Vivyan Ellacott.

Much of the work herein is from several invaluable research resources: the British Library, the BBC, the Imperial War Museum, and the BFI. All four institutions contain a veritable treasure trove of clippings, interviews, trade papers, cinema fan magazines, out of print biographies, audio interviews, Rank Organisation press releases, and other sources that were vital for this manuscript. I am also indebted to Bernard Morley for casting a careful eye over these pages during the editing stages.

1
OVERTURE

Actor, author, heart-throb, war hero, adventurer, movie icon, sailor: so many bits and pieces make up Kenneth More's persona that it is hard to know which defines him. 'He was an authentic British film star,' says Martin Jarvis, who never forgot as a schoolboy in the 1950s catching a glimpse of 'Mr More' during a day trip to London with his chum, Dave. The excitement began after he spotted a beige Rolls-Royce cruising slowly down the street near the Haymarket. As he recalls it, the passenger window had been wound down and a tanned figure in a Hawaiian shirt, arm resting casually half in and half out, was grinning and chatting loudly to the chauffeur. 'It was Kenneth More!' Jarvis exclaimed, transfixed in amazement. 'That ebullient, unmistakable voice, full of charm and humour. Dave and I were thrilled that we'd had this colourful glimpse of one of the nation's screen icons.' These words echo Alexander Korda's observation that 'Mr More' was 'every bit the star' – a man with an ineffable sparkle that 'never failed to turn heads'.

Though the first actor the family ever produced, Kenneth More could trace his descendants back to Sir Thomas More, the Lord Chancellor to Henry VIII. He was proud of his grandfather, who, he boasted, was a brilliant civil engineer, a 'man who built bridges and things all over the world, and a very clever man'. And before him, his great-grandfather – Major George More – had a distinguished military career cut short after being felled by cholera in 1859 in India.

As for himself, Kenneth Gilbert More belted out his first scream over a century ago at 'Raeden' house on 20 September 1914, a Sunday, just as the earliest shots of the First World War were fired. At home, the newborn was known as Ken, Kenneth, but mostly Kenny. The latter, his mother thought, suited him best. Living entirely on a family inheritance, the More family enjoyed a comfortable existence in the sleepy village of Gerrards Cross, a slice of Middle England, half an hour by train from Paddington. Between the late Victorian age and the coming of the railway, the settlement, known as the 'Brighton of Bucks', became a tranquil retreat for the upper classes, dotted with country estates. After 1906, the area was gobbled up into 'Metroland' and morphed into a commuter town for London's upper-middle class.

As was tradition in the family, Ken's arrival was announced in the *Bucks Herald* and *Reading Mercury*.[1] Over time, it became clear the child had inherited more than his father's thick brown hair and humour: he shared his love of life. So much so, that his maternal grandmother, known as 'Dear One', dubbed him 'Little Cherub', as he developed into a lively and curious child. 'My birth sign is Virgo, and they are meticulously tidy people as a rule – and I am true to type,' he once said, explaining his obsession with cleanliness. 'I also have an extraordinarily good memory. It goes right back to before I was one year old. When I hear songs from the First War, I can see the German Zeppelin airships picked out by the searchlights.'[2]

He had clear memories of his mother, Edith Winifred Watkins, as a slight woman 'with no brain in her head … but a lovely person'. The only daughter of R. J. Watkins, a moderately successful Cardiff solicitor, 'she was what I would call a fairy-tale mother', he said, generous in spirit and perceptive about people. Like most Victorians, she held a fascination with fairyland which vivified the literature of the time. *Hansel and Gretel, Little Red Riding Hood, Peter Pan, Aladdin,* and *Cinderella,* were among her bedtime stories, embellished with 'little touches' from her flamboyant imagination. 'She adored fairy tales, and knew them all, especially the Grimm works,' Ken remembered. 'Always before bed, we were told a fairy tale. I was brought up with my sister, Kate, in a fairy-tale world. The nursery meant everything to us, and we had a cupboard in the nursery on the wall, and if we were good at night, we had a sweet out of it, and if we weren't we didn't. I mean she was that kind of mother and I'll always remember her like that.'

Kate, eighteen months his senior and known as Kathleen or Katty, was a sensitive creature. In personality, she could not have been more different from her brother. When small, she was timid, but as she grew up, she became boisterous, 'loud and easily upset'. Ken had especially fond memories of his father, Charles Gilbert More, an outgoing and gregarious man. 'My father was a very clever mathematician, a very clever civil engineer,' he once said. 'Father ruled the roost' – he was a spirited chap full of joie de vivre with a good sense of humour and made friends easily. 'He could speak to a duke or a dustman and feel perfectly at ease.' Throughout his life, everybody liked Charles. Exactly how he made the acquaintance of Edith is unknown, but they loved each other with a rare intensity and tied the knot in 1910 during a 'fully choral' service at St Andrew's Church in Cardiff. 'The bride,' the local paper observed, 'was given away by her father, and looked charming in a gown of oyster white satin and pearl trimming, with full Court train, trimmed.' Edith radiated a glow which pulled all eyes towards her – but her gaze was fixed on Charles, a man she adored. In fact, Ken always thought they would have been happier without children, as 'they were totally as one, a devoted couple'. Together, they lived in a home with four bedrooms, a great brick chimney, south veranda, gables, greenhouse, stables, and rose garden. Unusually for the time, there were no strict rules in the household, as there generally were in British families. The More family wallowed in the age of Edwardian elegance, enhanced by the services of a parlourmaid, cook, butler, and a handyman who used to fall asleep behind the greenhouse. Sister Kate often woke him up by screaming at full throttle in his ear, 'nearly scaring the poor old bugger to death'. Though Miss Gessing, a buxom thirty-year-old nurse-cum-nanny, took care of the children's daily routine, the family often did things together, like piling into an old Ford for the annual 'jaunt to London' for the Bertram Mills Circus at Olympia to admire, as Ken said, the 'sparkling ladies in tights and sequins'. It was everything that reminded him of his father.[3] The family took special delight in visiting pantomimes, magic shows, jumble sales, fundraising bazaars, and garden fetes.

Overture

At home, Charles – or 'Bertie' as he was usually known – favoured friends who were professionals, engineers, or military types, especially aviators. And like many people, he welcomed the First World War, or at least accepted it as a harsh necessity when it arrived in 1914. Enlistment records show he was 'called up for hostilities' on 2 June 1915. His occupation lists him as a 'consulting civil engineer'. Four months later, on 12 October – just over a year after Kenny's birth – he sailed through a medical and was inducted into the Royal Navy Reserve's Air Service (RNAS) with the rank of temporary sub-lieutenant and posted on armaments duty to Eastbourne Air Station. Excellent remarks on his file testify that he got on famously with his superiors and was recommended for promotion. He moved to Dover, then Chingford, followed by a return to Eastbourne in June 1916 as a gunnery officer.

Interestingly, Bertie's record and performance reports – held in the National Archives – reveal a rare blot on his copybook. This hitherto unpublished 'blemish' occurred during a brief stint of active service at an RNAS flight gunnery school in Vendôme in France, where he arrived on 25 October 1916 but was swiftly ejected on 13 January 1917. A fascinating annotated five-line entry from his commanding officer in the 'confidential reports' section of his personal file (document 39060), reveals why:

> A/117746. Vendome: report of this officer's insubordination. I am sending him home immediately, as he is somewhat of a leader of a noisy clique who have been giving considerable trouble, and I consider strong measures are necessary.

It remains a mystery why there was no disciplinary action. However, after being posted home to Eastbourne, Bertie was 'medically surveyed' and declared 'unfit for flying duties', supposedly due to rheumatism and 'minor ailments'. Then, after being 're-surveyed' a month later, he was dispatched to Wormwood Scrubs Air Depot and deemed a most 'efficient armaments officer'. Finally, in January 1918, he was marked 'fit for active service' and offered a position in the Royal Flying Corps as a liaison officer.

With the advent of peace, he returned home to Edith and the kids and began dabbling – often despairingly – in inventing new contraptions, financed by a huge inheritance from his father. 'He was such a wonderful man,' Ken later chronicled. 'He had a marvellous personality, got through two fortunes ... gave all his money away. If you asked him for a fiver, he'd say "you can't manage on that, here's a tenner". He was a wonderful person but completely irresponsible.' Most days, Bertie could be found holed up in his workshop behind the house 'inventing things which never went right'. Ken often played the subject for laughs, and recalled one time, his father devised a liqueur called Vestpatrio by getting 'a bit of Benedictine, a bit of brandy and mixed them all together and said, "now we've got a new liqueur"'. Another innovation, Roomac, a seemingly harmless liquid supposed to make everything waterproof, actually made everything fall to pieces within two weeks. 'The house stank for months afterwards. It was awful.' Despite his often bumpy and frustrating pastime, Bertie remained a near mythical figure in Kenneth's memory. He often conjured up images of him covered in grease and oil, and credited him with inventing the carburettor – a device to control and mix air and fuel. As time passed, however, Bertie squandered his fortune on hare-brained inventions, and stock market gambles. For some reason, he even refused the offer of a lucrative partnership from Lord Nuffield, founder of Morris Motors, a man later discredited as a zealous anti-Semite and financer of Oswald Mosley's Blackshirts.

Then, at Bertie's insistence, the year 1920 saw Kenny, along with Kate, packed off to Steyne, a boarding school on the western fringes of Worthing. The house was in uproar. Edith burst into tears, Nanny Gessing fretted, and Kate had hysterics. 'It seemed incredible that such a kind man could make such a cruel decision,' Ken complained. Though considered a reasonable establishment, the school catered for the children of the middle classes. A period prospectus promises 'A thoroughly modern education for boarding and daily pupils.' Furthermore, fees were moderate and 'physical culture' a speciality. 'I wet my bed every night,' Ken said. 'I was very miserable ... very unhappy.'[4] The food, he claimed, was served on wooden tables around bare benches, and consisted of foul-tasting fish paste, cold shepherd's pie, yellow margarine, and black bread. He told one interviewer years later that the thought of carbolic soap, playground punch-ups, bullying, and cabbage water still gave him the shivers. 'To be thrown into such a place seemed like child abuse.' All too soon, life revolved around lessons beginning at dawn, lunch at 1 p.m. sharp, and lights-out being strictly observed at 7.30 p.m. Like the other boys, he was introduced to some different courses, including cadet training, and shooting lessons. As for Kate, she displayed little talent for hard work or the rigid curriculum of domestic management, music instruction and typing 'taught on modern machines'.

Thankfully, they did not stay long at Steyne. After two years, salvation arrived in the form of illness. First, Kate contracted diphtheria, followed soon after by Kenny breaking out in mumps. Alarmed, the headmaster, G. B. Bennett, sent the pair home, never to return. Though it was a blessed relief, gloom prevailed in the More household, a situation caused by Bertie's free spending accumulating massive debts. Almost daily, the postman brought letters from lawyers claiming monies owed, a situation made worse, Ken remembered, by Bertie's over-generous streak: 'I saw bailiffs come in. My father was always giving money away. A man only had to come and tell him he'd invented a new valve and he'd pay out thousands.' Suddenly, amid all this uncertainty, 'a miracle happened', when an elderly aunt settled a substantial sum of £30,000 as an inheritance. 'Our fortunes were revived by this windfall and the cloud of anxiety above our home vanished.' Better still, just shy of Kenny's tenth birthday, Bertie – fearful his fortune could evaporate again – accepted a £500-a-year position to run the Jersey Light Railway, beginning a phase of relative stability. With new prospects, the More family boarded the GWR's SS *Reindeer* on 29 July 1924 and sailed for a new life in the Channel Islands. Arriving under glorious summer sunshine, they headed straight to their new home – Ellangowan – a supposedly haunted property, nestled on the heather-covered coastline at Fauvic, east of St Helier. For the next few weeks, Kate and Ken walked around in a cloud of happiness, overwhelmed by their exposure to nature. From the front bedroom window, Bertie could watch the train pass on its eight-mile journey to La Corbière at the other end of the island. He found his new job both congenial and important as the railway, along with transport links to England, helped spark a boom in Jersey's tourism industry. Though considered inefficient by locals, Bertie was quick to replace antiquated engines, and get the trains running on time. As for Ken, he was enrolled at Victoria Preparatory School in St Helier and performed moderately well in art, history, and English, easily his favourite subject. He was a good reader, 'fair' in science, and his French was – and always remained – appalling; he achieved an average of two out of ten during his first term. Typical of the man he was to become, he promptly fell in love with Miss Bunny, the headmistress – a woman of 'big bosom' and even bigger heart.

To the outsider, the isle – especially in the winter – can seem bleak and uninviting, but away from the classroom, it provided Ken and Kate an 'island playground' surrounded by the sea, and nature, where springtime was usually sopping wet and summers sweltering. He had fond memories of carrying fishing gear, bait, snacks, and a bathing suit along the cliffs to St Aubin where he would spend the day casting for sprats from a wooden jetty. At the age of twelve, he transferred to Victoria College, a public school with 'classical and modern sides', where the atmosphere was more relaxed than regimented. A period prospectus boasts a successful army class, large cricket field and several Fives courts. By the age of thirteen, Ken had grown to a full height of 5 feet 9 inches. Photos show he had his father's thick brown wavy hair, a beaming smile and his weight seldom varied from 11.8 stone. A large part of his affection for Victoria College was devoted to 'the very wonderful headmaster', A. H. Warrell, who lived to be ninety-three. 'He once told me being a great classical scholar, that he read Gibbons' *Decline and Fall of the Roman Empire* from volume one to the end of whatever volume it was!'[5] (Warrell had also taught Bertie at Bradfield.)

Like most kids, he loved the rough-and-tumble of football and his musical taste extended to popular tunes of the day, but he must have had a good ear, for he took up the piano, becoming accomplished enough to plunk out hymns during morning assembly. It was during this time that his first foray on the stage took place. Before long, he clocked-up appearances in twelve school productions, including twice in the *Admirable Crichton*: 'As a schoolboy, I played the role of Tweeny,' he recounted. 'Then as a Victoria College schoolboy of 17, I graduated right up the social scale to the part of the portly, pompous Lord Loam.'[6] Whether he found his true calling after these experiences or not remains unknown; however, nothing at Victoria or at home seems to have given him a moment's worry. He certainly enjoyed watching his parents, Bertie and Edith embrace amateur theatricals and appear on stage at every given opportunity with the Jersey Green Room Club (as did Kate, who flung herself joyfully into song-and-dance routines). 'I might say my mother was an appalling actress – but she never thought she was,' Ken explained. Her limited artistic grasp was displayed in *Les cloches de Corneville*, a comic opera written in the latter half of the nineteenth century: 'My mother was playing a serving wench or something or one of the chorus girls or something. But she was absolutely appalling.' In fact:

She was so bad that my little chum sitting on my left in the front row of the dress circle – my school chum – said to me, 'Is that your mother, More?' and I denied it. I said, 'No, she has got nothing to do with me, whatsoever.' My father was a little better at it, but not much. However, I think in those days I had some leaning towards professionalism because I remember being struck by the performance of the Count Henry character in the play *Les cloches de Corneville*, and he was, in fact, a professional who had been hired, I was told later, for the week by the Green Room Club. And I was most impressed by his performance which was head and shoulders above the others.[7]

On another occasion, for some bizarre reason, Kate was cast as the plump cleric Cardinal Wolsey in a school play, and made her grand entrance by mincing on to the stage with her head held high, donned in silk scarlet robes. According to Ken, Bertie was heard to whisper, 'Good God! Did I give birth to that?' Around two years into the Jersey posting, Bertie's initial triumph at the railway preceded disappointment. Firstly, he began to find the pressure and long hours irksome as the line started to teeter on the brink, as passengers opted for cheaper bus services. And, as if that wasn't bad enough, more financial misfortunes followed, as his shares fell, and personal investments floundered. There were new lines of strain on his face, worsened by kidney troubles. He had long grumbled about pains in his back but refused the advice of doctors to take an X-ray. Not long after, he collapsed in his office and was rushed to hospital where doctors detected a huge, calcified kidney stone requiring prompt intervention. It would have been a comparatively simple operation if confronted earlier but was now much more complex. After surgery, Bertie never regained his strength and jolliness. Befogged by worries, his interest in the Jersey railway had gone as far as it could. So, in early 1926, he accepted a position with Sentinel-Cammell, an engineering firm based at a hulking factory in Shrewsbury turning out everything from steam-powered lorries, and railway locomotives, to buses. Recently, the company had shifted its emphasis to steam train carriages, and working on a two-year contract, Bertie was engaged to meet potential customers in Asia, a position made attractive by the fact he could take Edith on his travels through Ceylon, Singapore, and other outposts of the British Empire.

Too young to undertake such long journeys, Kenny and Kate remained in Jersey with friends. However, hopes that travelling would soothe Bertie's ailments were disappointed. Though he managed to clinch an important deal with Ceylon Government Railways to supply three steam railcars, after less than a year abroad, he returned to London where, to his horror, doctors discovered an untreatable infection had spread to both kidneys. When Ken saw him at the new family home in Malvern, Worcestershire, it was a horrible shock. 'Father,' he recalled, 'was a doomed man.'

Amid Bertie's increasingly out-of-focus life, Kenny left school with no ambitions other than a vague wish to 'do something creative'. Because of his limited academic ability, the idea of providing him with a university education never crossed Bertie's mind. Instead, one of his final fatherly acts was to fix him a position at Sentinel's in Shrewsbury. 'I'm afraid my scholastic record was appalling,' Ken admitted. 'I managed to achieve an all-time low, and that is I got 2.5 per cent in mathematics in the school certificate ... which of course qualifies you for absolutely nothing.' So, at the height of the Great Depression, he joined the British workforce as an apprentice on the shop floor earning a weekly salary of £1. Although there were some happy moments, his most potent memory was being paired with a sweet-natured Welshman, Wat Thomas, the most prodigious drinker in Shrewsbury. Kenny's task was to hold a metal spike against the end of a locking pin while Wat swung a sledgehammer and knocked axels free. However, because Wat was usually hungover, Ken lived in terror of suffering a gruesome hand injury. So, one morning, increasingly wary about his digits, he bet Wat a carton of cigarettes that he couldn't quit alcohol for a week. 'Sure enough, he did,' Ken beamed. Then, back in the workshop, the sober Wat took a swing at the spike, 'missed and took the nail off my right thumb'.

After six months, Ken became 'Master More' when he moved to the safety of the sales department. Outside work, like other young men, he looked for thrills – and loved the hunt which centred around the local pub, and the dancehalls of Shrewsbury – as well as, inevitably, the pictures. The Bull Inn on Butcher Row, which had hardly changed since the 1920s, was one of his favourite haunts. Over time, he enjoyed a series of brief, unserious encounters and lost his virginity after a fumble with a nurse. She was no distinct beauty, he regaled, and certainly not a wallflower at the local dance. 'She wanted sex ... I was to be the means of gratifying her need.' Until this moment, he confessed, he had never actually 'put it in' and in his unbounded excitement, it was 'all over' within seconds. For a while, he fretted that this 'unprotected union' may have spawned a pregnancy, but the days passed peacefully. So peacefully, in fact, he soon became an accomplished skirt chaser, jumping into bed with a 'hideously ugly' schoolteacher and indulging in other flings, but only vague outlines of his antics are clear.

Over time, he made many friends, but his heart wasn't in the job, nor Shrewsbury. 'I liked my engineering days – the practical side of it,' he recounted, 'but it just wasn't for me.'[8] In the end, Bertie never lived to see his son throw in the towel. 'He had so many worries before his death, all his money had run out – he was an ill man, a sick man. He couldn't think of me very much or my sister.'[9] Bertie died on 18 June 1932 at Middlesex Hospital, aged forty-five. If any experience marked the low point in young Ken's life, this was it. Shattered by the loss, he never forgot the funeral, where the church bell tolled loud and mourners, family, and friends came and went. 'His death, for me, was a brutally painful experience,' he admitted. Fortunately, a life insurance policy covered the family debts and Edith – distraught and inconsolable – dashed off to live with her mother in Weston-super-Mare. Happily, her veil of sadness was lifted by an offer to return to Malvern to run a hotel, but she resigned soon after when daughter, Kate, then a lively slip of a girl, was discovered stark-naked wrapped around Bobby Pinnegar, the owner's husband, a known Lothario. When the dust settled, Ken finalised his departure from Sentinel's, and with the help of a loan from Edith moved to London.

With none of the intellectual agility of his father, he attempted to enlist in the Royal Air Force but, after being spun from right to left on a swivel chair, failed the medical due to dizziness, and a balance disorder. Dejected and jobless, the theatre provided solace and he often turned up for afternoon matinees, and crept out after the evening performance. He loved comedies and drama, but was decidedly sniffy about Shakespeare and flamboyant actors churning out the classics. He adored Max Miller's turns at the Holborn Empire, an obsession of the moment, always viewed from the end of the second row in the balcony. Donned in a colourful suit with plus-fours, a kipper tie, trilby and correspondent shoes, Ken believed Miller was the greatest stand-up comic of his generation: 'His timing was absolute perfection. He was of course a blue comedian, but he left it to you, and he was never offensive, because his timing was so perfect, you just could not help laughing at Max Miller.' British films dominated his visits to the cinema, and later, when asked his opinion of the greatest movies he saw, he consistently mentioned *The Invisible Man* with Claude Rains and Charles Laughton, whom he would come to know personally. Decades after seeing *The Private Life of Henry VIII*, Ken could still describe the entire film, shot by shot from the opening credits to the fade.

Amid all this, as Ken looked for work of any kind, Edith suggested he take a job at Sainsbury's, the grocers, which, she insisted, was a 'safe and respectable profession'. And, though he swallowed the bait and began his 'first face-to-face encounters with the British public', the novelty soon wore off. While his good looks made him popular among the girls behind the fats-and-eggs counter – he was supremely ill-suited to retail and unable to add, subtract or do multiplication. Invoices were beyond his grasp and after a month, the manager showed him the exit.

While Edith continued to offer guidance and to follow her son's progress keenly from afar, she was horrified to learn about his latest venture. It all began while Ken was drowning his sorrows at The Bunch of Grapes, a little pub on the Brompton Road.

After a few pints, he struck up a conversation with Bill Manfield, a man of many words, who had long fantasised about 'earning a fortune' fur trapping in Canada, 'the land of opportunity'. With the aid of a couple of Navy Rum chasers, Bill opened a long recital claiming to have 'family contacts' at the Hudson Bay Company, the famous fur traders and – before the night ended – Ken agreed to form a partnership hunting foxes and moose in the Canadian wilderness. 'I was ripe for this kind of talk and could see myself leaping from ice floe to ice floe, gathering up furs and shooting grizzlies,' he confessed. Though appalled by the tin-pot scheme, Edith reluctantly parted with £200 for the pair to buy tents, snowshoes, sledges, breeches, puttees, Boer War rifles, and other paraphernalia. It was a massive undertaking, and when everything was arranged, they scraped together fares for three third-class passages – the third, and unexpected traveller, was Bill's twenty-eight-year-old doe-eyed girlfriend, Joan. 'We had to take Joan along too,' Ken explained, 'because she threatened to commit suicide if we left her behind.' Nonetheless, admiring her thick red lips, brown eyes, and ample cleavage was no hardship.

Armed with four suitcases and a crate of equipment, the three set off from Liverpool across the Atlantic on the Canadian and Pacific vessel *Montcalm*. Quartered in the steerage area, a 'dark, damp, stifling rat hole', the stench of vomit – lingering due to lack of ventilation – was the first surprise. The second, on docking at Quebec, was their immediate arrest and detention at an immigration prison. Though independent, Canada was part of the British Empire, but retained strict entry rules – neither Ken, Bill or Joan had the necessary visas, and authorities also discovered they had no money to launch their venture. Due to this 'unwitting infringement of the immigration laws' all Kenny saw was 'the Château Frontenac through the bars'.[10] Worse still, Joan, it seems, was married. 'By bringing her into Canada, Bill and I were guilty of smuggling a married woman across the Canadian border without her husband's consent, and with no appreciable means of support,' Ken explained. 'It was, said the official, a very serious charge.'[11] However, they had nothing against Ken personally, but Bill and Joan could not enter Canada. 'In a flood of loyalty, I said if they couldn't go in, neither would I. A decision which seemed perfectly acceptable to the official.'[12] Once marked for deportation, the trio faced the stinging indignity of boarding the same ship for the return journey, and with the fast-disappearing coast of Canada in the distance, they were escorted back to the 'rat hole' cabin in steerage.

Travel-strained, wearing army boots and carrying a tatty rucksack, Ken was forced to go down to Weston-super-Mare and confess failure to his mother. 'There wasn't a word of recrimination,' he said. 'She gave me her last available £50 to try and do some good.' As for Bill, he distinguished himself in the Second World War before being killed during the brutal Burma campaign.

Returning to London, Ken set up home in a poky basement room in Bayswater, large enough for his suitcase, a hat stand, iron-framed bed, and something akin to a closet. It was there, he vowed to pack in his drifting and two-bit schemes. And, as luck would have it, one of those 'seemingly unimportant quirks of fate' occurred when his mother wrote on 28 November 1932 to say that sister Kate had become engaged to comedian called John Tilley while working as a programme girl at London's

Windmill Theatre. As an emerging radio and variety star, Tilley's engagement warranted a small item in the press. Notably, the *Daily News* described Kate as 'the chief lounge attendant at the Windmill Theatre', where Mr Tilley was resident comedian. Interestingly, the *Era* added that no one was more pleased by the 'sudden and romantic love-match' than Vivian Van Damm, the Windmill's manager. 'Miss More is the daughter of Vivian Van Damm's oldest friend of thirty years' standing, who, largely through having been over-generous, and largely through the results of the financial crisis, died practically penniless. His daughter, brought up in luxury and refinement, had no ambition for the stage but Van Damm found her some employment at the Windmill, where since her father's death, she has been selling programmes.'

It is unclear if Kenny attended the wedding in January 1933, which – as reported in the press – turned out to be an unusual affair. Tilley, a man blighted by continuous ill-health, emerged from his sick bed at 10 a.m. with a temperature of 101 and was driven to Paddington Register Office for the service. At seven minutes after eleven, he was back in bed at his flat in Gloucester Terrace with a temperature of nearly 102. His bride tucked him in and gave him a hot drink. The couple were toasted by their friends at the bedside, and then Kate went to work. 'We had made the arrangements for the wedding long before John caught the flu,' she explained, 'and we did not see why a spot of temperature should interfere.'[13]

Kenny's own memoirs of this time aren't quite accurate – while he hints at joining the Windmill soon after Kate's engagement, it seems almost a year passed before he summoned enough gumption to meet Van Damm. 'I went to see him in desperation and said I'm no good as an engineer, I've failed for the Air Force, and I think I want to have something to do with the theatre,' was how he described the encounter. 'I had learned that my father had helped Van Damm out of a financial jam. It doesn't always follow that favours are repaid, but his opening words to me were: "Your father was one of the best I've met. He was very good to me once and I'm going to be very good to you."' What is certain is that Van Damm – known to his staff as 'V.D.' – hired him to shift scenery for £2 10s a week on the condition that he never asked to be an actor: 'I promised him faithfully that I never would.'

Perched on the corner of Archer Street and Great Windmill Street, near Piccadilly Circus, the club gained a saucy reputation given Van Damm's exploitation of a legal loophole that nude statues could not be banned on moral grounds. This led to his legendary 'Windmill Girls', naked women that remained motionless in the shadows and glare, as the Lord Chamberlain's ruling directed 'If you move, it's rude'. Underneath the misery of the Great Depression, London's nightlife was booming during the early 1930s. In Soho, the Windmill's giant neon sign became one of the city's glorious trademarks, signifying sauciness, and refined entertainment. By the time Ken arrived, the club had morphed from a fringe venture to enjoying good mainstream business. He remembered a 'well-organised factory', and from the offset, felt a warm feeling of 'belonging', like being at home. 'The theatre was the world for me,' he said as he got close to Van Damm and even enjoyed a 'platonic romance' with Betty, V.D's daughter – who worked as a model in the Windmill. Though a 'well-made girl', he always took pains to point out that they never slept together or 'anything like that'. Strangely, Sheila Van Damm, Betty's sister, recounted the two 'nearly got engaged'. She also remembered Ken 'played startlingly good football for the Windmill team, everyone liked him'.[14]

He devoted himself to his job and spent his free time nattering with the girls in a tightly packed dressing room beneath the stage referred to as the 'parlour'. Two floors up, V.D. could be found running the operation like a military campaign from an office with an 'aroma of leather and tobacco'. Van Damm looked every inch the part of the Svengali and prided himself on doing 'his own little bit' to create a more permissive society. 'I have one recipe for picking girls,' he often declared. 'Personality, youth, beauty, talent. In that order.' He had a genius for ballyhoo, and kept punters happy with comic turns, singers, and the occasional magician. 'This was 1934,' Ken gushed. 'I had the most marvellous ground training: I shifted scenery, I went on to the electrics board, I learned all about stage lighting, went to the front of the house, I learned about management, and eventually I became the assistant stage manager.' The most terrifying job at first, he reflected years later, was 'sweeping' the nudes offstage. 'I'd go crimson giving the girls their dressing gowns, their reaction was to giggle and tell me I'd get used to it and my school friends would turn up after the show astonished that I was paid for doing the job … it was all a great big schoolboy joke!' But 'it wasn't long before, instead of turning a bashful pink as "les girls" scurried past me, I was hustling them offstage with the best of them'.[15] The evening shows were fun, but he preferred watching the morning auditions, sitting quietly in the orchestra pit, casting an eye at turns ranging from bird whistlers, acrobats, jugglers, and cycle acts to vocalists and tap dancers. Occasionally, he saw Van Damm bury his face in his hands, and then, after a moment, bark 'next please' – pulling the plug on another showbiz dream.

Inevitably, when covering events at the Windmill, reporters mentioned the 'nude tableaux', but usually took care to stress they were 'artistically presented' and did not offend. Although there was occasional praise for the variety artists, the nudes remained the star attraction, though Van Damm – disingenuously – maintained they were never presented 'for the sake of a nude'. In truth, there was an erotic, almost grubby, tinge to everything, as customers sought a glimpse of exposed nipple, thigh or naked derrière. Moreover, Ken never forgot lines of men queuing up daily to secure front seats, passing a notice in the foyer reading: 'Will patrons kindly vacate their seats after the performance. The use of artificial visual aids is strictly forbidden!' There really wasn't much need for binoculars, as the theatre only seated around 300 and was so small that performers could see everybody beyond the footlights. Likewise, perched up above the auditorium, Kenny could conduct his daily 'wanker watch', a crucial chore which involved scouring the stalls for customers clandestinely masturbating under the cover of a raincoat, hat, or newspaper. Overstimulated by naked flesh, one frequent visitor, an old sea dog, always shuffled in equipped with a compact refracting telescope. Once seated, he clung to the instrument with his left hand 'and played with himself with his right'. Over time, Kenny developed a code to report 'suspicious activity' to the weary security guard: 'I would pick up the house telephone and say: "A4, Wanker, *Times*. C17, *Daily Mail*."' Once alerted, the old guard stumbled – quite literally – over the offenders to deliver a few sharp words and disdainful look.

For a while, Ken's own gaze shifted towards a girl in the show, Pearl Hackney, a five-foot-two, petite ballerina, with bobbed blonde hair and blue eyes. They appeared to have a 'good connection', and he often took her out but, before long, competition arrived in the form of Eric Barker, a slender, scholarly-looking chap who wrote comedy scripts for the show. Barker and Pearl got engaged and, soon after, tied the knot. 'I nearly married Kenneth More,' Pearl confessed in the 1970s. 'I don't know why I opted for Eric. Perhaps he gave me two chances and Ken only gave me one. He is still telling people how I gave him up for Eric.'[16]

Despite the knock, Kenny's self-confidence grew – and after six months on 'wanker watch' he was yearning to be before the spotlight rather than behind it. This change of heart all began, he recounted, one Saturday night when he was scheduled to be working the electric boards. However, comedian Gus Chevalier required help with a sketch: 'It needed a man dressed as a policeman and say to the people inside: "Is this your car outside?" I had a terrible policeman's helmet which came down over my nose and I forgot that in stage windows the glass is supposed to be there, so I stuck my head through the empty pane and caused a roar of laughter! And for the first time in my life, I tasted that sweet sound of laughter from the front. And that's how it all started …'[17]

'He was a great success,' Sheila Van Damm recalled. 'Much funnier than the comic – far too funny for the comic's liking, and he was quickly put back between the props and the lights.

But that was the first appearance of Kenneth More.'[18] Not long after, he landed a little film role and uttered a single line – 'They can't get in' – in Gracie Field's *Look up and Laugh*, 'a picture of riotous mirth' telling how Gracie battles to prevent the closure of a local market, with 'many humorous situations'. His two and a half seconds of screen time added a little prestige to his blank résumé and from here on, he referred to this blink-and-you-miss-it performance as his 'screen debut'.

In the Silver Jubilee year of King George V in 1935, opportunity knocked again when a Windmill singer sprained his ankle and, scrambling to find a quick replacement, Ken was pushed on stage in a costume several sizes too large and instructed to sing. To his elation, the audience met the end of his number with a roar of laughter. 'The stage-bug that Vivian Van Damm had warned me against had drawn blood,' he admitted, before spewing out his feelings to V.D. by confessing he was 'fond of the business side', but even fonder of the aroma of greasepaint. Perhaps out of affection, V.D. made some vague noises before throwing a few crumbs such as letting him feed comedians on stage. Before long, he was a general understudy, hovering in the wings, ready to step in for any cast member at any given time. A friend remembered the thing that truly distinguished him as a performer at this time was his plain likeability, and tangible sense of delight in what he was doing. 'It was the best training in the world for comic sketches,' Ken said. He didn't mind playing the straight man, a role usually unpopular among most comics, who disliked acting the sucker, the foil, or the mark. After a few months, the audience got to know him, and though initially performances were sporadic, he was soon on stage nightly alongside some of the biggest up-and-coming names on the comedy circuit, including Barry Lupino, Eddie Hooper, Doris Barry, David Dale, and Eric Woodburn:

> And watching comedians like Gus Chevalier, Dickie Murdoch and Eric Barker gave me the idea that I might, someday, be able to raise a laugh myself. I started off as a stooge, a feed … a fellow who says: 'Who was that lady I saw you with last night?' so that the star can crack swiftly back with 'That's no lady. That's my wife!'[19]

By this point, his sister Kate had long left the Windmill and was caring for her husband who – after enjoying a brief stint on the American stage and offers of film work – underwent an unspecified 'serious internal operation' in November 1934. Somehow, he managed to limp back to work after a few months in a nursing home but by June 1935 he was bedridden and died on 3 August 1935, leaving his wife £6,335 and a flat in Hemel Hempstead. 'I thought it was nothing more than kidney trouble,' Kate reportedly told the *Sunday Sun*, though she was named as 'Mrs Tilley' and not Kathleen Thomson, her marital name (John Tilley's real name was John Morrisey Thomson). 'I think he knew he was dying, but he was afraid of me knowing and nothing more was ever said about it between us. I gave him morphia, so he suffered no pain. It seems extraordinary to think that he was only some three years on the stage and made such a name. He crammed a lifetime of work into those three years.'

Amid this family turmoil, Kenny continued to develop comedic instincts, mainly as a pantomimic comedian – mugging became a specialty. And though he could play the piano, he abandoned a plan to pepper his routine with singing and dancing after Buddy Bradley, a well-known African-American hoofer, tried to teach him to tap dance before throwing in the towel. 'I didn't have two left feet,' Ken joked. 'I had two wrong feet.' He complained his legs went stiff; his shoes seemed full of lead. 'I felt like an idiot prancing about, and undoubtedly looked it.' Worse still, his attempts at crooning sentimental melodies, like 'Devon, Glorious Devon' and rousing ballads only brought discomfort to everyone in earshot. It was unanimously agreed that his singing voice could not be cultivated, as he simply did not possess one.

Sadly, not much publicity material from these early years survives, having been destroyed in a time when no one contemplated the possibility it would be of historic interest. We do, however, have a cutting from an *Era* critic, who (in the final paragraph of a review) noted Ken put in 'some good work in supporting comedy roles'. *The Dancing Times* also passed comment, noting that 'Mr Kenneth More showed remarkable versatility by turning from feeding comedians to partnering Mrs Doris Barry.'

Away from work, Ken became popular among the showbiz crowd and dived headfirst into the world of all-night restaurants, smoky pubs and, of course, showgirls. His reputation as a 'live wire' got around, and he soon could be found in the Grafton Arms or the Wellington pub on St Martin's Lane or holding court at Billy's Cafe near Wyndham's, a popular haunt for theatricals. He usually wore his brilliantined hair combed back, but there are photos where a small forelock gives him an unusually virile air. Like his time in Shrewsbury, there were many girlfriends but little emotional commitment. Instead, he continued to measure his manhood by a tally of one-night-stands. Worse still, he managed to blow a £600 inheritance during three 'glorious rip-roaring' months living on champagne, steaks, and caviar at Piccadilly's most expensive nightspots: 'It was an experience I'll never forget. When the money was gone, I was poorer but wiser.' Once when flush, he splashed out £90 on a green biscuit-box Morris and raced around Soho like an overgrown schoolboy. He also became, by his own admission, cockier, big-headed, and freer of speech – and dreamt the Windmill might serve as a launching pad for his career. Then, quite out of the blue, it all came crashing down when Van Damm stirred up a real hornet's nest by falsely accusing him of having slept with his favourite showgirl, a beautiful blonde. Though Ken denied the allegations, things went from bad to worse and an accumulation of grievances led to his dismissal. According to Bruce Forsyth, a Windmill comedian in the fifties, such firings were common, given V.D's autocratic style, penchant for venting his spleen and hate of staff dating the showgirls. 'If you did something he thought was wrong, he would dismiss you quicker than a click of his fingers.'

So, after nearly two years' continuous work, the unspoken bond between Kenneth More and Vivian Van Damm was severed. Unemployment came as a great shock. Worse still, Ken had just set up home with Anne, a girlfriend of the moment, and they'd leased an unfurnished flat in Maida Vale. However, with no money, he couldn't contribute a farthing towards the rent. 'I had not paid National Insurance stamp long enough to be able to draw the dole, so I had to live off Anne's bounty, a situation I disliked intensely.' Edith assisted by sending five-shilling postal orders but as money ran out, life became intolerable. 'I was flat, stony broke. There was very little to smile about.' After smartening himself up and making the round of agents trying to get a foot in their doors, salvation finally arrived in the form of Miriam Warner who fixed him an audition with Barry O'Brien's Repertory Company to tour with *Do You Remember?*, a comedy. His contract, signed on 2 September 1937, called for Warner's standard salary of £5 a week, payable on Friday evenings, with rehearsals slated to begin the following week. After bidding a final farewell to Anne, who was busily packing to pursue her own career in Scotland, Ken joined O'Brien's troupe. The company travelled by rail – as it didn't have enough people to justify a coach – and, over the coming weeks, passed through capacity houses at Eastbourne's Pier, Brighton, and the Wallasey Winter Gardens, before shuffling into the Theatre Royal, Birmingham. To his delight, Ken revelled in the unglamorous world of struggling actors, gruelling journeys, tatty theatrical lodgings, and peanut-sized dressing rooms. Better still, the tour worked wonders for his confidence, exposing him to graduates of the Royal Academy of Dramatic Art. 'I felt a rather poor relation,' he confessed. 'However, the ice was soon broken, and we got along fine.'[20] The pay-off came with several good reviews. 'Tribute for the success of this show must go to Kenneth More and Brenda Green,' noted the *Evening Dispatch* on 12 October 1937. 'If you are not too morbidly interested in pathos you will be swayed by its ebullient comedy and first-class characterisations.' Even better, Clarkson Rose from the prestigious *Stage* newspaper informed his readers that Ken's portrayal of Horace Fortesque 'gave to me what is a remarkable performance'. This insightful comment – providing a first draft of Kenny's stage career – adds the young talent made the audience like the obnoxious Fortesque 'without in any way whittling down the unpleasant traits of the character'. Interestingly, too, these glowing words came after Kenny's very first experience of performing in a straight play, without the opportunity to lark about. Clarkson Rose also supplies a fascinating glimpse of Miriam Warner. 'She loves life, and she loves people,' he observed. 'I have never heard her speak but well of a person.' What is certain is that Warner valued Ken. When *Do You Remember?* folded, she secured him a job in rotating repertory with Charles Denville at the Grand Theatre in Byker, 277 miles north in a suburb of Newcastle upon Tyne.

2
THE CALL OF THE STAGE

Newcastle was thrilling, a coming-of-age experience. Ken never tired of telling anecdotes about The Charles Denville Players, a typical shoestring operation existing on a diet of melodramas, mostly written by Denville himself and pulled together by E. Hamilton Jordan, a man of slightly neurotic temperament. 'I had a desperate itch to continue acting, so this seemed like heaven,' Ken explained. 'I acquired a new vitality. Byker was the starting line ... it was pure magic. A marvellous old Victorian blood-and-thunder theatre. It was a rough-and-tumble affair on the wrong side of the tracks.'[1]

Feeling very much a beginner, he didn't mind being billeted at cold-water digs on Falmouth Road, Heaton, one of the poorest working-class districts, replete with gas lighting and outside 'lavvy'. On that first day, buttoned up against the morning chill, he explored Newcastle's docklands along the Tyne, wandered the filthy back streets, and ate breakfast in a grimy cafe under the shadow of a slag heap. And, amid this smoke-stained landscape, sat The Grand – a majestic palace of entertainment providing a cheerful tonic for the hard-working locals. Boasting a long and storied history, the theatre opened in 1896 with a performance of *The Taming of the Shrew* with the famous company of F. E. Benson. The great days of variety had seen Florrie Ford at Byker several times and a young Charlie Chaplin performed there with *Eight Lancashire Lads,* a troupe of male clog dancers.

In this theatrical wilderness, E. Hamilton Jordan was the star turn, and despite being hampered by a set of ill-fitting dentures, he was one of the most recognisable local characters, togged up in a homburg, spats, and Prussian monocle. He 'delivered' his words – frequently with an undefined accent – but was good-humoured, and humorous. And – as Ken recounted – Jordan was unflappable in a crisis. In the course of a long career, his résumé expanded to include a stint as an agent, business manager and 'leading player'. At Byker, he pulled plays together in a hurry, performed twice nightly (with plenty of ad-libbing), and cobbled together a twice-weekly change of programme. 'Jordan could play hapless heroes and villains,' Ken said, half-admiringly. 'He was a beautiful actor, debonair performer. Whatever character he portrayed, he projected the air of the archetypal Englishman.'

Most of the other Byker actors – including Arthur Lane and Hugh Paddick – were not prosperous, but not that needy either. Everyone was paid £5 a week – which, even with a busy social life – went a long way. Fellow cast member George Henry Blackburn remembered, at first, Kenny was reserved, unsure how he would get on with Tyneside audiences: 'But he endeared himself to the people very quickly, not only by his personality, but by his understanding of the people. He had an old car which he used to drive to the theatre, and everybody knew it. On stage he always tried to help others, he was a good ad-libber and often livened the play with the unexpected.' Indeed, he thought audiences were a 'tough lot' as they worked hard for a living. 'Life wasn't easy for them,' Kenny said, 'and they had little cash to spare for fun. The theatre was the big event of their week, and they made the most of it. They joined in the situations on stage with enthusiasm, cheering the hero and booing the villain, and gave every performance a sympathetic hearing. They were very keen and came week after week. But they do not like changes. I had a thin time at first, but after they accepted me.' Over time, he enjoyed the run of the theatre and roles in *Sweeney Todd*, *The Prince and The Beggar Maid*, *A Sinner in Paradise*, *When Irish Eyes are Smiling*, *While Parents Sleep*, *The Coastguard's Daughter*, *Dr Jekyll and Mr Hyde* and *Dracula*. Fridays, he remembered, were fish and chips and bottle-of-beer night. 'No one listened to what went on on stage and we'd just mime our way through it. But every other night of the week they were most attentive.'[2]

During the last summer of peace, Ken had reason to feel flushed with pride as he developed into a natural actor, and enjoyed a rapport with the audience. 'I'm terribly thorough,' he said, looking back at those days. 'And I know I'm very professional. I'll be the first at rehearsal, that sort of thing. I also know enough not to get drunk at lunchtime because if I'm in the theatre, I'm tied to an audience that night and it's to give a good performance. It's as simple as that.' He did, however, concede to being 'genetically lazy', too lazy to be a perfectionist. 'I tend to settle for something that is just about good enough. I'm not a dedicated actor unless my blood is stirred and the real interest inside me is aroused.'

As the Sudeten Crisis rocked Europe, archives of the *Newcastle Chronicle* reveal Ken appeared in *The Face at the Window* – an ensemble effort – opening on 22 July 1938. 'They tell me it was a famous thriller 30 years ago, I don't remember it,' the critic complained, before conceding that every imaginable thrill was put into the show, the finish being a fight on the rooftops, rather a difficult thing to stage. Two weeks later, crowded houses showed their appreciation of *A Sinner in Paradise* – a production banned by the Lord Chamberlain, but later lifted. Presumably the same critic from the *Chronicle* praised Arthur Lane and Julie Boas for turning in 'their usual polished performances while Phyllis Baker and Kenneth More supply some excellent comedy relief'.[3] In fact, if Ken gained any comic ability, he owed it to Byker: 'It was no good forgetting your lines up there, customers would have struck you up to the nearest lamppost. So, you improvised like mad. Never since then have I been at for a loss for words on stage.'[4] His most memorable ad-libbing role came in an 'electrifying melodrama' requiring quick improvisation:

> I was in prison and the play ended with a warder bringing me a mug of water and a loaf of bread in which was a file. I tore the bread apart, found the file and began filing my way to freedom as the curtain came down to loud applause. One night, I realised there was no file, so I had to stuff the bread down my throat, stagger to the front of the stage, and say: 'My God, I've swallowed the file!'

Another oft-told anecdote involved a play featuring a gruesome murder in the final scene. As the action reached a crescendo, one actor aimed a gun at the other and shot him. However, one evening, the gun failed to fire, and the two panic-stricken actors gawped at each other. In an inspired moment of improvisation, the actor with the gun kicked the other guy up the arse. 'Arrgh,' screamed the other, 'the poisoned shoe!' and swiftly died.[5]

At Byker, the fun usually began even before the curtain went up. For a long time, Ken was puzzled about the origin of Charlie's fantastic storylines. Eventually – quite by accident – he learned that his shows were inspired by movies he had seen at the local cinema. If he enjoyed a film, he would dash home and thrash out an 'enhanced theatrical adaptation' of it in one of his precious notebooks. One of his most ambitious works, *The Sheik*, was loosely based on an exotic Middle Eastern folk tale and saw Denville empty fifty sacks of sawdust on the stage to simulate shimmering desert sands. Then, he marched on two horses, a goat, a half a dozen sheep, and a pitiful-looking camel to 'add real life' to 'Sheikh Kaled Ben Omar's encampment'. One whole hour later, this 'enchanted wilderness' stank to high heaven as animal excrement began matting the sawdust, sheep farted and pools of steaming hot urine seeped across the stage. Several versions of this anecdote have come down through the years, but they all mention a camel piddling during an important scene, leading to a squeal from the audience and someone bellowing, 'It's pissing, man!' As the cast struggled heroically, one of the horses threw the leading actor on the floor and ambled across the stage and off the other side. 'It refused to return,' Ken said, 'so our hero had to play the rest of the scene on foot.' Amidst the tumult, to cover backdrop changes, Kenny was instructed to stand on the ramparts and 'talk about something for five minutes' – never mind what – as the sets were changed behind him. No script, just 'the old ad-lib'.

Despite all this, he conferred excessive respect on Denville, found a reliable pal in Jordan and took an instant shine to Beryl Johnstone, a newcomer from Ellen Compton's Repertory Company in Cheltenham, lauded by the regional press as an 'artist of considerable promise'. Surviving sepia photographs show her to be a dark-haired beauty with long locks. At first, it seems, she was unresponsive to Kenny's assiduous wooing, but such obstacles never hampered his efforts. However, for all its enticements, after six months in Newcastle he yearned for better roles as thoughts of playing 'a bit of Ibsen or Shaw' dominated his thoughts. Strangely enough, his own accounts about his departure differ. In one narrative, published in the *Radio Times* in 1974, he admits to being sacked by Denville, but doesn't specify why. He does, however, note that Miriam Warner 'was not amused when I got myself fired from Newcastle'. The other explanation – proffered in his memoirs – has him quitting because he was 'in a rut' (and Denville expressing sadness at his departure).

What is known is that having managed to put aside a little savings, he headed south in July 1938 to try his hand at conventional repertory. Again, to the rescue, Warner fixed him a part in *Distinguished Gathering*, a three-act play of murder and blackmail at the King's Theatre, Hammersmith – a dream engagement. 'Remember his name,' one critic advised. 'He has a good sense for comedy.' With her ear cocked for any other jobs, Warner then found him work with Derek Salberg's repertory company in the West Midlands. A young man of attractive personality, Salberg had the double gift, rare even among London producers, of both foreseeing hit shows and handling delicate artists. Leonard Rossiter, John Alderton, John Le Mesurier, Peggy

Mount, Raymond Huntley, and Arthur Lowe were among the later-to-be-famous actors to gain experience with his company. Unusually, this new engagement meant Ken worked at the Grand Theatre in Wolverhampton and also, on occasion, at the Alexandra Theatre in Birmingham, known as 'the Alec'. Earning the mouth-watering salary of £7 per week, he quickly attracted new friends and found digs with Mrs Lowery 'a dear old thing' who charged thirty shillings, including laundry, hot meals, and motherly love. Even better, the job followed a similar pattern to Byker with rehearsals taking up most of his time before being sent on stage. Fellow actors – all of whom remained friends for life – included Althea Orr, Tommy Raynor and Bruce Walker. Alex Moller, the stage manager, became a close pal.

On the road to a successful career in the theatre by early 1939, Ken had reason to feel confident. In between rep seasons, short tours filled his diary with summer seaside stock and end-of-pier performances. Throughout this period, as Europe ignited with hate and violence, Wolverhampton remained positively tranquil. When the Grand was used for pantomimes in the winter of 1939, Ken briefly rejoined Barry O'Brien's company touring with *To Have and to Hold* featuring Phyllis Neilson-Terry, who later found fame in Terence Rattigan's *Separate Tables* on Broadway. It opened at the Winter Gardens, New Brighton in January to so-so reviews, with most of the praise going to Neilson-Terry. The show ran until March, taking in Southport, Blackpool, Wimbledon and Northampton. Back in Wolverhampton, he returned for a second season in April starting with *The Ghost Train*, Arnold Ridley's repertory favourite. 'Kenneth More,' wrote an admiring local reviewer, 'makes Teddie Deacon a vastly amusing character, though in the end not such a silly ass as he appears to be.' By some strange quirk of fate, that same month, Beryl Johnstone – the object of his desires from the Byker Grand – joined the Salberg company. The only spanner in the works, at least for the moment, was the fact she was engaged to Arthur Hewlett, an actor at the Ross Repertory Company in Weymouth. 'We have known each other about six months,' Hewlett told the *Manchester News* on 28 April. 'Now she is with the Wolverhampton Repertory Theatre, and we don't see so much of each other.'[6]

The engagement was officially announced in the *Birmingham Mail* on 1 May, but with Hewitt working down south, Ken promptly moved in for the kill. At a glitzy reception thrown by Salberg to hail a local dignitary, Beryl's resistance evaporated. Before long, they were stealthily evading her landlady during illicit – often noisy – late-night encounters (which saw Ken mount a drainpipe and, occasionally, hide under the bed). In spite of her nocturnal shenanigans, or maybe because of them, Beryl came fully into her own as a serious actress. Her first outing in Wolverhampton was in a revival of Shaw's comedy, *Candida*. 'The play proved once again its power to entertain,' the *Birmingham Daily Post* observed. 'Kenneth More gives a new glimpse of his capabilities as the rhapsodizing Marchbanks; he captures the petulant and ecstatic moods in a manner one had scarcely expected. Beryl Johnstone, in the name part, seizes her chance, too, and plays with freshness and disarming ease.'[7] Soon after, she won praise playing Lady Mary in *Fresh Fields*, a production heartily endorsed by the *Birmingham Mail* as a full-flavoured 'Novello vintage'. The production also starred Noel Johnson, an actor with a magnificent voice, who later found fame on radio as *Dan Dare* and *Dick Barton*. In *The Wind and the Rain*, the story of medical students at a Scottish university, Ken gave a magnificent performance as a moody young man discovering romance, prompting the *Birmingham Mail*'s reviewer to describe him as an engaging young actor, perfectly natural but with a grand sense of theatre with a 'frank boyishness and a charm' which could hardly be improved.

Remarkably, during the long hot August of 1939, as the fragile peace in Europe unravelled, Alex Moller convinced Ken to join him on holiday in Menton in the South of France for an excursion, which at first, had a last-fling gaiety about it. However, as they were ushered through Paris's Gare du Nord under a state of emergency – blacked out and under heavy guard – the looming menace of Hitler became very real. On the return leg in Boulogne, Kenny was struck by the visible signs of war after spotting rows of cars abandoned by fellow Brits hurriedly dashing home, desperate not to get stranded. 'The war,' he said, 'was suddenly real. I caught the smell of it for the first time.'

3
KENNY GOES TO WAR

When Kenneth remembered the beginning of the Second World War, what first came to his mind was the sense of embarrassment, even shame, at being rejected for service. However, his part in the conflict later became, by his own account, as dramatic as any movie and circled around several pivotal campaigns, including the Battle of the Atlantic, the Mediterranean and Middle East theatre and the fall of Japan.

When hostilities were declared in September 1939, he went 'tearing out of the theatre' for the nearest recruiting office to demand immediate navy enlistment. They refused – there were too many applicants. 'They gave me one of those pitying looks and took my name ... That knocked the edge of my enthusiasm.'[1] Instead, his first step for King and Country was as an ARP ambulance driver and warden, plodding the blacked-out streets of Wolverhampton. 'Well, at least I was in something,' he lamented. 'I hung about for so long waiting for someone to get a cut finger that I decided the best thing I could do was to go back into rep again.' For a brief period, the government closed theatres but when Nazi air raids failed to materialise, reopened them. During late summer, as German forces tore through Poland, the United Kingdom became a hive of activity. Street kerbs were whitened, car bumpers painted, and traffic lights were covered from above.

The first eight months of the war, the so-called phoney period, left Britain physically unscathed while the Nazis planned to carry out invasions in Northern Europe. In Wolverhampton, older actors from the Grand enlisted as spotters, scouring the sky for enemy raiders, sounding klaxons, and boasting about 'doing their bit'. Noel Johnson volunteered for the Royal Army Service Corps, while other Salberg players enlisted in the new, extravagantly named, Entertainment National Service Association – or ENSA – a unit producing concert parties and troop shows. Run by Basil Dean, the notoriously waspish theatrical producer, the organisation began life staging morale-building 'all-in wrestling' evenings, and ropey stage productions ranging from Shakespeare to Dickens, spawning the cruel translation of the acronym ENSA: 'Every Night Something Awful'.

In early 1940, Kenny was invited to join DEMS – Defence Equipped Merchant Ships, a unit protecting vessels on the Atlantic run. His blood was roused at the sound of the proposed duty – operating a deck gun against the threat from German submarines. 'This,' he rejoiced, 'sounded like a real job.' But before heading to war, he delivered a 'brilliant' last performance in *Thark*, an Aldwych farce. The press were quite enthusiastic: 'Gerald Cuff and Kenneth More have a flair for foolery, and in the parts created by Tom Walls and Ralph Lynn, carefully avoid any attempt at imitation,' the ever-attentive *Birmingham Daily* critic observed.

Ten days later, he married Beryl at Wolverhampton's Christ Church, the day before Hitler invaded Norway. 'With war coming up, the atmosphere heavy, and like so many young blokes at the time, I married the girlfriend of the time,' he explained. 'It was a cross between heroically preparing to go off and do battle and to get the marriage allowance!' That day, more than a hundred seats – including the choir stall – were filled with friends. And, like an old-fashioned melodrama, guests overheard Beryl's mother venting waspishly that 'this wasn't the life she wanted for her daughter'. Herbert Johnstone – the new father-in-law – shook Ken's hand, but his cheerful face fooled no one. In a tiny column, *The Birmingham Mail* reported, 'Next Monday, the bridegroom will join the navy as a gunner.' In the rush to tie up loose ends, Ken attempted to sell his Morris – already in an advanced state of neglect – but all he got was an offer of '30 bob' from a scrap merchant (£1.50 in today's money). 'I decided that was too bad a fate for her. So, I gave her a dignified sailor's farewell. I emptied a can of petrol over her and set it alight. It was all very sad.'[2] Parting from Beryl, it seems, wasn't half as explosive. With the glow of wedded bliss having already vanished, he lamented that she was 'getting on his nerves' and failing to deliver the 'sexual marathon' he'd anticipated.

By time he reported for duty at HMS *Victory*, a sprawling complex of naval buildings in Portsmouth, Beryl was a distant memory as a 'mental curtain' descended on his past life: 'I might have had no parents or wife; my experiences in London and Byker and Wolverhampton faded into oblivion.' At Portsmouth, his hair was cropped, he slept in a Nissen hut with fifty other men and existed on stodgy mess rations. Conditions were similar at Tiger Bay, Cardiff's dockland district, where he mastered the use of 4-inch guns against surfacing submarines and the operation of a PAC, an astonishing device designed to throw up a wire hundreds of feet to hit enemy aircraft. It was here, he learned about thousands of Jersey residents – including family friends and old school chums – being hurriedly evacuated to the mainland. Disturbingly, he overheard stifled gasps and frenzied talk about 'a Hitler victory', after a lightning German strike left British troops hemmed in along the French coast near Dunkirk, forcing 330,000 men to scramble home onboard small ships, private yachts, and fishing boats – transforming the disaster into a victory of sorts.

Amid all this gloom, he was assigned to the MV *Lobos*, a twenty-year-old freighter of the Pacific Steam Navigation Company bound for South America, shunting a cargo of cutlery and textiles. Scarred and worn from constant service, this ungainly Harland & Wolff workhorse had seen better days, but Kenny's enthusiasm wasn't dampened. In fact, he dashed along the gangplank to examine the gun. 'Whatever you do,' an officer barked from the top deck, 'don't fire it unless you really have to. Anything might happen. And there isn't much ammunition, anyway.'[3] After taking a closer look, Ken discovered, with some trepidation, that the weapon had been manufactured in 1898 – and made in Japan. 'I decided if U-boats took an interest in us, it might be more effective to get on my knees and pray.'[4] By teatime, he had mastered the skill of edging along rails to the bridge, using a foot-pump toilet and making a brew on a paraffin stove. From here on, every day brought a new experience; he found the sea air 'especially delightful', but detested food from the galley – mountainous heaps of bacon in white fat, oatmeal chunks, and dehydrated vegetables – all served with 'ghastly' sweet tea. When the day's duty was done, free time was spent reading under an oil lamp swinging on a hook or playing dominoes with the stokers. At first his fellow sailors did not know what to make of him – 'an actor!' – but his talent for composing 'sloppy handwritten love letters' soon made him popular as he knew he could articulate 'what some of the lads couldn't express'. Sincerity was the key 'but sometimes I could be a bit racy given the long periods of absence from their wives and sweethearts!' When 'on a roll', he could 'rattle-off' a dozen billets-doux in one sitting. 'I wrote hundreds of passionate letters to countless sweethearts. I always started off with a gentle salutation then it got more exciting from there on … some were for the more broad-minded.'

Not long after putting out to sea, this tranquillity ended as the convoy steamed through the southern Irish Sea; an area known as 'The Devil's Basin', given its exposure to enemy attack. It was there that a German submarine spied the tanker *Athellaird* – one of the ships under protection – and torpedoed it off the Irish coast. Squinting against a fierce explosion, Ken felt the blast and a feeling of dread in the pit of his stomach watching the *Athellaird* list to starboard and disappear beneath the waves. 'I was scared,' he later wrote. 'Enormous flames pillared into the sky.' The encounter lasted less than a minute. Remarkably, twenty survivors managed to row 400 miles to Britain in a lifeboat, existing on biscuits, corned beef, condensed milk, and rainwater.

Despite her vulnerability to Nazi U-boats, the *Lobos* crew remained good humoured and, as the watchkeepers kept their gaze, Ken sat above the stern clad in oilskins manning his antique Japanese weapon – which created small mushroom-like clouds when fired. After several weeks at sea, he was mesmerised by his first balmy glimpse of Cuba and took a taxi from the harbour for a whistle-stop tour of Havana. This, he thought, was paradise: the wonderful climate, the sun-kissed promenade, the palm trees, and olive-skinned beauties. All too soon, he was back on board the *Lobos* steaming through the Panama Canal where US guards – all armed to the teeth – swarmed aboard. 'The Americans were not yet in the war, but they were highly suspicious of every ship passing through the canal in case Japanese saboteurs were on board,' he explained. 'The guards examined and picked over little *Lobos* as thoroughly as an agent reading the small print in an actor's contract and did not leave us until we got to the Pacific.'

A shiver of anxiety ran through the crew as the *Lobos* nosed down the American coast calling at fifty-two different ports on the way, including Valparaiso in Chile, a major harbour for commercial freighters. With a maximum of haste, the ship's company hurried ashore to make every moment of their freedom count. In fact, if anything would toughen up a young sailor more than a Nazi torpedo, it was the streets of Valparaiso. Like many riverfront towns, the city was a hotbed of cheap hooch, smuggling, prostitution, gambling parlours, pool halls, and crime. Beyond the dockyard, Ken – along with his best pal, Bert, the fifth engineer – were keen to womanise, see the sights and taste the local beer, which turned out to be a 'thinnish but deadly watery substance'. Bert, an unprincipled adventurer, knew the best joints for pleasure, perversion, and punch-ups. 'We had a fantastic time, I just wanted to savour every moment,' Kenny said, recounting that the crew's main delight was baiting the Germans they met. 'The town was packed with Nazi sailors on account one of our battleships was prowling nearby.' During a nine week stay, while the *Lobos* was overhauled – the crew found sweethearts – Ken was briefly attached to a girl named Eliza Munis – a toothless sexpot, who refused to take his money and even escorted him back to the *Lobos* after a night of passion. Throughout, he was in the middle of all the action, the 'life and soul', always up for fun, always with an eye on a skirt. One time, he was embroiled in a 'Wild West style' brawl at the *Graf Zeppelin* pub when chairs were thrown, and bottles used as weapons. He never forgot staggering over bodies through the shadows and noise to 'land a final punch at the chap I was after. We had some magnificent bust-ups. It was a riot.' But as bloody as it all sounds, he received his real baptism by fire from the Germans on the return home eastward across the North Atlantic when the little *Lobos* navigated rough seas and poor visibility as part of HX84, a convoy of thirty-eight merchant ships.

What happened on 5 November is history. With little warning, all hell broke loose when the *Admiral Scheer*, a Nazi battleship, attacked the convoy – causing startled confusion aboard the *Lobos*. 'Suddenly,' Ken said, 'the captain ordered "general quarters"', meaning all hands had to sprint to their individual battle stations. 'We became embroiled in the Battle of the Atlantic.' Though in a state of bewilderment, he remembered – in horrific detail – how explosions roared like thunderclaps, the ships scattered, and *Lobos* managed to slip away to safety under a thick smokescreen. It was a savage attack – five ships were lost including the merchant cruiser *Jarvis Bay* – armed with ancient and inadequate guns – which bravely engaged with the *Scheer*, drawing her fire. Only sixty-five men survived from a crew of 250. As this was happening, the petrol tanker *San Demetrio* was torpedoed, leaving her crew with the impossible task of bringing her back to Britain – a few years later, this true-life adventure was made into a film at Ealing Studios, starring Robert Beatty and Mervyn Johns.

Amid the smoke and confusion, the *Lobos* guzzled along determinedly, rolling, and pitching so much that Kenny thought she would never right herself. What concerned the crew most, he remembered, was pondering what horrors they would find at home. 'We'd heard all sorts of reports that Liverpool had been completely wiped out and that London was in ruins. As it was, when we docked at Liverpool, we found it virtually undamaged.'[5] A few days after returning, he thumbed a ride to the Midlands for a brief reunion with Beryl, but it did nothing to lift his spirits. Worse still, she had been frittering away the joint 'marriage allowance' on clothes, gifts, and cigarettes (she smoked forty a day) – and was stony broke. During this brief leave, they quarrelled, and reconciled but the breach was near complete. During the few high spots when they were flush – he was his old charismatic self – the joker, charmer and romantic. But it was one of a million unhappy wartime marriages. 'At the time, it was a huge disappointment to us,' he later confessed.

The outlook, however, was not entirely bleak. His activity in the Atlantic was enough for the navy to approve an application for a commission and in January 1941, he shot off to Lancing

College in Sussex for five weeks' training before reporting to HMS *King Alfred*, a shore base in Hove. The tale goes that he followed fellow actor Robert Newton before a commission interview board. Though versions of the story percolated for years, Ken's adaptation tells how ordinary seaman Newton, a habitual drinker, was celebrated with great enthusiasm in Portsmouth where he held officers enthralled at the Goat with boozy stories. 'But the Officer Selection Board were not fans of his as he often returned to barracks so drunk that he climbed over the walls rather than try and get past the sentry. He had been caught several times and taken before the officer-of-the-night for punishment.' On the day of the important interviews, beet-red Newton addressed the assembled brass by nonchalantly informing them he 'may consider' any offer of promotion. 'He would, he said, be doing the navy a great favour by accepting a commission.'[6] Unfortunately, Ken was ushered before the same brass moments after Newton stumbled out. 'When I went in, I heard one of them say: "Oh, my God, not another actor."' Still, proceedings went well. After an admiral ran his eye over a folder of glowing testimonials, he emerged with the rank of Temporary Acting Sub-Lieutenant, RNVR (Royal Navy Volunteer Reserve).

Surviving naval records show the date of his seniority was confirmed on 13 March 1941.[7] However, the glow of promotion soon vanished with a shore posting to HMS *Mersey* in Birkenhead, tasked with training merchant navy officers in anti-aircraft gunnery. 'My delight quickly turned to depression as I wanted to see some real action.' In fact, he didn't have to wait long as the iron-hard realities of war struck Liverpool in May 1941 when Nazi bombers launched the most concentrated series of air attacks outside London. The skies were red when 681 Luftwaffe planes unloaded 870 tons of explosives, destroying the docks, and leaving much of the metropolis in ruins. Ken never forgot windows blowing in, walls blowing out, and stretcher parties running across streets amid the incessant wail of air-raid sirens. Unsurprisingly, a lack of sleep, rescuing people from collapsed buildings and living in a labyrinth of tunnels beneath HMS *Mersey* took a toll. The bombardment, he recounted, resulted in over 6,500 homes being demolished and 72,000 people left homeless. On the night of the 3rd and 4th of May alone, as 400 fires raged, Kenny marvelled at how Scousers, with their legendary fortitude, didn't show fear however much they felt it. He had a close shave during one heavy raid in the cellar of the Liver Building when it was hit by a bomb which failed to go off. 'I was mesmerised' by the bomb, he recounted. It was 'the biggest I had ever seen. My bones turned to water.' Soon after, having inspected the explosive, a cheerful disposal expert declared that the device was safe. Yet when the bomb was taken to Southport, it exploded killing the expert.

Amid the raids and drudgery of daily life, Ken became impatient to return to sea. 'I wanted action, you see,' he told author Michael Munn, 'so I asked my CO for a transfer, but he just said I was too valuable where I was. Then I asked the advice of an old chief gunner's mate, a retired petty officer who always had good advice, and he told me to have a sudden attack of appendicitis and have them whipped out because after being on sick leave they would inevitably post me somewhere else.'[8] So, he found a medical book, and 'after an hour or two there wasn't anything I didn't know about this little bit of nonsense they call your appendix. Then, when I had what I considered to be a really good audience, I went through the whole works, the sickness, the pain in the tummy, the yell when the MO touched the spot.'[9]

The ruse worked, and as Liverpool stuttered back into life, Temporary Acting Sub-Lieutenant More marched aboard HMS *Aurora*, a light cruiser, as a watch keeping officer. 'Finally, I was going to sea. The *Aurora*, when I saw her, looked superb, sleek, aggressive and altogether magnificent,' he recounted. Indeed, this 5,270-ton vessel attracted plenty of attention, later gaining the nickname 'Silver Phantom' in admiration of her Mediterranean exploits, coupled with daring missions hunting for the German battleships *Scharnhorst* and *Gneisenau*.

The officers, Ken remembered, were a 'grand bunch' and 'forgave me for being an actor, and we got along together extremely well'. Like every junior officer, he worshipped the stately figure of Captain 'Bill' Agnew, an outwardly serene man renowned for his hatred of sloppiness. Educated at the Royal Naval College, Agnew had joined the navy in 1911 and served aboard the battleships HMS *Glory* and HMS *Royal Oak* during the First World War.

Beryl, in the meantime, had given birth to a daughter, Susan Jane. And increasingly concerned about the war, she left Wolverhampton to live with her parents in Cheltenham 'for the duration'. Meanwhile, as a result of his good performance, Ken was elevated to the rank of lieutenant in May 1942 before *Aurora* sailed down the Mersey on the evening of 4 July, passing the north of Ireland to act as an escort for minelayers. 'The aim was to block the route by which U-boats were sneaking from the North Sea into the Atlantic to get Allied convoys,' he explained.

Though violent waves came fiercely down on her decks, he remembered 'we had a memorable time; icebergs were about, a thick fog settled down. Nevertheless, we belted along at 15 knots in tight formation. It was cold and decidedly dodgy – especially when the mines were being chucked overboard. One in ten of the blasted things exploded, breaking the eerie silence with a most awful, shattering bang.'

The story of the *Aurora* is one of continuous activity combined with periods of stillness. From the icy reaches of the North Sea – battered by rain and sleet – she skirted to Land's End escorting a convoy of Cameron Highlanders heading to reinforce Montgomery's effort in North Africa. Their route to the Middle East was via the Cape, 'but we were only going part of the way to Freetown in Sierra Leone, on the west coast of Africa,' Ken said. 'The hotter the weather became, the more clothes we took off. But when Captain Agnew spotted some of us at action stations in shorts, he promptly sent out a reminder that our bodies had to be covered,' making conditions extremely uncomfortable. The order, though, was not malicious but to protect the men against flash-burns from the guns. From Freetown, *Aurora* steamed to the Mediterranean to support Operation Torch, the Allied invasion of North Africa. As the Nazi grip began to give way, Allied forces inflicted a series of victories over the Germans, reaching a climax at the Second Battle of El Alamein. A few days later, on 8 November 1942, off Oran, a port in the north-west of Algeria, *Aurora* engaged the Vichy French destroyers *Tramontane* and *Tornade*, sinking the latter and damaging the former so badly that she had to be beached. During all this, Ken took charge of the anti-aircraft guns. 'At dawn,' he recounted, 'a big French destroyer – her battle ensign at full top – steamed proudly out of the harbour obviously determined to make a dash for it. We didn't want to fight the French but had our orders. We went after her. Twenty minutes later, the French captain decided that he'd had enough. He beached his ship, a pathetic wreck burning furiously. It made an unforgettable instruction to the swiftness, noise, tenseness, and savagery of a naval action. Even though many of the shells were hair-raisingly close, I found to my surprise I wasn't scared. I was too busy. Also, we weren't hit, and I had no real idea of the horror it would involve. That was an experience yet to come.' Later that morning, as the sea swarmed with enemy submarines, twenty-five torpedoes were fired at *Aurora*, but by the grace of God, all missed. As the morning progressed, the shadowy outlines of more ships came into view as two other French destroyers tried to escape. 'One of them was a large-funnelled job, the other rather smaller,' Ken remembered. 'At once another life and death fight broke out. Bursting shells spouted up in fountains from the water. Two shells straddled us neatly. But the *Aurora* could do at least 29 knots and Captain Agnew swung her sharply out of the way. When the shell came whistling down, it very nearly scraped the paint from the stern, 20 yards from the control platform. With the help of a British destroyer, the *Boadicea*, we knocked out the small French ship. The larger one fled for cover behind a promontory of rock, pulling down an enormous umbrella of thick black smoke over her. And that took care of the naval operation at Oran.'

Lieutenant Paymaster E. J. 'Jock' Offord, a gunnery officer and Kenny's cabin mate for two years, remembered Admiral Sir Andrew

Cunningham, the Naval Commander of the Expeditionary Force, came on board the following morning glowing with praise for the crew. 'Also, we had two American correspondents and a *Times* man (Ure) and (Ken) More gave them a story,' he noted in a letter home. 'As they were leaving, they asked More and I to look them up. That evening Sam and I and More looked them up and of course we had a terrific evening. Incidentally, we were to have gone home but the captain saw Cunningham and said he thought it a black show to send us home (to Scapa) when there was fighting to be done, so we are still in the warm.'[10]

In fact, the crew availed themselves of an opportunity to revel in the luxury of Algiers, an 'Aladdin's cave' where Ken bought lipsticks, stockings, and perfumes – presumably for Beryl – before *Aurora* was elevated to the flagship of the 10th Cruiser Squadron under Sir Cecil Harcourt and began targeting Rommel's supply lines between Sicily and Tripoli. Using Bone in Algeria as a base, she led 'Q Force', with the *Sirius*, *Argonaut*, *Quiberon* and *Quentin*. It was an effective outfit – and sank two Nazi destroyers and four troop carriers, and, thereafter, *Aurora* was continually dive-bombed. On one occasion, Douglas H. J. Hardy, a cameraman for *British Paramount News*, was on board during a German attack. 'Well, I remembered it very well, because it was a terrifying moment,' Ken explained. 'Our anti-aircraft armament had been knocked out and we couldn't shoot back. Then he (Hardy) said to me, "shove up a bit", so I shoved up a bit and where my head would have been his head was! And a piece of shrapnel came through the ship's side and took a lump out of his head instead of mine! And when I looked round, he was all covered in blood and I said, "Well you are a bloody fool, that should have been me!"'

Time and again in his life, Ken remained modest about his contribution to the war effort. It was not the case, as he insisted years later, that he was a 'hopeless gunner' – stories were often invented for comedy effect. In another yarn, he claimed to be the 'only man who ever succeeded in shooting down one of our own planes' after the invasion of North Africa. 'I thought it was a German FW109. But there was a happy ending. The pilot broke his leg and came on board. The broken leg gave him six months in Blighty!' The tale is, alas, nonsense. There is no documentary evidence that any such incident took place, nor of any blot on his copybook (elements of reality mixed with considerable doses of bravado exist in each version of this story, regaled on countless occasions). In fact, accounts in the archives of the Imperial War Museum tell a different story, with testimony from a senior officer stating that 'If More is interested in something, there's nobody I'd rather have do the job. If he isn't, there's nobody I'd rather not do the job.' More importantly, as an officer, he seems to have been remembered as a fair man by the ratings. For example, Seaman Howard Burris never forgot 'having a quiet cigarette on the mess deck, and I felt a tap on my shoulder and then was asked if I'd "got a light, mate". And I turned round. It was Kenneth More. He said: "Don't let me bloody catch you doing that again!"'[11]

Though now and again he helped arrange sporadic entertainment evenings, and organised occasional Silver Phantom concert parties, Ken tried to keep his profession entirely apart. 'I was a naval officer on active duty and entertainment had no part of it,' he expounded. Nevertheless, his theatrical experience led to a 'very special job' as a commentator. Whenever the ship went into action, he was given a microphone and had to stand on the back of the bridge and describe exactly what was happening. 'If there were torpedo bombers coming on the port side, I had to tell the crew. There is nothing worse than being in the engine room during action – and you're hearing all these explosions – but you don't know what's going on.'[12] Thanks to a wire antenna, the ship was in earshot of the BBC, meaning the crew could hear news from the rest of the world. That summer, over the Tannoy, broadcasts relayed events in what turned out to be a vital turning point in the Second World War. In Europe, where a second front was in the making, Germany was on the defensive fighting an increasingly futile battle against the Soviet Union. Meanwhile, the RAF and US Air Force had established aerial supremacy in Western Europe, making it impossible for German industry to function properly. And in the Pacific, the tide of war was beginning to turn against Japan.

One particularly memorable thing for Ken happened in June 1943 when, after visiting North Africa, King George VI made an impromptu decision to visit Malta. After rearranging his schedule, the monarch was transported to the island onboard *Aurora* and his arrival on Sunday, 20 June 1943 was a day never to be forgotten. At nine o'clock on that glorious summer morning, the sleek grey lines of the *Aurora*, flanked by a destroyer escort and with fighter planes overhead, entered the Grand Harbour at Valetta. 'The Royal Standard fluttered at our main and the King, in full whites, stood on a special saluting platform, just forward of the bridge,' Ken recounted. As *Aurora*'s anchors went down, Malta's church bells rang out a joyous peal.

After the invasion of Sicily, the Germans remained restless on the high seas. Though unaware of it at the time – Ken's future chum, Alec Guinness, was also navigating the dangerous Mediterranean. In letters to his wife, Guinness, a naval lieutenant, gave a vivid – but gruesome – snapshot of life in those treacherous waters. 'I've seen a few dead lads floating about, all blown up, unimaginable,' he wrote. 'One is supposed to go and chop off their identity discs and search their pockets, if any. I simply couldn't.'

Meanwhile, escorting British destroyers reinforcing troops on the island of Leros, *Aurora* was involved in a 'bad fracas' on 30 October 1943 when Nazi Junkers Ju 87 and Ju 88 aircraft attacked her in the Aegean off Castellorizo, causing massive damage when a 500 kg (1,100 lb) bomb hit the funnel. There was a terrific impact, the ship shuddered and was engulfed in clouds of black, acrid smoke and fumes. The explosion and subsequent fire killed forty-seven crew. One of Ken's subordinates, Petty Officer Frank Cowen, flashed a torch into the night and immediately caught a glimpse of dead shipmates. He thought it was a miracle that anybody survived. After the raiders left, Kenny helped clean up the mess. The deceased were buried at sea as the captain and crew looked on. After this bleak episode, the *Aurora* withdrew to Taranto for repairs which lasted until April 1944. Two months later, in June 1944, D-Day saw Allied troops land along the Normandy coastline. From here on, the British and their partners drove the German army back from the beaches of Normandy, across France, through the Low Countries and into the wastelands of Germany.

By Christmas 1944, with victory finally in sight, Kenny cast his eye toward a home posting and successfully volunteered for training as a flight direction officer (FDO). On arriving at the school in Somerset, he was thrilled to discover fellow actor Michael Hordern was his commanding officer. Even better, given his appalling grasp of maths, a dalliance with a young Wren with access to the exam papers ensured he passed with flying colours. After that, the talk was of civvy street, ordinary life, and his longing for it. Hordern recalled Ken worried incessantly about returning to the theatre and pleaded to be sent to a naval base in the British Isles, but 'I had no choice but to send him out to the Far East. He was rather cross about that. He didn't want to be stuck out in the Pacific.'[13] In fact, Ken was beside himself. With little time to spare, he briefly met with his mother, sister Kate and held another unremarkable reunion with Beryl, before boarding the *New Amsterdam* troopship destined for the Red Sea to join HMS *Victorious*, part of the British Fleet in the Indian Ocean and Pacific. Though dispirited, he made the most of his predicament. He explored *Victorious* just as he had *Aurora* – alone, unhurried and with a sense of wonder. This Illustrious-class aircraft carrier had been laid down at the Vickers-Armstrong shipyard at Newcastle in 1937 and, by the time he boarded her, had seen action against the *Bismarck*, taken part in Arctic convoys, and in Operation Pedestal, the British mission to supply Malta. As the flight direction officer, he continued to witness history, and became a participant in the American bombardment of Japan, enduring the nerve-racking wail of projectiles and the crash of bombs. As Hirohito's empire crumbled, the *Victorious* helped neutralise enemy air strength, as the Americans focused on Okinawa. 'It was a fantastic operation, refuelling at sea miles from anywhere,' he recounted. 'In fact, we were 50 days without seeing any land apart from the occasional smudge on the horizon.'

Though he didn't realise the significance at the time, Ken was on duty when atomic bombs obliterated Hiroshima and Nagasaki on 6 August and 9 August respectively.[14] For four days there followed a frightening silence, then, news of Japan's surrender swept through the ship prompting him to join scores of pilots drinking themselves 'silly in a phenomenal party' before stripping naked and hanging from the bulkheads, singing, boozing and 'enjoying every delirious moment'.

After that, there was no real work, as *Victorious* sailed through a non-combatant zone. The crew were bored and some were homesick by the war's end. We are given an outsider's glimpse of life by RAF pilot Donald Chute, a shipmate, who remembered everybody knew Ken because he was such a character who got 'very much involved' in the ship's entertainment. 'He could do anything,' Chute said. 'Perhaps his biggest forte was being able to play the piano so well, if you could sing it, he could play it!'[15] At the end of his impromptu 'concerts', the audience were often invited to perform. One night, a midshipman with a stutter did an impression of Churchill, a watchman warbled 'Happy Days Are Here Again', and two stokers sang a romantic duet to roars of laughter. Ken always finished the show with a rousing rendition of 'God Save the King'. As the end of Ken's war approached, the *Victorious* made a stop in Sydney – where the ship's company took part in the Victory Parade – before finally sailing for home waters, arriving in Portsmouth in late October 1945.

The war had exasperated everyone. At the age of thirty-one, Kenneth More was demobbed with a gratuity of £146 and a 'ghastly orange tweed sports jacket, flannels, shoes, a raincoat, a blue and white tie and a green pork-pie hat'. The conflict, he once confessed, taught him a lot about human emotions. 'I saw dead people and live people, apprehension, joy and fear.'[16] Surviving photos from the period reveal his boyish looks and slender frame remained unchanged, but his eyes showed his age. Again, there was a reunion with Beryl, who had just returned from her own brief adventures with ENSA, but despite warm words and declarations of friendship, there was no romantic rekindling, and, for the sake of peace, they went their separate ways.

4
BREAKTHROUGH

With his marriage in shambles, Kenny persuaded himself that his future lay in London. Using his own savings, bolstered by a demob payment, he opened a bank account, took out a life insurance policy and found digs at a basement flat on Westbourne Grove, not far from Kensington Park, before meeting up with old acquaintances to swap information about securing work. Though victory had left the country insolvent, his transition to civilian life proved seamless, pushed along by a series of lucky encounters. Within fifteen days of arriving in London, Equity directed him to Geoffrey Robinson, a 'useful contact man' who introduced him to Abraham Adolph Dubens, a Ukrainian-born agent representing ex-Forces actors. Hailing from Odessa, Dubens – known as 'Harry' – was an original – having arrived in Britain at the age of fourteen, he embraced the whiff of greasepaint before working as a scenic designer at the Metropolitan Opera House, New York for Oscar Hammerstein, and then joining the Diaghilev company as designer in Paris. By the time he met Ken, he was focused on management and had a knack for discovering and cultivating unknown talent. With young male performers thin on the ground, he specialised in helping demobbed actors get back to work by opening a department to deal with their problems, run by his son, Stanley, a former prisoner-of-war. After a brief meeting, he became Kenneth's agent for all his work and remained so until he died fourteen years later. The two enjoyed a genuine rapport. 'He got me a job in *Crimson Harvest* at the Gateway Theatre, Paddington,' Ken explained, remembering it opened to so-so reviews. 'It was a terrible melodrama, but I had a showy little part! It was my first appearance on the post-war stage.'

There was another bright bit of news. During the run of the show, Michael Barry, later the head of BBC TV drama, approached him to appear in a series of closed-circuit test broadcasts, beginning a long and fruitful association. Back then, television was such a novelty that some actors found it difficult to make the transition, but Kenny proved a willing collaborator performing in dramas at Alexandra Palace, the major production centre for BBC television, where gaffes were seen live. For instance, on one unforgettable occasion, when playing Captain Peter Niles in *Mourning Becomes Electra*, he was required to break an embrace between Marjorie Mars and Andrew Osborn, her passionate suitor. 'The two of them clasped each other, sprang apart when I entered and revealed a ghastly accident. Half of Andrew Osborn's moustache had stuck to Marjorie Mars's upper lip. The result was fantastic. Grotesque. I nearly burst out laughing.' Like a true pro, Mars brushed off her half of the moustache with enormous style, as Osborn 'stormed through the rest of the scene with one hand covering his bare top side of lip'. Thankfully, the audience was tiny – only 1,343 TV Licence-holders lived within range of the London transmitter.

From the outset, the BBC adopted a high culture approach by focusing on solid drama to gain 'cultural legitimacy' on the new medium. In fact, Ken's opening role came in *The Silence of the Sea*, the first play televised after the end of the war, telling of how a French pensioner and his niece showed resistance against the German residents by ignoring the officer who was occupying their house (Ken). His character, a former composer, had dreamt of brotherhood between the French and German nations, but became deluded by Nazi propaganda. As the story progressed, he realised the real goal of Hitler's army was to wreck and exploit. Written by Jean Bruller, the story was first published in France in 1942, much to the irritation of Nazi occupation authorities. The following year, it was released in the United States and by the time of the BBC broadcast, *The Silence of the Sea* had sold more than a million copies. 'It was terrifying,' Ken recalled, certain it would be a one-shot engagement. 'I played the German officer, and it was the only speaking part in a 90-minute transmission.' Interestingly, BBC archives reveal the script was chosen as a 'practice exercise' prior to television's reopening and then – to everyone's surprise – as the main attraction on the big night. Peter Sallis, who later found fame as 'Cleggy' in *Last of the Summer Wine*, saw the live transmission on 7 June 1946. 'It was a very touching and moving play and years later, when I was working with Kenny, I told him that I had seen it, and he could hardly believe it. I think I was the only person, apart from close members of his family, who had ever seen *The Silence of the Sea*.' Thankfully, his performance was good enough to warrant inclusion in the official 'BBC Artists

Index' and he 'went on to do fourteen similar productions for TV during the next three years'.[1] Among them was a starring role in Jan de Hartog's *Death of a Rat*, which the *Tatler* lauded as 'one of the most striking plays of early post-war television' concerning a sick man's hallucinations foreseeing the onset of the atom bomb. 'It was superbly acted by Mr Kenneth More and Miss Rene Ray in the leading parts.' A lighter engagement came playing 'Mr Badger', one of the main characters in A. A. Milne's *The Wind in the Willows*, adapted by Michael Barry. Alan Reid played Toad, Andrew Osborn was Water Rat, and Jack Newmark portrayed Mole; Victor Woolf and John Thomas played Alfred the horse, while Jon Pertwee – who later found fame as Dr Who – starred as the Judge.

He had better exposure when Dubens – trying his hand as a producer with his partner Bill O'Bryen – handed him the part of a vicar in *And No Birds Sing*. The ensemble effort – featuring Elizabeth Allan and Harold Warrender – was greeted warmly in Newcastle, Aberdeen, and Norwich and received a Command Performance in July 1946 before The King and Queen at Edinburgh's Lyceum Theatre. Speaking to reporters that night, Dubens expressed pride that seven cast members were ex-Service people: like Kenny, Warrender had served as lieutenant in the RNVR, Nigel Stock as a major in the Indian Army in Burma, Derek Tansley was a sergeant in the Royal Tank Regiment, Natalie Jordan was in the ATS and Pat Nye was a superintendent in the WRNS. However, despite a promising start, the play closed at London's Aldwych Theatre just three months after failing to find a sufficient audience, a situation caused, in part, by an atrocious winter.

The early months of 1947 experienced the lowest temperatures in years, with foul weather persisting well into March. Six weeks of snow led to thousands of people being cut off, forcing the army to clear roads and railways of snowdrifts. Disheartened by the harsh weather and power outages, the public lacked the motivation to venture outdoors. Somehow, though, *And No Birds Sing* embarked on a second provincial tour, yet Ken was growing despondent, plagued by doubts regarding his own abilities. The press wasn't too encouraging either. *Theatre World* deemed the play entertaining, but failing 'to grip in its entirety because the authors' aim was never made clear'. Desperate to supplement his income, his anxiety was stoked further after he made a brief appearance in *School for Secrets*, a flick about wartime scientists produced by Two Cities Films at Denham Studios. Though audiences found much to admire in the film, Ken didn't. 'Peter Ustinov directed and wrote it,' he explained. 'Dicky Attenborough was the star – a young air force man, and I had a marvellous part, only one snag. I was a bomb aimer in a Lancaster over Berlin and there was an oxygen mask all over my face, all you could see was my two eyes. And the only line I had was, I remember it to this day, "Left a bit, left a bit, steady, bombs away skipper, get the hell out of here." But unfortunately, it sounded as if I was speaking through rows and rows of rhubarb!' Uttering a mouthful of unintelligible dialogue was demoralizing, and as he approached the age of thirty-three, Ken pondered whether he possessed the luck and talent to succeed. At times, he groused freely at Dubens and was beset with nagging doubts about his ability as an agent. However, Dubens prided himself on knowing what was best for Ken; and persuaded Chloe Gibson, a young actress making her directorial debut, to offer him a part in *Power Without Glory* – marking a turning point in his luck. That winter, Gibson secured a cast of unknowns, including Dandy Nichols, Maureen Pook, Beatrice Varley and Dirk Bogarde, a newly demobbed captain, who, Kenny remembered, sat forlornly, smoking, staring at the floor between his legs.

Power Without Glory tells the story of a soldier who returned from the war to find that his fiancée was in love with his brother, who, in turn, was seeing another woman who was later found murdered. After gaining permission to stage the play in The New Lindsay at 81 Palace Gardens Terrace in Notting Hill – a basement venue used most evenings by an Arts Club – rehearsals turned out to be a delight, filled with excitement and anticipation. Despite its dirty appearance, the Lindsay held a certain charm that many performers found hard to resist. In fact, the brief period Ken spent there marked some of the happiest and most fulfilling moments of his career, especially as he shared a dingy dressing room with Bogarde, 'sparsely furnished with a shelf, two wooden chairs, and a washbowl'. Bogarde, he recounted, spoke in quick bursts of conversation, and spent much of his time lamenting his lack of confidence and experience. For his part, Bogarde never forgot Ken turning up for run throughs in an ex-naval overcoat, 'badges of rank long since ripped off, a string bag beside him with a packet of cornflakes and a pint of milk. He'd collected his rations in the break.' Throughout this period, Gibson worked at an intense speed, swiftly moving back and forth from the stage to the stalls, barking directions. And, as the cast established themselves as a tight unit, Dirk – playing the murderer – came into his own as a stage personality; the tense story, it seems, stiffened his spine.

On the first night, 25 February 1947, Bogarde remembered 'not much happened' when the curtain fell, prompting Ken to quietly remark, 'They've all pissed off ...' Then – like a bolt from the blue – 'the place erupted'. Ken celebrated the success by enjoying a brief fling with Dandy Nichols – the actress who later found fame in *Till Death Us Do Part*. They were still 'carrying on' by early April when the play moved to the larger Fortune Theatre. It was there, a critic from the *Daily Mirror* 'sat electrified' before heralding a minor masterpiece:

> Mary Horn, Beatrice Varley, Dandy Nichols, Kenneth More, Dirk Bogarde, Maureen Pook, Trevor Ward. Note these names. They form the full cast of Michael Hutton's *Power Without Glory*, and because all richly deserve a mention I have ensured that they get it. Hutton has written a psychological murder play that might have happened next door, and Chloe Gibson's production helps to make it one of the most moving, most gripping pieces of theatre that we have seen for a long time. Please see this show.[2]

Attracted by the glowing notices, Noël Coward – the most influential name in British theatre – dashed across London to watch a special run-through. 'He was profoundly moved, and his enthusiasm touched me deeply,' producer Peter Daubney reflected years later. So much so, that Coward even wrote an article stating that anyone who 'cared for vital, true, and exciting acting, must see *Power Without Glory*'. It was, he declared, 'a most moving and finely written play and on all counts an enthralling evening in the theatre'. But in these troubled times even such powerful support couldn't stop the play losing money and folding at the end of April. 'We were nevertheless able to keep it going for a limited run of eight weeks,' Daubney explained, before penning a discreet closure announcement for the London papers. 'I was obliged, therefore, to write the venture off as an "artistic" flutter, a gesture which, I hoped, had brought pleasure to the public.' Nonetheless, talk about *Power Without Glory* had been extremely positive in the United States where Lee Shubert, a New York impresario, requested Chloe Gibson retain the entire cast – including Kenneth – for a Broadway run. As all this was taking place, Noël Coward was putting the final touches to his hotly anticipated West End war drama, *Peace in Our Time*. Shrewdly, on hearing about Shubert's plan, Coward offered the entire *Power Without Glory* cast parts in his play. And to his surprise, they all accepted with the exception of Bogarde who had already signed a five-year contract with Wessex Films. 'I never read it, but was told, by him (Coward), in the most intense detail, what it was all about,' Bogarde confessed. 'I privately thought it was pretty frightful but did not say so.' Though disappointed not to have a crack at Broadway, Kenny's enthusiasm for the Coward project was, however, beyond question. He seized the role of George Bourne, a young resistance hero, and recounted 'Coward made it seem as if I'd be doing him a personal favour, I was so overwhelmed at meeting him that I'd have agreed to anything.'[3] The play, as it happened, was his meat, the kind of melodrama with big moments that he had perfected in his years of repertory in Newcastle and Wolverhampton.

Meanwhile, despite stiff setbacks, nothing dampened Gibson's enthusiasm for getting *Power Without Glory* to New York. With Ken, Horn, Varley, Nichols, and Pook all now working for Coward, she was forced to entirely recast and auditioned over 300 actors at her Notting Hill flat. It was October before she got everything arranged. In the end, Lewis Stringer, a well-known radio player, took Kenny's part, and Pete Murray filled the Bogarde role. Sadly, it ran for just thirty-one performances at the Booth Theatre, New York in early 1948, with Gibson directing. 'The press murdered us,' Pete Murray recounted in his memoirs.

Kenny arrived for the first day of rehearsals, on 12 June 1947, thrilled at the opportunity of playing in a Noël Coward production. *Peace in Our Time* is set in The Shy Gazelle, a pub nestled among the mews and squares of Belgravia, and tells the tale of what might have happened had the Nazis occupied Britain in 1940. The pub's regulars, some arty, or a little theatrical, and the cordial publican (Bernard Lee) and his homely wife (Beatrice Varley), gather round the radio set for the nine o'clock news, as was then customary. As Big Ben chimes, the publican's wife remarks, 'It's funny that they can still hear that all over the world.' By this point, the Battle of Britain had been lost, Churchill shot, the royal family interned, and Parliament ceremoniously opened by Hitler.

With time on his hands, Coward had conceived the idea during a holiday in Paris shortly after the Liberation when the city appeared to be unharmed by the horrors of Nazi occupation. It didn't take him long, however, to grasp that, behind the facade, a great deal had changed, 'the sense of immediate relief had faded, and there was an atmosphere of subtle disintegration, lassitude and above all suspicion'. This led him to ponder what would have happened if the Germans had successfully invaded Britain, which they very nearly did. To his surprise, he became consumed by the whole experience.

During a week's try-out of *Peace in Our Time* in Brighton, Kenny received his first exposure of Coward's social whirl, witticisms, and acerbic tongue. He often dined out on the story of a young cast member buttonholing 'The Master' to ask about his chances as an actor. Withering with distain …

> Noël looked at him for a moment, then replied, 'Slender, dear boy, slender. To succeed in this profession, one must have the voice of Laurence Olivier, the looks of Evelyn Laye, and a modicum of my talent. You have none of these things. I suggest you write to Sainsbury's.

After a few chops and changes, warm curtain calls greeted the opening of *Peace in Our Time* at London's Lyric Theatre where critics praised its salty humour, pungent patriotism, suspense, and ugly tragedy. 'It led to everything,' Ken said. 'I will always be indebted to Noël. So many British actors owe their start to him and I'm glad that I'm one of them.'[4] From here on, Coward took a proprietary interest in Kenny's career, and the two remained close. Just prior to rehearsals, Ken had moved to a residence befitting an actor of stature, leaving Westbourne Grove for 'a new pad' at 105A Eaton Terrace Mews, Belgravia, priced at the exorbitant weekly rate of five-and-a-half-guineas. During a little housewarming party, leading lady, Elspeth March, the wife of screen heart-throb Stewart Granger, enquired why he wasn't making films. 'I told her that frankly no one would give me the right chance,' Ken replied. 'Too small, not good-looking enough, the list of reasons was endless.' He was, predictably, infuriated at Ben Lyon, the casting director of Fox, who had cackhandedly confided to Dubens that 'his client' had a face like a 'full moon and hadn't a hope of succeeding in pictures'. Funnily enough, Maude Spector, a well-known casting agent, did occasionally offer bits of work – but, apparently, at a price. Actress Erin Geraghty recounted a story Kenny had told her in 1979. 'When he was young, he and an actor called Geoffrey Keen used to buy silk stockings for Spector,' she explained. 'And she would insist that they rolled the stockings up her legs. That was their casting couch experience. Anything to get the gig. I don't think Geoffrey and Kenny were traumatised by it. I think they thought it was a jolly good wheeze to get cast!'

Back then, actors, Ken theorised, had to look like Stewart Granger to succeed in romantic roles. 'You had to be tall and dark and thin – what I call cigar shaped. There are two types of actors – there is the cigar shape and the square shape – I'm a square. I'm not Rex Harrison,' he explained. 'Therefore, I never got romantic roles. I had two assets to fall back on, comedy and emotion. Women either want to be knocked off their feet by an actor – they want to be pulled into bed by a romantic actor – or they want to take that actor to bed themselves and cuddle him. That's what I call the "small boy" line. I knew I stood much more chance in that direction than in the cigar shaped direction. So, I went for that.'[5]

Ken was enormously pleased with his work in *Peace in Our Time* and thrilled when it transferred to the Aldwych. However, when a gust of rumours quickly spread about the viability of the production, W. A. Darlington, the leading *Telegraph* (and *New York Times*) critic assured his readers the play could not possibly fail. 'It is too moving, too exciting, too deft – and too timely,' he expounded. 'We need to be reminded, just now, that we are people of spirit.' In truth, while this made for good promotion, the reality was that after the initial enthusiasm, the box office recorded a sudden slump and *Peace in Our Time* closed on 14 December 1947 (making way for *Macbeth* with Michael Redgrave in the title role). 'A flop – it came too soon after the war,' Kenny theorised. 'Another one the critics killed. The people who came to see it loved it, but there weren't enough of them.'[6] Dirk Bogarde was blunter, reckoning Coward, the man who once was exuberantly the toast of London, had lost his way. 'His time was over, and it bewildered him greatly.'

Short-lived though it was, the play had far-reaching consequences for Kenneth More. Not least, it led to a cablegram from film producer Michael Balcon who was busily assembling a cast for *Scott of the Antarctic*, an epic portraying Captain Scott's ill-fated expedition to the South Pole. After a screen test at Ealing Studios conducted by Henry Cornelius, Ken landed the part of Lieutenant 'Teddy' Evans. 'It was like striking oil,' he recounted, 'a bit of welcome news in a very difficult period.' This good fortune, he later learned, came after Elspeth March spoke to her husband, Stewart Granger, who then 'bullied John Mills' into giving him a part. The contract stipulated he would earn £20 a day, with a minimum of £500 and was to be on set at 7.30 a.m. and could be required for 'up to 12 hours, possibly longer'. Just prior to shooting, Mills described the project as the most responsible thing he'd ever embarked on. 'I was only about four when the tragedy happened,' he explained, 'but Scott has always been one of my heroes and it's jolly satisfying to feel that the job of helping to bring the great story of British enterprise and grit to the screen has fallen to me.'

Relieved momentarily of financial worries, Kenny spent many hours supping pints with James Robertson Justice, a chap he described as an entirely untheatrical 'mountain of a man' resembling Henry VIII. Playing the role of Petty Officer 'Taff' Evans, Justice carried himself with the air of someone who'd seen a thing or two. During breaks in filming, he claimed to have worked as a gold miner, fruit farmer, lumberjack, insurance salesman, photographer, journalist, and teacher. Around Ealing, he forged a reputation as a 'prize bullshit artist' as his tall tales were so plentiful that biographers still debate his actual place of birth. On one occasion, between takes, Kenny ribbed him by giving a graphic description of an exotic – but fictional – 'blue spotted' butterfly. Though it was a deliberate leg pull, Justice took the bait. With a little devil look, he couldn't resist boasting that his relatives once caught this 'rare species' in Tibet. The laughs provided a distraction from what was a difficult shoot as director Charles Frend tried to create an atmospheric journey through snowdrifts toward the Pole. The cast abhorred the artificial ice mounds created with jagged plaster which caused painful cuts when they stumbled on them, and worse still, synthetic fog triggered violent coughing fits compounded by 'hideous' pellets the actors had to suck to give the impression they were in the bitter cold. In the end, the film was not unpopular, but it was by no means the smash Ealing had anticipated, and it did nothing for Ken's career. And like with *School for Secrets*, he was disappointed – there were a few good shots, but most were obscured by his beard and goggles. 'It was a big prestige film, and although I was paid £500 for it, it did me no good at all. We all looked the same, 14 Johnny Millses huddled up in beards and snow.' He also believed the script wasn't up to scratch. 'Scott was a bad film – despite John Mills' magnificent performance – and certainly it was not the happiest to work on.' Mills disagreed. In fact, in his memoirs he opined that Ken had made such a 'marvellous impression' that he was sure 'one day he would become a highly successful actor'. Conversely, at this point, such a prospect looked extremely remote.

During a long period of idleness, Ken found time for a brief visit to meet old friends in Wolverhampton, including Beryl. When they amicably divorced two years earlier, she had won custody of their child and Ken agreed to stay out of his daughter's life until she was fifteen. 'Susan had a new father,' he reasoned. 'She owed her first love and loyalty to him.' In fact, the new father was Arthur Hewlett, the actor Beryl had been briefly engaged to in 1939. Looking back at this period, Beryl once said it was obvious even then, that Ken would eventually enjoy great success. 'He was a very good actor – and the pushing type. I'm afraid I'm not the pushing type at all. Throughout my life other people have pushed me forward.'[7] Elaborating, she added, 'I had a daughter to bring up and I didn't want to leave her for too long. My home is in Cheltenham and playing in repertory in the Midlands suited me domestically.'[8]

One of the first things Ken did on returning to London was to meet director Lawrence Huntington, who was casting an eye around for his forthcoming feature for the Associated British Picture Corporation. It was a good meeting, and just after celebrating his thirty-fourth birthday, he found himself back before the camera in *Man on the Run*, an action flick with Derek Farr as a deserter on the run only to be discovered by Newman (Ken), an ex-corporal from his old regiment, who demanded 'hush money'. He threw himself wholeheartedly into the role and in his few minutes of screen time, revealed a dark nastiness that he rarely had a chance to display. Luckily, it led to another unsavoury character part in Anatole de Grunwald's *Now Barabbas*, the 'inside story of the men inside – and the women who put them there!' The unusual title refers to a character from the Bible who was picked over Jesus by the crowd in Jerusalem to be pardoned and released. In another notable departure from his cheery style, Ken pops up several times as Spencer, a small-time pickpocket masquerading as an RAF officer. On set, he struck up a friendship with actor Richard Burton, who shared his love for whisky-soaked nights at a pub near Teddington Studios. Occasionally, Burton's flatmate, Stanley Baker joined the fun, and equalled Burton in his reputation for drinking and appetite for the fairer sex. After *Barabbas*, to his joy, Kenny's kitty was boosted by two days' work playing a policeman in *Stop Press Girl*, a tissue-thin yarn about a teenager with a strange power to stop machinery, a flick best remembered for bringing Sally Ann Howes to the public's attention. Another bit-part followed in *For Them That Trespass*, starring Richard Todd.

During this time, Kenny enjoyed a close attachment to Elspeth March, who was by now recovering from a split with her husband, Stewart Granger. It is more than probable that they were enmeshed in a chaste affair, and were often spotted holding hands at Caprice, sparking a gust of rumours.[9] While this made for good gossip, the nature of the mutual attraction between the thirty-five-year-old Kenny and the thirty-eight-year-old March was most likely nothing more than shared common interests. A graduate of the Central School of Speech and Drama, she was known for her wicked humour and sense of adventure. In fact, during the war, she suspended her acting career to drive an ambulance for the American Red Cross, dispensing 'coffee and doughnuts, love and friendship' all over England in a converted Green Line bus. According to her own account, she had a hair-raising time navigating the vehicle along winding country lanes and narrowly missing exploding shells during air raids, but recalled feeling no qualms about being hit by bombs, feeling safe in her insulated driving cab as long as she kept moving! With the completion of *For Them That Trespass*, they saw more of each other, and it's likely March encouraged him to test for the part of a foreman in the comedy-cum-drama *Chance of a Lifetime*, a commentary on 1940s' Britain – highlighting unionism, socialism, and strikes. Kenny never forgot walking up Regent Street to meet the director, Bernard Miles, a man known for playing rural-type character roles. Thinking he didn't stand much of a chance, he sauntered into Miles's office in an open-necked shirt, flannel slacks, and bomber jacket. 'When I happened to breeze in, looking as if I'd just come off a machine shop floor, he decided in my favour,' Ken recounted. For Miles,

Chance of a Lifetime was a very personal project. He wrote the script in collaboration with Walter Greenwood (*Love on the Dole*) and, after scouring the country for a location, chose to conduct the entire eight-week shoot in the Cotswolds during March and April 1949.

Based on the mood of a nation blighted by austerity, the story essentially traces factory life in post-war Britain. Not enough pay, a hard-driving management, ineffective union officials and the dismissal of a worker serves to provoke a brief strike that leads to the workers running the factory. Basil Radford plays the owner of an agricultural implement factory, while Kenny – looking like the boy next door – gave a sympathetic performance as a keen young foreman rising to unexpected heights. Most of the other actors chosen for the ensemble were relatively unknown, although some – including Hattie Jacques, Geoffrey Keen and Patrick Troughton – went on to a certain measure of stardom. Even Compton Mackenzie, the novelist best known for *Whisky Galore* and *The Monarch of the Glen*, made an unexpected appearance as the banker. Sadly, though, during filming, the cast witnessed Radford bathed in alcohol, shaking, stuttering, and fluffing lines. 'It wasn't an easy film to make,' Ken explained. 'There were 27 takes for one scene.' Only with the aid of Scotch was Radford able to perform. 'Then he was ebullient. There was not one false note.' In fact, his powerful performance was as impressive as the picture that surrounds it, and Kenny recalled an extremely happy film, which earned him a fee of £1,250. 'There was no quibbling about overtime,' he said. 'Never has a unit been more loyal to the director. Bernard is a truly remarkable man. He has a knack of getting the best out of everyone. The finished product wasn't a bad little picture; we had worked hard and felt pleased with ourselves.' However, in an unusual twist, because of its stark socialist theme, *Chance of a Lifetime* was turned down by all the big distributors. Eventually, Harold Wilson, then the chairman of the Board of Trade, persuaded the cabinet to approve the film's release, using the 1948 Film Act to ensure it was shown on the major cinema circuit, in this case the Odeon.

Possibly because the public was so tired of politics, *Picturegoer* described a 'clumsy and self-conscious piece of work' and, with a minimum of tact, declined to promote it. Most damningly, *The Daily Film Renter*, an industry journal, thought it propaganda to encourage the idea that 'the workers should also be the bosses'. The public, it added, 'does not regard soap-box sermons as entertainment'. A few newspapers were kind, including the *Daily Herald*'s Paul Holt who thought Radford as the deposed boss was 'the best that I've seen so far this year'. Sadly, *Chance of a Lifetime* sank without a trace, despite being selected by the British Film Academy as one of the movies of the year. 'After that,' Ken said, 'I was teetering on the brink of absolute disaster. I couldn't get a job. Nobody wanted me. I even considered re-joining the navy. I needed some kind of work to prove that I was still an actor.' Privately, among other anxieties, he feared Dubens was adopting a cocky habit of demanding too much for his services, thinking it was a good business strategy. Another blow around this time came when director Roul Walsh rejected him for a part in *Captain Horatio Hornblower*. Utterly disillusioned and demoralised, it proved to be the final straw. Though he never alluded to this in either of his memoirs, Kenny decided to throw in the towel and move to Australia under an emigration scheme calling for British workers. During this time, thousands of ex-servicemen, disinclined to return to their old jobs or struggling to find new ones, took up government offers to carve out new careers in the Dominions. And Kenneth More – it seems – was one of them, but just twenty-four hours before his scheduled departure for Melbourne, an encounter at the Caprice with actor Bernard Braden changed everything. Elspeth March, who was present, recounted events for Braden's memoirs. 'I remember it only too well. Kenny had his one-way ticket to Australia and was supposed to leave the next day,' she explained. 'We were having a farewell evening. First, we went to the theatre to see *A Streetcar Named Desire* then on to dinner. While we were sitting there you (Braden) and Barbara came in, and Kenny said we should pay our respects. After our long conversation you left and Kenny said, "That settles it. I'm not leaving." Wish I could tell you he tore up the ticket, but he didn't. He needed the refund.'[10]

In the event, work soon arrived with small part in *Morning Departure*, a John Mills epic about a muster of Royal Navy sailors facing death at a depth of fifteen fathoms in a sunken submarine. Again, like in *Scott of the Antarctic*, it is almost certain the job was fixed by Elspeth March, who happened to be the oldest friend of Mary Hayley Bell, the wife of John Mills. The pair had attended Sherborne School for Girls together and remained close ever since.

Morning Departure tells how the sub heads out to sea on a routine operation off the coast of Britain. However, shortly after diving, she hits an old floating mine, igniting two huge blasts leaving her bow and stern destroyed. With twelve crewmen alive in watertight compartments, she slowly sinks to the ocean floor. And then begins the melodrama of waiting for rescue and of testing the crew. Describing it as 'an exercise in Britishness and stoicism', director Roy Ward Baker – a realistic storyteller – chose Nigel Patrick to play the first lieutenant; Richard Attenborough as a young stoker who goes crazy with claustrophobia, and James Haytor as a happy-go-lucky cook. 'I kept my feet dry,' Ken recounted. 'I wasn't in the thick of the action – or even onboard the submarine – I did a few onshore scenes with Bernie Lee. But it provided a very good shop window for me, especially being in uniform and with the publicity it later received.' Indeed, as the *Evening Standard* noted, the agony of the trapped sailors was shared by the audience: 'Oh, the gentleness of the Englishmen in peril! It would be interesting to hear how a foreigner would react if confronted with a dialogue so charged with unspoken undertone, with silences so simple, and yet so complicated.' The paper said it revived in any doubting mind 'the sure knowledge that there are no people on earth as dear and wonderful as the British'. Remarkably, the film was nearly shelved when the Royal Navy's HMS *Truculent* sank in the Thames in vaguely similar circumstances in January 1950, just months before the planned release. 'The tragedy of the *Truculent* made us very concerned about the impact of our screen story on the public,' producer Jay Lewis said. 'But the censor has passed it.' Most papers praised the films terrifying psychological realism, adding it was impossible to watch without thinking of the sixty-four *Truculent* men who lost their lives. As a tribute to the bravery of Royal Naval personnel, the film opened with the following prologue:

> This film was completed before the tragic loss of H.M.S. *Truculent*, and earnest consideration has been given as to the desirability of presenting it so soon after this grievous disaster. The producers have decided to offer the film in the spirit in which it was made, as a tribute to the officers and men of H.M. Submarines, and to the Royal Navy of which they form a part.

5
THE EMERGING STAR

In later life Ken tended to suggest that he was still little known in 1950. In fact, the new year was scarcely underway before he landed a plum part in *The Way Things Go*, a Frederick Lonsdale comedy starring Glynis Johns, Michael Gough and Ronald Squire, an actor famed for playing upper-crust types. Though underwhelmed by the story – an Edwardian era yarn about a bankrupt aristocratic family facing the prospect of working for a living – the production signalled the beginning of Kenny's long love affair with the West End. Strangely enough, he had been turned down for the role a month earlier by Lonsdale. As the story goes, even before being able to utter a word of greeting before the audition, the author swiftly dismissed him, stating that he was 'not a suitable candidate'. Ken recounted standing in silence, utterly speechless. The encounter ended abruptly, leaving him bewildered as he was escorted from the room after a mere thirty seconds. In the end, Lonsdale hired Edmund Purdom, but during rehearsals, Purdom failed to deliver a comic performance.

Then, in a panic, he summoned Ken to take his place. An urgent telegram sent to Dubens read, 'Can Kenny come immediately to take over part of John. Stop. Agree to terms thirty-five pounds a week.'

Though Michael Gough privately 'never rated Ken as very good actor', he applauded his strikingly athletic performance as Squire's nephew and, before long, the two became firm chums.[1] And by the time the play had found a rhythm, Ken and Squire also became good friends. Born in Tiverton in 1886, Squire was an actor who could set off the fireworks 'without appearing to even notice them', a critic once noted. Having quit his job as a journalist for the stage, he quickly found his footing as one of the best light comedians in the country. 'Ronnie taught me a lot about comedy,' Ken explained, recalling how on one occasion, Squire – twenty-nine years his senior – advised him to 'throw the ball about a bit' on stage – meaning to make sure everybody, even the smallest characters, got a chance to shine. 'I've always stuck to it. It would be absolute nonsense to do otherwise because the audience needs a complete picture.' Inevitably, Squire became a role model of sorts, and his magisterial voice lent weight, at least vocally, to the aristocratic figures he often portrayed. He went out of his way to plug *The Way Things Go* and was in 'full voice' at the London opening in March 1950 when Mary, the eighty-three-year-old Queen Mother, 'dressed all in white, diamonds flashing … sipping a cocktail' received a tremendous reception from the Phoenix audience. After stepping out to take their bows, the cast were also treated to backstage visits from Tyrone Power and Stewart Granger. Even better, *The Spectator* called it a dexterous and entertaining comedy exhibiting Lonsdale's old mastery

The Emerging Star

of the theatre. 'The whole cast make the most of the plentiful opportunities which the author has given them.'

The only dark spot on Ken's horizon came when news arrived from Wales of Edith's death; she was just sixty, the doctor said it was probably coronary thrombosis. At the cremation, he saw the 'most dreadful final curtain anyone can have'. It was probably his idea to bury her ashes in the hills near Cardiff, not far from Landaff, a gesture typical of his sentimentality. For the next two days, in a cold drizzle, Ken and Kate revisited the places their mother had lived and grown up. He was fractionally cheered up back in London after enjoying several quick infatuations, followed by a 'heavy affair' with a vivacious married woman (known as Barbara, not her real name) – who he considered 'fair game', given 'an estrangement' from her husband. (Ken asserted his 'rather elastic code' prevented him from interrupting a happy marriage.) Other distractions included playing Willy Shepley, a secret service agent in *The Clouded Yellow* alongside Trevor Howard and Jean Simmons – both stars at the local box office. It was a credible picture, with Simmons portraying a suspected murderess and Howard helping her elude the police. The job involved location filming in Liverpool and the Lake District – assignments Kenny squeezed in between Phoenix performances. Financial advantages aside, he got a kick out of sharing drinks with the stars and thought Simmons a 'beautifully unspoilt young lady', and Howard had 'none of that condescension that a star could have shown me in my smaller part'. He was far from idle in the following weeks, appearing, briefly, at Elstree in *The Franchise Affair*, a low-budget thriller starring Michael Denison, dismissed by *The New York Times* as an 'hour and a half of sheer boredom, unrelieved by any action or surprise'. Another 'spit and cough' role followed in *The Galloping Major* with Basil Radford, the first independent feature made by Henry 'Corny' Cornelius, the South African who had conducted his screen test for *Scott of the Antarctic*. On set, Corny was sympathetic toward Radford, who still sought solace in alcohol, but remained charming. Though the all-star cast, including Janette Scott and Jimmy Hanley, spun a funny yarn about residents of a London backwater clubbing together to buy a racehorse to enter for the Derby, the critics weren't thrilled by the picture. Watched today, it retains a grainy appeal, but sadly, Radford didn't live much longer and died at St George's Hospital, Westminster, in October 1952 from liver failure due to cirrhosis.

Back in the West End, Ken needed no convincing to extend his contract on *The Way Things Go*, which continued to be a happy production. 'When anybody is lucky enough to have a bit of success in life, all one's friends and acquaintances claim to have put you on the road or had a share in your discovery,' he pontificated. 'But I really think it was just a question of hard slogging paying off, you know – going from strength to strength, ever so little perhaps, year after year. *The Way Things Go* gave me a chance to play comedy. I think that probably opened new fields for me.' New pastures also opened in his personal life when he met 'a slim, delightfully elegant woman' who introduced herself as 'Bill'. Sensitive to using her real name – Mabel Edith Barkby – she explained that 'Bill' was a childhood nickname, which 'had fortunately' stuck. Sleek, and impeccably tailored, she had just divorced after her husband – Arnold Barkby – petitioned for dissolution, alleging she deserted him. It seems she had much to offer Ken. She was well-travelled, educated, an experienced hostess, and extremely wealthy. Her family itself also provided a fascinating background. During research for this book, it became clear that this five-foot-five brunette probably used the name 'Bill' to disguise her connection with her late father, Frederick William Porter, a roguish businessman who shot himself in 1942 leaving an estate valued at £574,029. A series of ugly headlines revealed his fortune was made by Admiralty contracts and his suicide occurred during police enquiries into his company, mainly involving fraud and conspiracy. To her horror, Mabel's name was splashed in the papers when it transpired her father had been swindling the government by dishonestly charging for wages for more men than were employed, making a fortune in the process. On one occasion, he stuffed £10,000 into a bank deposit box telling Mabel, 'It was for emergencies.' In the end, his crimes led to the conviction of several others and prompted a judge to remark: 'Porter, no doubt, was as wicked a man as ever lived in Liverpool and a very rich man.'[2] For that reason – the name Mabel Edith Barkby never appeared in print again. There is no record of whether the scandal made its way to Kenny's ears, but it is more than likely given his ensuing friendship with Bill's brother, Cyril.

Though two years his senior, Bill's combination of sophistication, wealth and lifestyle proved irresistible: 'That was the start of a relationship that was to become very dear to me,' Ken said. Presumably, his dalliance with the unhappily married 'Barbara' had fizzled by the time he turned on his famous charm for his new infatuation. Before long, they were seen everywhere – at fine restaurants like Caprice and at the best parties. They even started spending Sundays together, enjoying a few rounds of golf, a pastime she bore courageously. By the time *The Way Things Go* packed up on 15 July 1950, they were 'going steady'. So steady, in fact, that she was invited to Denham studios to watch him perform a small uncredited part as a navigator in Nevil Shute's bestseller *No Highway in the Sky*, a film drama about a scientist convinced a new plane would crash after travelling a certain distance, starring James Stewart, Marlene Dietrich and Glynis Johns. The picture was especially memorable, Ken said, because it marked the first time he'd had a canvas chair with his name painted on it. Dietrich had the role of Monica Teasdale, the glitzy Hollywood star; Stewart played Theodore Honey, the aeronautical boffin who realises, while the plane is over the Atlantic, that it could lose its tail through metal fatigue; Glynis was Marjorie Corder, a pretty air hostess, and Kenny had the smallish part of Dobson, the co-pilot. Also featuring in the film were Jack Hawkins and Janette Scott. Production hit many setbacks, including when every airline refused to lend a plane – fearful of the dreadful publicity of being associated with a disaster movie. So, at the last minute, a wooden fuselage was crafted from plywood and for the location shots, a full-sized prototype of a passenger plane was knocked together on the airstrip at Blackbushe Airport in Hampshire. Ken remembered James Stewart as being 'easy-going but reserved' and 'the German' Dietrich – 'full up with penicillin to ward off a cold' – turning up wearing Dior, mink, and smoking cigarettes 'through special holders'. To prevent getting a chill, she wore gossamer panties made of angora wool.

The Emerging Star

The production posed no problems other than spending 'endless hours' sitting in a mock cockpit at Denham, the UK's largest studio. 'Kenny was great fun,' remembered fellow 'aviator' Pete Murray. 'He played the co-pilot and always seemed to be climbing into the cockpit of the aircraft and making 'vroom-vroom' noises like a kid with his first toy racing car.' In contrast, filming proved an unhappy experience for Stewart, who was recovering from an appendectomy. 'The poor man was far from fit and looked done in, but he carried on without a grumble,' Ken recounted, saying Stewart's mood wasn't helped by Dietrich's attempts to hog the best shots to compensate for her dull, secondary part. Stewart's wife Gloria, thought the German's problem was that she was so much the ageing film star that even the character Jim played didn't fall in love with her, 'he fell for the stewardess, who was much younger and prettier'. The past few years hadn't been particularly kind to Dietrich whose fortunes were on a downward slope. She genuinely felt she didn't have enough exciting or impressive scenes. As a result, Ken later told author Michael Munn, her frustration materialised with difficult behaviour, including 'an episode' during a bitterly cold location shoot in December at Blackbushe, when she held up production:

> James Stewart had come out of hospital and gamely stood and froze with the rest of us, waiting for Marlene Dietrich to come out of her trailer. She always had to look absolutely perfect, and as soon as she stepped out into the wind, her hair, which was pretty well lacquered anyway, would blow out of place and she had to go back inside. Finally, Jimmy said, 'This has gone on for long enough,' and he strode over to her trailer and went inside. About

five minutes later, he reappeared with Marlene in tow. I have no idea what he said to her, but it worked; it got her out so we could get on with the scene. Marlene wasn't a bitch, but she did think only of herself.

In this rancid soup, filming plodded on until 26 January 1951. Years later, he again reminisced about 'what a nasty German cow she (Dietrich) was and what a difficult old bat she was'. In the end, for all the expense and effort, the film performed poorly at the box office, despite a handful of glowing reviews. On the plus side, the monetary shortfalls and anxieties Ken had experienced during the 1940s were over and done by 1951. His salary was rising steadily, and there was more film work. He was distraught to miss out on the plum part of Flight Lieutenant 'Batchy' Salter in the RAF drama *Angels-One-Five,* after being tied to playing Lionel Fallaize in *Appointment with Venus*, a wartime yarn about a plan to pinch a pedigree cow from underneath the noses of the Nazis, shot on the craggy isle of Sark (standing in for the fictitious island of Armorel) in April 1951. His character, a gentle, pacifist painter, enjoyed a few memorable scenes, including a pivotal moment when he was slapped by a thuggish German sergeant, named Vogel. With wet eyes, he glared at his abuser: 'What a very nasty child you must have been Mr Vogel. And still are for that matter.'

Though the Channel Islands sojourn was brief, he revelled in the jovial atmosphere under the direction of Ralph Thomas, who later enjoyed success with the *Doctor* farces. There was certainly plenty of adventure. At the hotel, the film's star David Niven claimed he was cohabiting with a spirit as a mischievous ghost scattered his belongings around his room. 'The owner of the place confirmed that an active poltergeist was said to be in the room, and I was inclined to believe her,' Ken said. Aside from the unearthly happenings, the Sark air, he remembered, 'was like champagne' allowing the crew to booze all night and be on location the following day 'feeling and looking fresh'. The only sour note came after the shoot when Niven – enduring a slump in his faltering career – ordered Kenny's best scene be cut, fearing unwelcome competition. It is unclear which scene was cut, but it is likely Thomas shot a longer fight sequence between Kenny and his German abuser later in the picture – in the final print, the confrontation lasts a few seconds. Speaking years later, Bill said she was appalled. 'Everyone says how wonderful David was, and he was to his friends,' she told Niven's biographer Graham Lord. 'He was a most amusing man and a wonderful friend to the people he liked, and at first he and Kenny were bosom friends, but my husband was a beautiful comedy actor, as good as David was, and although he was just beginning his career, he was competition.'

Back on the mainland, Ken's disappointment was compounded after being rejected for a part in David Lean's *Sound Barrier*. Finally, his luck changed during July when work started at Southall Studios on *Brandy for the Parson*, a tepid comedy about a couple getting unwittingly involved with a French smuggling racket run by Tony Rackham, a man of loud words, played by Kenny. Made by the government-financed Group 3, the project was intended to unearth new filmmakers, trying to prove that good full-length feature films could be made on sensible budgets. Unsure at first, Ken finally agreed for a flat fee of

£750 – a princely sum for an emerging talent. He was, however, disappointed that the shoestring budget of £40,000 meant Torquay would depict a French seaside town, meaning there would be no foreign locations. Interestingly, as the project took shape, an unknown young actress named Audrey Hepburn was considered to play the lead. 'Although Audrey loved our script, she soon received another tempting offer of a musical picture to be shot in Monte Carlo,' scriptwriter Alfred Shaughnessy remembered. 'Because our budget had not yet been agreed by the National Film Finance Corporation, my bosses, Group 3, would not allow me to contract her for *Brandy for the Parson*. So, we lost one future star, but gained another in the relatively unknown Kenneth More, who had his name over the title on *Brandy* for the first time in his career, which pleased him a lot.' While most pictures of the time took a few months to shoot, *Brandy* was filmed in seventeen days covering four weeks, including a weekend break. Unsurprisingly, the actual filming was a terrible botch: poorly photographed, and shot with none of the visual spirit of Ken's first few films. Within a fortnight of wrapping, it was edited and ready for distribution. Despite its flaws, the finished picture garnered emphatically mixed reviews. 'Mark the names of James Donald, Kenneth More and Jean Lodge,' the *Fulham Chronicle* enthusiastically advised. 'You will be hearing more of them in the future.' However, the critic for the *Tatler* put his finger on one of the film's inherent flaws – it wasn't very funny and didn't contain a single memorable sequence. 'The best thing about the British film, *Brandy for the Parson*, is its title,' he grumped. Though not without merit, even Kenny conceded it could have had more laughs, but revelled in being 'treated like a star' for the first time which made him feel 'on top of the world'. To the public at large, however, he was still almost entirely unknown, and like after *Scott of the Antarctic*, despite all the publicity, there was no immediate flood of offers.

Then came his break. It was stroke of luck on the golf course that changed everything. It all happened at the eighteenth hole during a natter with Jeremy Hawk and Roland 'Roly' Culver sometime in December 1951. The latter, lighting-up, casually mentioned that Ken might be the right fit for the role of a 'young air force type' in Terence Rattigan's new melodrama *The Deep Blue Sea*, set to feature Peggy Ashcroft. In the play – presented by H. M. Tennent, the biggest theatrical producers in Britain – tensions are established immediately with the discovery of Hester Collyer in her flat, after a botched suicide attempt. Her life lay in ruins after she had left her husband, a High Court judge, for a boozy former RAF pilot, Freddie Page. At first, their relationship was passionate, but his ardour soon cooled, leaving her desperate.

The playwright, Roly explained, had an eye toward casting Jimmy Handley for the Freddie Page part, but remained undecided. Duly, he put in a 'good word' with Rattigan. 'I was very insistent,' Culver recounted in his memoirs, adding the role was 'tailor made' for Ken and 'they would arrange an audition the following week'. When it happened, the try-out turned out to be a disaster, when Kenny – suffering from a bout of nerves and fiddling with notes – read the lines like a bad actor having a 'pot at Hamlet'. Yet, Rattigan saw potential and, a few weeks later, arranged a second audition at his flat in Chester Square. In preparation, Kenny knocked back two stiff drinks and producer Frith Banbury, who was initially sceptical, was persuaded, though privately unsure. However, during rehearsals, he helped his young star develop a talent for creating 'bits of business' – displaying downturned lips, doleful eyes or flicking his cigarette butt on to the floor to show nonchalance. When Ken found something that worked, he memorised it and added it to his 'acting armoury'. 'I gained many new experiences,' he admitted, 'and tried many new things.' A few weeks later, as the year 1952 got underway, the play had its world premiere at Brighton's Theatre Royal prior to a big, old-fashioned West End opening at the Duchess.

The play's London opening was magnificent. Writing in *The Guardian*, Philip Hope-Wallace observed it was greeted with 'that unmistakable hush with which a first night audience, though calloused by current trash, still knows how to honour a finely written and superbly acted piece of emotional drama'. Much to Rattigan's relief, Kenny carried his role off beautifully, playing the young pilot brimming with sexuality but failing to fully return Ashcroft's passion. In fact, the More-Ashcroft pairing turned out to be inspired, and even Kenneth Tynan, one of the great theatre critics of the period, thought it a 'most absorbing' production. 'In Kenneth More, we have acquired an actor who may become our best retort to Marlon Brando, with the same doubting proviso: can he do anything else?' The *Daily Mirror* hailed a play of 'distinction', while the author of the syndicated 'London Notes' thought Ashcroft gave the performance of her life. It is difficult for even the hardened playgoer, the scribe observed, 'not to be moved by the deep intensity of her acting'. Furthermore, 'Kenneth More, as the waster, Roland Culver as the husband and Peter Illing as the broken ex-doctor who encourages her to live give perfect support.' Even Noël Coward noted in his diary that it was a beautiful production superbly played. 'Peggy Ashcroft perfectly wonderful – Kenneth More, Roland Culver, all impeccable.' Kenny couldn't believe what he was reading. 'I had to pinch myself,' he later recalled. 'It was magnificent.' So, the young actor who'd been reluctantly signed after a second audition became absolutely the hottest thing in London. But stage success did not make him blasé – far from it. He was happy to accept thirteen days' work playing a warm-hearted father in *Yellow Balloon*, a psychological drama about a boy made to believe he has murdered his friend. Though a small role, it proved an exceptionally pleasurable experience and introduced him to J. Lee Thompson, a director who later played an important part in his career. He also struck up a friendship with Kathleen Ryan, who portrayed his wife. 'She was an adorable girl,' he gushed. Ryan had been discovered just a few years earlier by Carol Reed and placed in *Odd Man Out*, the noir classic with James Mason and Robert Newton. 'Kath was a typical Irish girl. Talented, funny, and sweet tempered. We had great fun making that picture, but we were both stunned when censors gave it an X-certificate,' which, he recounted, 'shook us more than somewhat.' The fact that no person under the age of sixteen was admitted to screenings meant that even the child star of the film, Andrew Ray, was not allowed to see it. Although some of its thunder was stolen by the censors, it still managed to earn well at the box office and was praised as one of the finest British pictures that year. 'Altogether this is a tightly packed parcel,' the *Evening Post* noted. 'It is delivered with no time wasting and stamped with an X-certificate which here stands for excitement rather than excess sex.'

Kenny's workload briefly increased with a series of new rehearsals at the Duchess when Celia Johnson replaced Peggy Ashcroft in September 1952 and offered a fresh take on Hester Collyer. 'I had got used to Peggy Ashcroft's lips being in a certain place when I had to kiss her,' he said. 'Then Celia Johnson took over the role. She's much taller. It was disconcerting at first to find her face on a different level. You put your face in one place to be kissed and you find hers is somewhere else. But you get used to it. I'm very adaptable.' Johnson – who defined the refined, middle-class housewife – had shot to national fame alongside Trevor Howard in *Brief Encounter* a decade earlier. However, by this point, she was acting sporadically while her children were growing up, preferring to devote her attention to home life. Frith Banbury thought she provided 'a sense of utter desolation which tore at one's heart' and was devastated when she left the role after just five months. Googie Withers, exhibiting her own brand of subtlety and sorrow, replaced Johnson on the stage and in a special television version of the play.[3] It was hardly unexpected when the telecast raised the issue of broadcasting the 'sordidness of real life', resulting in a bookings surge after scenes showing Hester attempting to gas herself aired, despite 'strong calls' to tone it down. The scene was so shocking that the then-righteous BBC placed a stiff religious epilogue at the end of the play, presented by Canon Bryan Green. 'It was the equivalent of stationing a preacher in the foyer of a theatre as the audience is leaving,' the *Birmingham Mail* opined. However, such controversies were a blessing for a show. 'That certainly helped put bottoms on seats,' Ken mused. 'We were thrilled about it.' To his further surprise, amid all this, Dubens secured an audition for a small but pivotal role in *Never Let Me Go*, a derring-do Cold War thriller with pretensions of Hitchcock, designed as a showcase for its American star, Clark Gable, set to be shot at Elstree. From the outset, Gable expressed unease about the 'crummy story' depicting him sneaking behind the Iron Curtain to rescue his captive bride and deliver her to a life of freedom and happiness in America. But despite his misgivings, he was too busy pursuing Gene Tierney, the leading lady, to make any serious complaints.

At Ken's first meeting with Gable, ostensibly the audition, the American looked him up and down, and handed him the role of Steve Quillan, a Moscow-based radio journalist. Though Dubens negotiated a plump contract, Ken found dashing between the film studio and the theatre exhausting. 'Even with my strong constitution I found it far too much,' he told journalist Neville Nisse. 'It was terribly difficult to concentrate on either role and even though I fought against it, I cracked up inside. I felt rough for nearly three years afterwards.' In fact, visiting the cast backstage one night at the Duchess, Charlie Chaplin was 'quite horrified' to hear about him appearing in films and on stage at the same time. 'He took my hand,' Ken said, 'placed it on my heart and made me swear that I wouldn't do the two together again.'

After filming wrapped, Ken prayed *Never Let Me Go* might open doors to America but, again, was left scratching for answers when his big scene was deleted. Perhaps, he pondered, the American felt upstaged? After experiencing David Niven's insecurities, he was not totally surprised. 'When Clark Gable had my scene cut out of his movie it made a nonsense of the whole story because that scene was a key point,' he recalled. 'And what on earth could I have done to Clark Gable? I was no threat.' So, in a period when Gable suffered a stack of misfires, *Never Let Me Go* proved no exception. Adding embarrassment, critics and preview audiences thought it too comical to take seriously. In fact, the flick was so far out of the mainstream that it died outright. 'The Russians are so remarkably naive and stupid,' *The Sketch* observed, while 'the Western Allies are so comfortingly bold and clever.' Worse reviews followed. *The New Yorker* said Gable's facial dimples resembled craters on the moon: 'Mr Gable, at this point in his career, is grizzled, not withered', and *The New York Times* reviewer was just as shrill, describing the star as being as a 'little older, a little fatter, a little shrewder and more cynical'. In fact, MGM were so disappointed that they relegated it to second billing below *Metroscopix*, a 3D horror. And, as is known, Gable's career continued to flounder and, after several bouts of bad health, he died in November 1960, aged just fifty-nine.

In retrospect, it was probably best that Kenny's 'big scene' in *Never Let Me Go* was cut, and thankfully the film sank without doing much damage. By the time he'd accepted the situation, he was busily focused on securing Bill as a wife. Though they had already started to see more of each other, they both remained independent, afraid of repeating past mistakes. Both had been previously married 'and our marriages had ended in disaster', Ken lamented. 'We knew too keenly the misery of an unhappy relationship.'[4] In a remarkably frank talk, he privately admitted to Ronnie Squire that his code of sexual morality remained 'somewhat elastic' and confessed that he didn't love

Bill. Squire listened with endless sympathy as he agonised about accumulating in-laws (and a stepson), and having chains placed upon his sexual appetites. Nevertheless, he 'could do nothing about' a seismic urge to tie the knot. The odd thing is that – much later – Ken asserted that Bill 'understood' his feelings and assured him 'love would eventually come'. There would be flings, he warned, and sought her guarantee for a swift divorce should he fall for another woman (she agreed, apparently). In the end, his proposal to Bill was hardly romantic. He had originally pictured popping the question at a fancy restaurant, or maybe a beach at sunset. In fact, it happened at Bill's flat over a 'particularly delicious plate of her steak and fried Spanish onions'. By this point, it seems, they were both more interested in realistic plans than romantic gestures. A great deal of care was needed in Ken's handling of Jonathan, Bill's sensitive teenage son from her previous marriage. 'I was proud when he let me know that he wouldn't object to having me around the house permanently.' Relieved and excited, Kenneth Gilbert More and Mabel Edith Barkby tied the knot on 18 August 1952 at Oxford Registry Office, with a reception lunch held at a hotel in Sonning-on-Thames. Details of the nuptials were not released to the press, but Betty Box threw a party back in London, and eighty guests joined another celebration a few days later.

After the wedding, Kenny moved into his complaisant wife's apartment at Kingston House, Princes Gate – a luxurious eight-bedroomed, five-bathroomed abode overlooking Hyde Park. To the outside world, it seemed a union made in heaven. And in many ways, it was, at first. From the outset, Bill brought him considerable happiness and took a keen interest in his career. She listened as he spouted his latest plans – and demanded the same attention from her as he did from the studio. Better still, she shone at intimate dinner parties, film galas and charity banquets. Over time, they gained a reputation as generous and appealing hosts, especially as Ken's huge stock of anecdotes never failed to keep guests in fits of laughter. And even as their social status grew, Bill's view of her husband remained gentle. For her, he would forever be an 'average Joe Bloggs', loafing about in old slacks and pullovers. Though she smoothed his rough edges, his taste in clothes remained casual. He liked to wear shirts of bold colours and designs, with sweaters of brown or burgundy on top. He had a passion for flat caps, the more colourful, the better.

During this time, apart from golf and Bill, there was little to divert him from his profession. The routine of films, 'with those free weekends', meant 'Saturdays were reserved for the missus, and Sundays for golf!' His hobbies were limited. Beyond a few paperback books and trashy thrillers, he rarely indulged in heavy literature, and never ventured beyond the *Daily Express* or *Daily Mirror*. Politics meant little to him. He claimed to play golf best with a hangover. Though just an average player, a fifteen-handicap man, he kept his 'head down and eye on the ball'. He hated cricket, watched a bit of TV and adored jaunts to the coast. 'Oh, he's very gay about the house,' Bill divulged. 'But he is also very quiet and thoughtful. And he hardly ever goes to the local for a pint.' That's not to say he didn't like a tipple; his fondness for continental wines was well known, especially Chambolle-Musigny 1933 from the Côte-d'Or. He also puffed Craven A cigarettes prodigiously, especially when meeting people for the first time. 'I try to make them smile,' he confessed. 'If their smile is sincere, they're OK. But if they give me one of those lightning on-and-off grimaces, then they've failed the More test.' Like most people, he was capable of displaying the occasional fit of temper, 'usually sparked by red tape and too many people telling me I must do this and that'. He never tired of talking about his grudge for casting directors. 'For years,' he often expounded, 'I stayed on the stage because they told me I wasn't enough of a glamour boy for films. But I get my own back these days. To casting directors that used to turn me down on these grounds and now want me for films I return their scripts saying I don't think the role is suitable for a short, spotty actor.' For a while, he was nervous about publicity concerning his taste for the highlife, so much so, that he wrote an article for *Men Only* taking pains to emphasise his 'average bloke' credentials:

Elegant living? Who me? This will give my wife something to chortle about. All right, let me admit straight away that I'm not really elegant in the generally accepted sense of that term – and I never shall be. My favourite clothes are blue jeans and a sweater. Anyway, there's precious little elegance in being a film actor these days – getting up at six in the morning, sweating all day in a studio, and being called 'Charley Boy' by all and sundry. Mind you, I prefer it that way. At heart, I'm a simple soul with no pretensions. And if I presume to lecture you on the art of elegant living, you'll have to accept my own definition of the words. Elegance in itself, for its own sake, is very apt to develop into pomposity – and that is something one should avoid. It makes me see red. If I meet anyone trying to be pompous, then I go into a bat. I pull 'em down, I attack with every weapon I can muster. We humans are insignificant creatures really, and only fools think they're not.

There was nothing pompous, he insisted, about his purchase of Lock End in Shiplake, 'a little piece of heaven' near Henley-on-Thames, hidden in woodland, a stone's throw from the river, near the Royal Regatta Course. The property had been built in 1880 and owned by the Dobbs family, the London furriers, who fashioned a stunning Italian garden, once featured in *Country Life*. Embracing the beauty of its surroundings, the house contained rustic walnut furniture and stencilled rose motifs adorned the kitchen tiles, while stone walls and a wrought-iron gate encased the garden. It was 'without a doubt the most tasteful, elegant, and habitable film-star home' writer Donald Zec had ever seen 'including all the lush, Technicolored palaces of Hollywood'. In reality, Ken harboured strongly mixed feelings about the property, which quickly became a chore to maintain. 'We were forty miles from London, and our domestics weren't keen on the prospect of a winter in the outbacks of Henley,' he lamented. Cooks and maids came and went with frightening speed, 'nearly reducing Bill to hysterics'.[5] During a period of messy renovations, he was coaxed back to London by Henry Cornelius who approached him to play Ambrose Claverhouse in *Genevieve,* after practically every actor on Rank's payroll, including Dirk Bogarde, refused the part. Ken, though, was quick on the uptake. It promised yet another pleasant payday – £3,500 – though it wasn't a picture he wanted to make. On the plus side, solid support came from Kay Kendall, John Gregson, and Dinah Sheridan – each a unique personality. Speaking to film historian Brian McFarlane some years later, Sheridan remembered asking Dirk Bogarde for his advice on taking the role. 'He told me to take *Genevieve* if I got it. He had turned it down because he didn't want to do comedy again,' she said. 'They didn't want Kenneth More, they wanted Guy Middleton; they wanted Dirk instead of John Gregson, Claire Bloom instead of me and I can't remember who they wanted instead of Kay Kendall.'[6]

Set to be filmed in colour, *Genevieve* chronicles the rivalry between the owners of vintage cars and an uproarious race back from Brighton. Alan McKim (Gregson) drives his adored 1904 automobile, named Genevieve, while Ambrose Claverhouse (Kenny), a raucous bounding type, takes his classic Spyker car. Alan and Ambrose bring their wives (Sheridan, Kendall) along for the ride, but the trek soon turns fiercely competitive, each driver inventing clever ways to sabotage the other in hopes of winning the race. As Claverhouse, Ken managed to look like a cad and behave like a gentleman. To women, one observer noted, the combination proved irresistible. 'They love the thrill of danger while feeling safe. It is like swimming when you know you can touch the bottom.'

The formula for Rank films in the early 1950s was straightforward: keep the productions as cheap as possible, shoot them quickly, and use the actors to promote them. However, delays plagued the project from the first day on 8 October 1952. 'Everything went wrong, even the weather,' Ken said. 'Having to rush to the theatre every night was bad enough, but the shooting of the picture was hell.' Compensations came when he pursued a fling with Kay Kendall – a tall, slim, Yorkshire-born actress, with a lively spirit and colourful vocabulary. Like himself, Kay was no shrinking violet. The sex, he later confided, wasn't great because they were too busy giggling.[7] An affair developed that raged on and off for the entire shoot. Dinah Sheridan remembered they weren't discreet about their ardour, and even shared a dressing room and arrived each morning clutching a bottle of champagne. 'Kay, you know,' Ken revealed, was 'as funny off as on screen. Once when she was tired of re-takes on one shot in *Genevieve*, she whipped up a big parasol and clobbered the director on the head, saying she'd do no more work that day.'[8]

During their dalliance, its doubtful Ken knew Kendall was pregnant with the child of her lover James Sainsbury, and even underwent an abortion during their off-set fling. The affair, apparently, generated little, if any, emotional heat, and didn't extend beyond the film. Off set, though, there were many parties and impromptu 'booze ups'. However, according to Kendall's biographer, Eve Golden, not everyone enjoyed Kenny's earthy humour. At one party, John Gregson's wife, Thea, was appalled by his off-colour stories, and lost her temper when – slightly tipsy – he told her to 'come on, smile!'. 'She slapped his face, leaving two ugly scratch marks down one cheek.' That night, Gregson wound up sleeping on Kenny's sofa, and the two arrived on set the next morning nursing hangovers only to encounter John Davis – J. Arthur Rank's right-hand man – who chose that day to inspect the shoot. A stern-faced, hard-working man, intolerant of contradiction, Davis was the very picture of a 'stuffed shirt'. His staff either loved or loathed him, but Ken's relationship with him was friendly but not especially warm. A 1952 book on the film industry notes he ruled Rank with a strict hand.

> He does not understand people I have heard it said, and people do not understand him. He suffered from the jealousy and envy which always accompanies spectacular success; and from the resentment of men who had been in the forces during the war and came back to find him on top.[9]

Thankfully, that morning on the set of *Genevieve*, American screenwriter William Rose, a cricket-loving Anglophile, was on hand to charm Davis with his fund of anecdotes. Everybody loved Rose, a man who'd spent his career creating fantasy out of imagination. In real life, he had fought for the Finns against the Russians, and took part in the ill-fated Dieppe Raid. On set, Rose became so popular that Dinah Sheridan spent her spare moments knitting him a scarf. During the last days of production, the film neared calamity as costs spiralled out of control and Cornelius was blamed for a £20,000 overrun. Known as a nitpicker, he would re-shoot scenes endlessly until the cast and crew were exasperated. At one point, things got so bad that Hugh Stewart – a producer working at Rank – said it was considered one of the most despised films ever shot at Pinewood. And Olive Dodds, a senior member of the casting department, listened patiently when Kenny, Kendall, and Gregson, all came to her at one time or another and said, 'I want to be out of it.'[10]

Rumour has it that by the end of shooting Cornelius collapsed in tears. What is certain, Ken was 'tired, depressed and fed up with the whole thing' by the time his freedom from this chore arrived on 12 February 1953, the day he made his last shot. A few hours later, he was on a flight with Bill bound for Switzerland for a retreat to a rented villa. Convinced that *Genevieve* would be a flop, he reflected, 'When they showed it to John Davis and all the bigwigs in Rank, they said: "Oh no, we must never show this, it is terrible, a ghastly mistake."'

6
CELEBRITY FULFILLED

In a strange trick of fate, *Genevieve* became a genuine phenomenon and changed the course of Kenny's career. Simply put, the film was a smash hit. No one was more relieved than the 'nitpicker' Henry Cornelius, who maintained he 'always knew' he was crafting a movie 'destined to be a classic'. And, after surveying mammoth box-office profits, he claimed the secret of *Genevieve*'s success was its non-topical, timeless story: 'People went to see it three, four and five times. You see, basically, people are just interested in people.' In the event, *Genevieve* paved the way for a cycle of comedy flicks, all with predictable storylines. Even William Whitebait, the sniffy critic at the *New Statesman*, thought the picture achieved 'that rarest of qualities in an English film – spontaneity'. When it opened after a trade show at the Gaumont, Haymarket, in May 1953, Kenny said the reaction came as rather a surprise. 'I don't really try to be funny; you know. It just seems to come out that way.'

Upon its initial release, others clambered aboard the *Genevieve* bandwagon, including Lone Star Toys which churned out 25,000 'accurate scale models of the famous veteran car' moulded from plastic and metal, and Columbia Records issued a recording of Larry Adler's soundtrack. At the same time, Rank's marketers scrambled to rope in contract artists – who always did as they were told – to join the ongoing publicity jig. Dirk Bogarde did his bit by lauding Kenny's success as being based on integrity, sincerity, and taste. 'And besides he's the only actor in Britain who could have successfully pulled off a role such as the one in *Genevieve*. He really does act and talk off-screen like the people he plays on the screen. Some critics say it's only Kenny playing himself. But that's the most difficult thing for an actor to do.' For some reason, even Bill joined the chorus of praise, saying it was only because her husband was 'so fundamentally kind' that he could play 'that rakish fellow' Claverhouse without losing sympathy. Better still, when Oscar time rolled around, it was nominated for two top awards: Best Screenplay, and Best Music Score. In the end, it picked up a British Academy Film Award for Best Picture, and collected a Golden Globe for Best Foreign Film.

As Ken's fame grew, he attracted wide publicity and appeared on the cover of *Picturegoer*, the movie periodical, marking the beginning of a long relationship with its publishers. At first, the media hype was fun and *Picturegoer* asserted he was 'coming along very comfortably in the race to establish himself as a light comedian of the Naunton Wayne school'. He must have sniggered when a follow-up profile praised his 'Niven touch and Cary Grant candour'. Not so funny, however, was an unflattering sentence describing him as 'a not very tall, not very handsome man in his mid-thirties' but it soothingly added, he was 'the newest thing in debonair comedy' – a natural born light comedian. 'There is a polish about his playing that exact attention to detail that is the quintessence of humorous, not quite caricature. He could become as much as a British screen institution as Alistair Sim.'

From here on, Kenneth More sought a more relaxed working atmosphere, and time to enjoy the pleasures of golf, leisure, and money. However, even before *Genevieve*'s success became apparent, George Minter, the director at Renown Films, pencilled out the best offer he could make on a five-week contract for Ken to feature in *Our Girl Friday,* a lame tale about a woman shipwrecked with three men on a deserted island, alongside Joan Collins, George Cole, and Robertson Hare. Renown had planned the picture as a Jane Russell vehicle in 1950 under the title *The Girl on the Island* but ran into financial problems. Desperate to revive the project, Minter proposed a fee of £2,000, but Kenny was noncommittal, holding out for a better deal. In the end, Dubens secured a payment of £4,500 and Ken signed on to play an Irish stoker and set about 'perfecting' a Dublin accent. And to please Minter, who had detailed shot-by-shot sketches traced on a storyboard, he agreed to have his hair lightly permed and dyed blond. As the project was pulled together, plans for filming in Majorca turned out to be a mammoth operation involving an advance party of eight lorries loaded with technical equipment driving from London to Barcelona before making a 155-mile sea trip. Before production began on 4 June 1953, Ken also insisted on driving, and with Bill journeyed into Spain by car. Thankfully, filming turned out to be a leisurely affair, shot mostly on the beaches of Peguera where Joan Collins could be found most days wearing a bikini and no make-up. 'It was quite restful and more like a holiday than work,' she recounted. 'The script was hilarious and the three actors who were in it were important stars.' The 'rather silly story' may not have appealed to Ken, but nevertheless he and the crew found a kinship, like a little band of Brits abroad. As the thermometer rose, everyone helped with the cooking, and collectively mucked in to build a beach shelter using palm tree leaves. 'We thoroughly enjoyed making it,' Ken beamed. 'Robertson Hare, he's got a very bald head, the temperature was about 108°C in the shade, and we had to make mats constantly to protect his head otherwise Bunny would have boiled!'

The only hiccup, according to George Cole, came when he and Ken were asked to swim naked. For authenticity, director Noel Langley insisted they shoot a scene without shorts – exposing their bottoms on camera. 'Ken More wanted nothing to do with this and protested vehemently and the issue resulted in a major confrontation involving the whole crew, all of whom seemed to have an opinion on the matter,' Cole remembered. 'Eventually, I said, "I'm game," and Ken had no alternative but to go along with it.' According to legend, a Spanish extra looked up from her knitting – spied Kenneth frolicking stark naked in the ocean – and fainted.

Despite its flaws, *Our Girl Friday* proved a success both in Britain and America, but not all reviews were positive. *The Monthly Film Bulletin* labelled it a humourless comedy which made little of its situation. 'The jokes are largely about Robertson Hare wearing a grass skirt and peeping at Sadie bathing in the sea.' Likewise, *The New York Times* critic didn't care for the film, reckoning that Collins made 'no impression as an actress'.

Graham Lord, her biographer, savaged her performance saying she sounded like Princess Margaret and her pouty mouth resembled that of a 'gormless goldfish'. And if that wasn't bad enough, he reckoned Kenny's Irish accent was about as Celtic as 'Japanese whisky and managed to incorporate traces of cockney and Zummerzet'. However, the virtue of *Our Girl Friday* was that Collins had the last laugh when Daryl Zanuck, the head of 20th Century Fox, waved a Hollywood contract before her eyes.

The completion of *Our Girl Friday* dovetailed neatly with Bill's pregnancy. Though absenting herself from London's social scene, she gamely let her husband impose his work on their home life and often observed him holding court before journalists in Kingston House. In contrast to some celebrities who maintained some degree of privacy, Kenny opened his abode to all-out exposure and ensured publicity agents, as well as the press, knew what he was up to personally and professionally. 'Gossip columnists started to come and see me at home,' he said. 'And they entered my front door with eyes cast in every direction, picking up details with a passionate suction for information.'[1] His pursuits were often covered by the major newspapers, including the *Daily Express, Daily Mail, Daily Mirror,* and *Daily Herald*. The sheer volume of his off-screen appearances also led to consistent coverage by fan magazines such as *Picturegoer, Picture Post, ABC Movie Guide,* and a plethora of European film magazines. A part of the chore was to be photographed engaging in traditional leisure activities – playing golf, watching tennis, at the races in Newmarket, or socialising with friends. Period publicity continued to marvel at his 'everyday bloke' persona – a view shared by *Picturegoer*'s Dorothy Alison who 'discovered' a man of warmth and 'delightful modesty' on her visit to Kingston House. 'He listens with the same intensity as he talks. And he has a flattering characteristic of sitting forward in his chair – it gives importance not only to what he's saying, but also to what you're saying.' During such encounters, he could be brash, outspoken, syrupy and sentimental. On one occasion, pontificating on the female sex, he gave a hopelessly outdated view that the 'perfect woman' was a cross between a 'saint and a drayhorse, a diplomat and an automatic washing machine, a psychiatrist and a bulldozer, a sanitary engineer and a mannequin'. These opinions, Dorothy cooed, were 'refreshing as a harbour breeze and buoyant as the yachts that sail it'. Furthermore, she insisted he was an 'actor by accident rather than instinct' and couldn't help sharing her big scoop: Ken had accepted the part of Richard Grimsdyke in Betty Box's *Doctor in the House*, a new film romp based on the best-selling novel – and (another) natural follow-up to *Genevieve*. Getting the contract signed wasn't easy – Box asserted Ken drove a hard bargain financially: 'But who blames him for that?' she reasoned. 'This is a business, after all. And besides, he deserves it.' In fact, he needed a good film after *Our Girl Friday* to consolidate his growing status and *Doctor in the House* – a hotchpotch in the life of rowdy, workshy medical students – teamed him with Dirk Bogarde, Donald Sinden, and his old flame Kay Kendall. 'Without a doubt, comedy is something I understand most,' he said wistfully. 'I feel, too, that there's this point: if you're lucky enough to have a sense of comedy, and if picturegoers, viewers and playgoers are made happy by seeing you expressing it, you're a bit of a cheat to go away from that and say "Now, I want to play Macbeth."'

Doctor in the House – stuffed with guffaws and gags – chimed with a mood of optimism as Britain headed toward a new Elizabethan age. However, Bogarde, it seems, had become petulant about working conditions, and only appeared on the understanding that Kenny's screentime was reduced, or drastically watered down. And at times, his sheer ego kept him from being as pleasant as he might have been to the crew. Donald Sinden – who had never worked with Bogarde – was struck by his lack of contact with others and remembered during breaks, the cast – including Ken – could be found laughing and joking near the fountain at University College, but Dirk always vanished to the back of his Rolls-Royce, and sat alone. Despite such preciousness – or because of it – writer Nicholas Phipps inflated Ken's character of a perpetually failing student. In fact, the part was so good that he nearly walked off with the film but, alas, James Robertson Justice stole the show with his effortless performance as the surgeon, Sir Lancelot Spratt. And luckily for Rank, the idea of gags in a hospital would spawn other lucrative medical comedies, including *Doctor at Sea*, *Doctor at Large*, *Doctor in Love*, *Doctor in Distress* and *Doctor in Trouble*.

Off screen, Kenny was briefly preoccupied when, after a difficult delivery, Bill gave birth to a baby girl, christened Sarah, at King's College Hospital. Three days later, the child was brought home to luxury and comfort. Though 'slightly disappointed' it wasn't a boy, Ken was soon spotted happily pushing a pram in the park, with his poodle, Buster, in tow. In looks, Sarah was like her father, hazel eyed and moon faced, with wavy chestnut hair. She left babyhood rapidly, learning to walk by thirteen months, and talk soon after. 'Nanny and the baby and the missus are a wonderful sheet anchor,' Ken said, when talking about life during this period. 'Worries all go when I'm sitting in the nursery.' The most vivid picture of the More household at this time comes from Geoffrey Winn, a star columnist for the *Daily Mirror*. After visiting Kingston House, he considered the nanny 'formidable and friendly' as she beavered away in a nursery overlooking Hyde Park. As for Sarah, she had her mother's 'fairness and delicacy of bone and skin and her father's complete unselfconsciousness and lack of affection'. Winn – who noted Ken 'spent his life studying people' – dined with the More's at Les Ambassadeurs on Park Lane, where he perceived that Ken either liked someone instinctively or he didn't: 'What they do, what they earn, what power they possess leaves absolutely no impression on him whatsoever.'[2]

The joys of fatherhood did not lessen Kenneth More's attention to work. In fact, around this time, nothing drew a clearer line under the irrevocability of his newfound status than when Alexander Korda – the Hungarian film mogul – touted him as the 'boy wonder of British cinema' and pushed a five-year contract under his nose. Korda was a rare commodity in the film industry: both a producer and talented studio boss. By this point, his name was a byword for lavish cinema, he lived in 'Millionaires Row', Kensington, ran a luxury yacht and directed his empire from the former home of the late king. Though by no means a genius, he knew what the public wanted and imported stars from the USA and Europe, introduced foreign cameramen, and had a magnificent set designer in his brother Vincent, and another director in Zoltan. His fame was secured in 1941 after making

Lady Hamilton, which Winston Churchill saw eight times. On each occasion, it brought tears to his eyes. The Hungarian was knighted the following year.

At their first meeting, Ken never forgot being ushered into Korda's magnificent office where the mogul sat perched on a Chesterfield chair, puffing a cigar. 'Korda could charm the birds off the trees, I adored that man,' he recounted. 'I loved him. This is a magic business and you've got to have magic personalities running it. Big hearted, extravagant, spendthrifts. Korda came into my life with big cigars, and a marvellous Hungarian personality! He'd say "Come in, Kenny. Sit down, have a cigar." And he'd offer you one a foot long! And immediately you felt important. I loved him, he was a big, warm hearted, marvellous showman. He made me feel like a star.'[3]

The name of Kenneth Gilbert More entered Korda's British Lion files on Saturday 23 January 1954. Strictly speaking, though, the contract was a personal agreement with Korda. Three days later, when it was agreed he would be paid the phenomenal sum of £10,000 a year, Korda threw a party, a black-tie affair of lavish merit to celebrate, where Rex Harrison, Graham Greene, and Terence Rattigan toasted 'Britain's newest star'. 'This is the life,' Ken told journalists, munching on smoked sturgeon, topped with layers of caviar. A few days later, a note arrived confirming his membership of the Garrick Club, the haunt of gentlemen and actors (once described as a quiet sub-branch of a pensioners' retirement home). On most days, the snores, coughs, and grunts discharged by older members resting after lunch could be heard as far as the lobby. Located in an impressive-looking building near Covent Garden, it boasted a mahogany-panelled library, handsomely appointed restaurant, and lounges providing members a luxurious retreat where life's pressures rarely intruded. Commander Satterthwaite RN (retd), the club's secretary, recalled Kenny's membership was approved along with Rex Harrison's application. 'There was inevitably a long, noisy discussion, but in the end, there was only one dissenting vote, a lawyer,' he recounted. 'Appropriately, Kenneth More was to decorate this bar almost daily when in London. So was Rex Harrison, but we did not see so much of him.' Other 'theatrical members' included Peter Ustinov, John Mills, Douglas Fairbanks Jr, Alec Guinness, Robert Morley, and Michael Hordern. (The Green Room on Adam Street became another of Ken's perches.)

Having achieved fame, Kenny insisted on all its prerequisites, including a coffee-coloured chauffeured Rolls-Royce. Soon after, a Steinway baby grand, custom-built book-lined study, and Georgian drinks cabinet were added to his growing list of home improvements. And by the time Sarah was learning to speak her first words, a sixty-five-year-old white-tie-and-tails butler, Charles Coupland, was engaged to supplement the services of a 'live in' maid. In a business where ego and competition ran high, Kenny's parties at Kingston House took on a mythical aura as guests were plied with the best booze, and hobnobbed with illustrious figures. Occasional binges of extravagance saw him splurge on grouse and exotic delicacies. 'The other night,' he confessed, 'six of us sat down and ate our way through six pounds' worth of caviar' to celebrate the British opening of *Doctor in the House*. Still, the celebration was worth it – the film set a record by being seen by more people in its first year of release than any previous movie: 17 million tickets were sold. Even more astounding, in the fourth week of its run at the Leicester Square Odeon – London's premier theatre – it took more money than any other film since 1937. '*Doctor in the House* was probably the most successful film for a very long time,' Betty Box beamed. Better still, having accumulated many champions among the fraternity of film critics, Ken was endorsed in his nomination (and win) for a British Film Award. 'I was rather pleased about that, actually,' he confessed. 'Everybody disregards comedy. I don't know why. The greatest classical actors look down on what I consider to be the greatest comedy actors – men like Charles Hawtrey, Gerald du Maurier, Ronald Squire, A. E. Matthews.'[4] Casting a golden glow over his prospects, *Picturegoer* said it was a wonder that after years of small parts, Ken's flair for belly-laughs and humour helped make him one of Britain's favourite comedy actors. 'More gives a first-class performance as the only medical student in the faculty who has some money in his pocket. It bubbles and babbles with the sheer joy of living, like a spring brook in sunshine. It is carefree, it is gay; it is as light-hearted as a breeze.' The review set the pattern for notices that continued in the United States where it packed theatres and even received a standing ovation.

At the time of the film's release, author Kingsley Amis had just published *Lucky Jim*, his satire about college life and had agreed to have it adapted into a motion picture. Having seen *Doctor in the House*, he was convinced Kenny should play the lead role of Jim Dixon. 'I'm sure Kenneth More would be a killer in the part if it ever gets to that,' Amis wrote to Hilary Rubenstein, one of Britain's premier literary agents, on 4 April 1954. 'I must coach him in face making.'[5] However, Korda had grandiose plans to put his newest star in an epic about Alcock and Brown, two

Englishmen that flew the Atlantic in 1919. Provisionally titled *The Long Hop*, Kenny was cast for the part of Sir Arthur Whitten-Brown, while Denholm Elliott was to play the other half of the flying partnership, Ken Annakin was slated to direct. The whole thing was incredibly audacious, and as things got moving, Kenny took lessons in handling a Vickers Vimy aircraft, memorised his lines and was all set for shooting when – out of the blue – plans were suddenly dropped in June 1954. 'It was a shattering blow,' Kenneth wrote in his first memoir. 'I was flabbergasted.' As Ken Annakin explained, Korda faced financial disaster and had 'been forced into bankruptcy and the receiver refused to allow us to continue production even though over a hundred thousand pounds had been spent'. In fact, the situation was dire. Though Korda had enjoyed success with *The Third Man*, *The Sound Barrier* and *The Fallen Idol*, British Lion profits were countered by flops including *Tales of Hoffman* and *The Beggar's Opera*. When the crash came, the government took over British Lion by appointing a receiver and manager from the National Film Finance Corporation – the organisation controlling state loans to the industry. Then, when it transpired that British Lion had lost over £2 million of taxpayers' money the contracts of all producers, directors, and stars – including Kenny, Margaret Leighton, Moira Shearer, and Claire Bloom were terminated and placed in the hands of the receiver. 'We were in shock for quite a while,' Ken remembered. 'I really wanted to make this picture.'

After weeks of speculation, production resumed but the Alcock unit – including Ken – were reassigned to Ian Dalrymple's low-budget comedy, *Raising a Riot*. Ken Annakin, however, refused to direct as Wendy Toye, a former dancer with ambitions to become a director, had been toiling on the project for months. 'It seemed to me highly immoral that because I had a valid contract, I should push out someone who had been hoping to make her debut as a director.' Thus, in the end, Toye directed *Raising a Riot* on location during September 1954. As she took a major new step in her career, Toye later said that 'among the many people in the film industry who showed faith in me was Ian Dalrymple – he really put his head on the block. So did Kenneth More.'

> Ian found the story for *Raising a Riot* and liked it and showed it to me, and said, 'Do you think you could get Kenneth More to play in this?' I said, 'Well, I don't know. Do you mean with me directing?' He said yes. 'Well,' I said, 'I doubt it. I've only made one or two films before. Why should he bother with me?' So, I had lunch with Kenny, who I didn't know at all at the time. I admired him a lot. But he knew of me and said yes straight away.[6]

Filmed on the cheap along the Thames Estuary in Kent, the story pivots on a dilapidated windmill where Ken played a young naval officer forced to become nursemaid, cook, and laundress to three youngsters and a dog while his wife was away visiting a sick relation. Like in the old Denville days, he displayed a gift for slapstick, and was ably helped by co-stars Mandy Miller, as his daughter, and his old chum Ronald Squire, playing a not-too-helpful granddad. The uncertainty that reigned during this period certainly didn't affect the shoot. At one point, L. S. Lowry, the painter who recorded twentieth-century industrial life with his paintings, spent a few days on set, and as Ken recalled, sketched him lying down for a nap after lunch, surrounded by the crew beavering away at their jobs. 'So, I joined the band of his famous matchstalk men and matchstalk cats and dogs.' Altogether it was a well-mounted production. The *Daily Herald* hailed a 'simple film, amateurish, good-tempered, and sunny.' The reviewer of the *South China Morning Post* reported there were so many laughs, that he almost ached, 'Kenneth More as the officer is no less than perfect.'

Before Kenny looked around for other ventures, Alexander Korda bobbed up again, armed with £5 million from the City Investment Corporation of New York to finance five films. The Hungarian was full of ideas – but as Kenneth told it – they didn't always appeal. 'While nosing around for a new project Alex offered me *The Four Feathers*, a remake of his hit from the thirties. I politely declined. It was a rotten idea.' Interestingly, at the same time, David Lean wanted him to play the hero, Quinn, in *The Wind Cannot Read* but, according to Lean's biographer, Korda told the director, 'You're not going to have Kenneth More. I'll tell him not to do it and he won't do it if I tell him not to.' In his memoirs, Kenny tells a slightly different story by claiming that having been within an ace of accepting the Quinn role, he formed his own doubts and, to his eternal regret, turned down the part. (He also notes Korda pushed him to accept the role.) As rumours swirled in and out of the newspapers about his next projects, it was claimed he was considered for the part of General Montgomery in *I Was Monty's Double* – but plans stalled, and the role eventually fell to Meyrick Edward Clifton James, Monty's real-life decoy. Another, more intriguing, albeit unsuccessful pitch, came from John Sutro who failed to persuade Korda to cast Ken in L. P. Hartley's novel *The Go-Between*. Korda did, however, purchase the rights in the hope of selling them for a profit, thus infuriating Hartley, who was so annoyed 'that I put a curse on him, and he died, almost the next morning'.

After much wavering, Kenny was finally placed in a screen version of *The Deep Blue Sea*, budgeted at £400,000 and adapted – lengthily – by Terence Rattigan. Despite Korda's good intentions, it was a poor choice and required Rattigan to alter dialogue, make major cuts, tweak timing, and add scenes such as location shots in Switzerland to showcase CinemaScope, the widescreen format. 'I wasn't too pleased about that,' Ken confessed. It was also a bad sign when he blew a gasket at Korda's 'ridiculous decision' to cast Vivien Leigh, whom he disliked intensely, as Hester Collyer, and wasn't afraid about saying so. She was, he thought, an overpowering 'strange woman' who told bawdy stories and displayed the temperament of a man. Worse still, he 'could never really trust her' and suspected her overwhelming friendliness. Very few people who saw Kenny at this time were favourably impressed. Having made an enemy of Leigh, he turned up at a production meeting scowling before launching into an excruciating monologue about deficiencies in the script. The only success in this mess, as far as he could see, was the casting of Eric Portman as the weary doctor. Having said his piece, he snubbed director Anatole Litvak, but that was more likely due to the fact that he proved as much an attraction as the stars (and had enjoyed many exotic affairs, including with screen siren Bette Davis). Despite an air of uncertainty about the enterprise, filming in Switzerland proceeded crisply. In fact, Kenny was pushed before journalists outside the Hotel

Walserhof in Klosters and lied through his teeth about Rattigan and Litvak 'turning in a first-class script'. Asked why he took on such a serious part, he remarked, 'I'm portraying Freddie, not doing a Macbeth. Freddie is a light-hearted bloke who happens to be caught up in a dramatic situation. He's a hail-fellow type, unable to understand deep emotion. It's just his bad luck that he gets caught up with a neurotic woman.' By the time *The Deep Blue Sea* was released, its box-office fate was sealed by a string of negative notices. Other than Dilys Powell, who praised 'the flawless performance we expected' from Kenneth, reviews were muted. 'What has Mr Rattigan done?' Alexander Walker asked rhetorically. 'He has opened out his play to all the breadth of the CinemaScope screen, he has broadened his deep blue sea and inevitably he has made it shallow.' Though he thought Leigh 'battled bravely', she was never sensual enough to play Hester. In contrast, Kenneth, he opined, was 'impeccable'. (It is important to note that Walker landed his job at the *Evening Standard* when Kenny sent a letter of approval to the editor, having been moved by one of his reviews. He remained at the paper for forty-three years.) Even Leigh's close chum, Alan Dent, said no amount of integrity could make her realistic in the part of Hester in which Peggy Ashcroft had perfected on stage. 'Vivien's beauty and elegance were against her from the start. She did nothing – or was asked by her director to do nothing – to modify the impression she gave of a dazzling young woman of the world who would be extremely unlikely to ever find herself in Hester's predicament.' In the end, Ken never wrote or spoke fondly of Leigh, even following her death in 1967: 'I thought she was petulant, spoilt, over praised and over loved.' For her part, Vivien was just as graceless. Once, when asked about the movie, she responded, 'Oh, Kenneth More, was he in that film?'

To his amazement, Ken was nominated for a BAFTA and won the Venice Film Festival Best Actor award for *The Deep Blue Sea*. 'I was never so surprised,' he recounted. 'I didn't even know they were giving anything away at Venice. A journalist telephoned me with the news. He also told me that the announcement of my win was received in hostile silence.'

For the final act in the saga of *The Deep Blue Sea*, Ken sailed to New York for the American premiere and promotional activities. To start with, events began well when Bosley Crowther, the famed film critic of *The New York Times*, celebrated Kenny's 'giddy performance' as Freddie Page, and even reserved praise for Leigh's 'adroit emotional acting'. But despite Crowther's encouragement, the reception was generally muted. 'It was a tricky subject for American audiences,' Ken reasoned. 'The film just didn't come off.' In fact, he didn't help matters during a press soirée by taking a swipe at Grace Kelly and James Mason: 'How could they give that Oscar award to Grace Kelly over Judy Garland in *A Star is Born*? What a performance that girl gave! We were flabbergasted,' he said offhand, referring to Kelly's win for *The Country Girl*. 'Yes, Mason was all right [in *A Star is Born*] but he couldn't touch Freddie March in the original.' Such outspoken remarks – to which the American press was not accustomed – were badly received. After an hour, journalists filed out of the soirée muttering about this 'rude and ungracious' British actor. Luckily, the rest of the jaunt passed peacefully. 'If I'd been wiser,' Ken said, 'I suppose I would have pushed my mug inside Hollywood producers' doors and been seen at the proper night clubs.' Instead, after leaving New York, Bill engineered a trip to Chicago to meet her close friend Eleanor Page, the society editor of the *Chicago Tribune*. In the 'windy city', there were endless cocktail parties, baseball games (he watched the Yankees beat the White Sox) and a couple of press interviews. 'Would you like to leave London and live in the States, Mr More?' asked one reporter. 'No,' Ken snapped. 'I won't fall for the dollar. I shan't uproot. My home is there. I like my golf there on Sundays. Everything I know and understand is there.' By the end of the American tour, he was literally too tired to conduct any more appearances, prompting Bill to arrange a holiday in the South of France to laze on the beach, and frequent little cafes. During this break, he brooded at newspaper reports about producer Danny Angel, the husband of his old Windmill flame Betty Van Damm, preparing to work with Richard Burton on *Reach for the Sky*, a film based on Paul Brickhill's bestseller about the fabulous exploits of the legless fighter ace, Wing Commander Douglas Bader. Considered one of 'the most coveted screen roles' of recent years, Ken had already devoured the book, and insisted the 'whole attitude of Bader's life' resembled his own and was 'immediately impressed' by its potential for cinematic treatment. Only Kenneth More, he privately thought, could do complete justice to the role. It is entirely possible, even probable, that he communicated this opinion to Betty Van Damm.

With the exception of the moderate success of *The Sea Shall Not Have Them*, Danny Angel hadn't had a hit in years, but placed all his hopes in the Bader film. He also had a personal interest, having been invalided during the Second World War in

Burma where he contracted polio and was told he would never walk again. However, over time, he learned to move around in a wheelchair and taught himself to walk using a cane. Angel was in low spirits through the winter and spring of 1955, as *Reach for the Sky* was blighted by a series of upsets, and disappointments. For starters, finding a writer to transform the book into a screenplay proved a challenge. 'We tried to get all sorts of people – Rattigan, he wouldn't do it – then, A. G. Bates started on it and gave it up,' director Lewis Gilbert remembered. 'William Douglas-Home had a go on it and gave it up. And finally, Danny Angel said, "look they are all giving it up, why don't you do it yourself?"' With those instructions, Gilbert boarded the first BOAC Comet to Florence to help Brickhill, who was fed up with the project, and with Bader in particular. At one point, he confessed to suffering several nervous breakdowns because 'Douglas [Bader] was very, very difficult.' By the time they got around to sketching the screen treatment, Angel was on the phone with the news that Richard Burton had pulled out, after accepting a plum part in *Alexander the Great*. In an attempt to pull the frayed situation together, Gilbert pitched the Bader role to Laurence Olivier, which he later thought 'a bit daft – we were panicking by then'. In fact, Olivier retorted by saying only Bader could play the part. 'Finally,' Gilbert remembered, 'I had a great idea – and that was Kenneth More.' Unsurprisingly, by this point, Betty had also been banding Kenny's name about. Despite thinking Ken was neither 'versatile nor physically attractive', contracts were inked on Wednesday 6 July 1955 much to the dismay of Alexander Korda who insisted that Ken – 'a man with two good legs' – was mad to 'play a legless hero'. Never one to accept advice counter to his instincts, Ken was not to be put off, especially as Angel promised a £25,000 payday: 'Korda gave me his honest, albeit mistaken opinion as did Noël Coward, who also thought I would be mad to play Bader.'

Between pre-production and the shoot, Ken forged a lucrative sideline writing (or rather giving his name to) potted biographical pieces for periodicals including the *Daily Sketch* and *Woman's Own*, charging £50 for a thousand words. At the same time, he met officials from the Associated Broadcasting Company (ABC), the new ITV contractor in Birmingham to discuss presenting a show 'designed to offer the variety of a Sunday newspaper' (this never happened).[7] Then, he turned down a £5,000 offer to record a TV commercial, saying it would be 'demeaning,' but accepted £10 to appear on *What's My Line?* because 'everyone and their aunt watched it!' Amid all this, he appears to have expressed indifference at ongoing efforts to adapt Kingsley Amis's novel *Lucky Jim* – which, as noted, had started a year earlier. By 22 July 1955, Amis was still struggling to get a straight answer about Ken's availability. In a letter to Philip Larkin, the author noted that producers had 'certainly done a lot of work on the script, written to me a good deal, discussed casting etc. It all rather depends, as I understand it, whether Kenneth More can be got for Jim or not. If he can be, then the chances of the film being actually made are almost 100 per cent. If not, much less than 50 per cent.'[8] In the end, talks extended through the summer – but after another year on the drawing board, the Jim role went to Ian Carmichael, who, later admitted that Amis 'wasn't really happy with the way *Lucky Jim* had been performed and presented ... Looking back, analysing, being self-critical, I think possibly I was miscast.'[9]

Celebrity Fulfilled

Meanwhile, as the start-up date for *Reach for the Sky* approached, Lewis Gilbert returned from Florence clutching the final screenplay, stuffed with drama and heroics. Duly, he presented it to Douglas Bader, who 'absolutely hated it' and vainly lobbied to get his friends featured in the storyline. Despite this little face-off, the script remained intact, and Gilbert yelled 'Action' on 2 August 1955. The screenplay does a very neat job of detailing Bader's battle using 'tin legs', and blatantly magnifies his wartime adventures, his return to flying after losing his legs, leadership of a fighter wing in the Battle of Britain, and finally, his landing in a German prison camp, and his pluck against his Nazi captors. Predictably, the real Bader snubbed the production team and – by the time the cameras were rolling – he was embroiled in a nasty spat with Brickhill over book royalties. Ken liked Bader, but also was close with Gilbert – so played a difficult balancing act. 'I've had two meetings with him [Bader] and the way he has overcome his enormous disability just staggers me,' he said. 'We played golf at Gleneagles, and he practically drove me off the course. When we'd finished, he was ten times fresher than I was and quite ready to go round again.' Bader, he said, gave the impression of a tough and driven egotist. 'He cracks the whip, and the world must follow. He might be hard for some men to take. But that was the way he got over his problem.' At one point, the rumour mill had it that Bader himself had an itch to play the part, 'but he never gave me that impression'. But he did give some straight-from-the-shoulder revelations about the agony of walking on artificial legs, 'how he kept falling and kept getting up to master things, and how he was determined not to let them prevent him from doing anything he wanted to do'.

For the most part, filming continued without incident, except for Kenny complaining about being 'pretty mad' at not being allowed to fly. 'I took 15 lessons and then the insurance people stopped me because they said the risk was too great. It makes me feel like a little prairie flower.'[10] In fact, his wings were clipped after a near accident during his first solo flight with instructor Joan Hughes – one of Britain's first female test pilots. He completed a circuit, made one landing and went up again, according to reporter Gail Pedrick who witnessed events unfold. 'When they next looked down it was to see an ambulance, a fire engine and a man holding up a wheel. They leaned out to see a strut swinging from the undercarriage, but they landed on one wheel with some damage to the plane. It was a desperate moment – but I knew there were complications about insurance and so on, with possible trouble for Kenny, so I resisted the temptation to run to the nearest telephone.' Worried about a budget that had already shot up during preproduction, Gilbert also faced continuous headaches finding planes for the action sequences, as Hurricanes and Spitfires were proving difficult to obtain. In the end, the Chadwick Trust, an old airplane repository, provided a few aircraft, as did the Science Museum, though most flying scenes were created in a studio. Stills from the Rank archives show Ken sitting immersed in a dummy Hurricane, lurching, bumping, and swinging it left and right under blazing arc lights. Watching filming at close quarters, journalist John Stratton saw the 'strain of 18 weeks concentrated effort beginning to show' and recounted a combination of headache, dust, stale air, and sheer fatigue leaving Kenny with a shocking dose of catarrh. 'In fact,' he wrote, 'you'd never recognise the merry blade

Celebrity Fulfilled

of *Genevieve* in this tired, choky-voiced man in air force blue.' On another occasion, a columnist from *Reveille* reported there was hardly a dry eye during a hospital scene when Bader learned his legs had been amputated. 'Dressed in blue and white striped pyjamas and lying in bed, Kenneth More, as Bader, played the scene so movingly that even the toughest technician had tears in his eyes.' Then, the reporter noted, amid all this tension, the director called for a break in filming: 'The atmosphere was shattered by Ken sitting bolt upright and shouting: "Frank, ask them if they've got any bread and dripping, I'm hungry!"'

After shooting, the most urgent item on Rank's agenda was convincing Bader to attend the premiere. He refused, saying that no man should look at himself as a hero in his lifetime. 'I don't think I could stand it. I should feel embarrassed sitting among my old flying comrades and seeing them make such a hero of me up there on the screen.' So, as a way out of this impasse, Lewis Gilbert arranged a swanky private viewing for Bader at the Dorchester, along with Rank's top brass:

> John Davis loved the film and so did everyone who had seen it, so we were all pretty confident. So, Douglas sees the film with his wife, and John Davis and the chief distributor and there's around ten people sitting round a big table. Then suddenly at the end of the meal, John Davis says, 'Well Douglas, I think you can be proud of this film.' And Douglas just looked at him and said: 'Well I'm glad you think so, because I don't!' And John Davis went red in the face – his veins stood out on his neck – I thought, Jesus, he's going to explode. But with a tremendous effort of will, he said: 'I don't know why you say that, Douglas, because everybody thinks it's a great film.'

Bader was still stewing over his objections when *Reach for the Sky* faced the critics in July 1956. However, by this time, Rank recognised the film as a remarkable achievement and Earl St John, the man in charge of production, declared Kenneth gave a fantastic performance, 'one which cannot fail to win awards'. Then, as Gilbert recounts, the day before the premiere – which Bader still refused to attend – Rank arranged a press showing for domestic and foreign journalists:

> That evening, at about 11 p.m., Danny Angel said to Kenny and me, 'Look, why don't we go down to Fleet Street and get the morning papers?' So, we went down Fleet Street and the *Daily Express* then was the really big one, where Leonard Mosely was the film critic. I ran back to the car with a paper and there was Kenny More, Danny and myself. And we quickly opened the pages and the headline – in a full-page notice – was 'You are wrong Douglas Bader; you should have attended'. And they gave the film the most fantastic notice. I read it out to them, and Kenny was just ecstatic! There were so many quotes in it that were great. The interesting thing was the next week, the manager of the Odeon in Southampton rang head office out of the blue and said Douglas had been in with ten people to see the film!

In retrospect, it's hard to see how this modest little studio-based film produced such a rapturous response. But on its release, Ken's depiction of Bader was lauded as one of the great screen portrayals in British cinema. 'A very moving, stirring picture,' one critic noted, 'made all the better by Kenneth More's underplaying of the character.' *Picturegoer*'s Elizabeth Forrest surmised that playing a live hero wasn't every star's idea of bliss. 'But More played it. And he not only made good in the part, but he also enhanced his many-sided reputation even further.' In a full page 'plea', she also pushed Kenny to reconsider remarks he had made about avoiding starring in 'period features' and costume dramas:

> There isn't the slightest doubt that he is potentially our biggest screen actor and a likely top international star as well. Yet, when it comes to his career, More is showing an uncharacteristic streak of nervousness. For reasons no picturegoer would accept, he has stated publicly that he is essentially a contemporary actor. He feels he lacks the scope to tackle any of the classical period roles of Shakespeare, or Restoration comedy, for instance. And now, I hear, he's turned down a role in a period action drama. This is madness. All right, no one blames him for turning down a role that perhaps he feels isn't right. But it's more than that, it's a whole field of film-making More is shunning. But, unless he changes his ideas drastically, we'll have to wait for ever. And on behalf of picturegoers let me say this timidity is not only unrealistic – it's also criminal![11]

While the overall British reception of *Reach for the Sky* pleased Kenny, it was followed by a painful performance in America where Bosley Crowther, the *New York Times* scribe, found it shocking how 'brazenly and bleakly' Lewis Gilbert plied clichés: 'Outside of Mr More, the cast is routine.'

Worse still, during a US publicity trip – which saw Ken pose on top of the Empire State building, lecture at Yale and appear on radio talk shows – he delivered his usual shtick, beginning with an attack on the American film business during a press breakfast in New York. Speaking to a half-filled room from a podium set up in front of the Rank gong, he opened his monologue by naming two American pictures which 'should never have been made'. As he saw it, *Baby Doll* – the story of a child bride – was 'magnificent but very dangerous and encouraged juvenile delinquency'. He saved his special wrath, though, for Marlon Brando's *On the Waterfront*, the gritty story of graft and murder on the New York docks. It's no great secret that he despised American film noir, with its gloomy photography, world-weary private eyes, people turning up dead, thick accents, sleuthing, curt dialogue, and seedy storylines. As the engagement wore on, he lectured his listeners about feeling 'morally bound' to stay in Britain and make 'good, healthy pictures'. For good measure, proceedings ended with a swipe at the screen star Deborah Kerr: 'She wasn't a British actress any longer,' he mused. 'She has swallowed the Hollywood pill beautifully.' In fact, Kerr had moved to California in 1946, and scored a huge success in a string of pictures, including *The King and I*. Unsurprisingly, the media – both in the US and UK – gave the story national attention. From their perspective, Britain's foremost cinema idol in a public spat with America was a sensational story, and they played it to the hilt. The *Daily Mirror* ran a front-page banner 'Star in Revolt', then, Deborah Kerr stepped into the fray by expressing surprise and disappointment: 'Fancy Kenneth being so nasty. I admire him as an actor, and I have told half of Hollywood not to miss *Reach for the Sky*. It is silly of him to antagonise Americans when his picture is just about to be premiered in New York.' The only faint murmur of support came from reporter John Stratton who thought Kenny was 'so very much' a man's man. 'He speaks his mind freely in a world where most actors keep one eye uneasily on the studio publicist. His comments are always pungent and to the point.' Ken never doubted that his reputation would survive any tabloid scrutiny and he would emerge unblemished in the eyes of the public. 'My remarks had been so ordinary,' he later insisted. 'When I was shown these headlines I roared with laughter.' However, almost without trying, he returned home as the most sought-after screen actor, with the possible exception of Alec Guinness, and even claimed Hollywood producers had called with an offer to do two films with Marilyn Monroe, followed by a tempting proposal from MGM but he 'saw no reason for going there when I had plenty of work in Britain'.[12]

But however heartfelt his utterances about loving Blighty were, he chose to spend Christmas with Bill in Austria to celebrate a 'remarkable year in our lives'.

7
THE FILM STAR

By 1956, as *Genevieve* enjoyed its third reissue at cinemas, Kenneth More bore little relation to the man who arrived in London a decade earlier. That year, when the average annual income in Britain was a little over £700, he earned £26,000 – there was no end in sight to his magnificent lifestyle. Not long after purchasing a £3,000 turquoise Thunderbolt sports car (a real 'bobby dazzler', he called it), press interviews showed him in a new self-reflective mood. On one occasion, he unburdened himself saying celebrity was a mixed blessing and complained about 'unfortunately' having the sort of face that's identical off screen and on it, meaning the end of privacy. 'That's the greatest penalty of being me ... sometimes it can be quite unbearable,' he said. 'No private life.' He continued to decry being unable to stroll down the street, window shop, walk in the park with his daughter, get on a bus, or even sup a pint at the local. 'All impossible now.' Whatever the reason, autograph seekers were also something he found hard to fathom. 'It gives people happiness to have my autograph, that's fine but I'll just be walking down the street and people come up and shove old envelopes at me ...'

On the plus side, having proved his box-office mettle, he became choosier about the parts he played and was confident enough to turn down Alexander Korda's suggestion to film *The Admirable Crichton* – an old yarn about a group of shipwrecked Edwardian aristocrats. Before asking Ken to play Crichton, a snobbish butler, Korda had spent four years struggling to adapt the play, initially with Rex Harrison in mind. 'So, when I said no, Korda dropped the idea,' Ken remembered. 'He knew the temperament of the actors he dealt with and if a story suggestion didn't appeal to any particular one – he'd drop it.' However, things changed when Lewis Gilbert thought it might be a winner. 'Anyway,' Ken said, 'Lewis and I got more and more excited. I said I would tell Alex I'll do it if he let Gilbert direct.' In the upshot, Lewis rang Alex. 'He picked up the phone. I saw his face drop ... Alex had died the night before. My sense of loss was tremendous; Alex had been not only my employer, but a very good friend and adviser.'

A few nights later, hosting a BBC tribute, Ken joined Charles Laughton, Robert Donat, Laurence Olivier, and Ralph Richardson in lauding Korda as an impresario, poet, showman and philosopher: 'The film industry will miss him terribly,' he said. 'There is no one to take his place. He was the life blood of the cinema. He was unique, he put his work before anything and when warned he should take things easily, he just carried on.'

A few days after Korda's funeral, feeling the need to move quickly on *The Admirable Crichton*, Mike Frankovich, the director of Columbia Pictures in the UK, promised backing for the film. With Columbia's money behind it, preproduction work then advanced under Ian Dalrymple – Ken's chum from *Raising a Riot* – and shooting schedules were set for Bermuda for September, October, and early November. At the same time, Lewis Gilbert secured all the talent he could muster by signing Diane Cilento, Cecil Parker, and Sally Ann Howes for supporting roles. Gilbert also delivered a brilliantly crafted script, oozing all the pageantry and glamour of the Edwardian age. 'It is something to see, especially in colour,' Ken told *Picturegoer*. 'And you've got the down-to-earth side of it when the action switches to the island.'

Before shooting, Ken even took instruction from Charles Coupland, his own part-time butler, who had been in service since 1898. Having worked for the aristocracy in the grandest homes, he knew everything that made Crichton so utterly unflustered. 'It comes as second nature to him,' Ken explained. 'He understands exactly how silver should be arranged on a breakfast tray ... when to speak, when not to speak.' And in a typical gesture, Ken even invited a Keystone press photographer to snap Coupland explaining how to polish the silver. 'But he is so good,' Ken said, 'that I can't get him full time. I have to share him with Robertson Hare.' During this flurry of pre-production activity, Kenny set out on a brand-new venture by forming 'Kenneth More Productions Ltd', ostensibly to back Ronald Culver's play *A River Breeze* at the Phoenix Theatre, a joint project with H. M. Tennant, starring Culver, Naunton Wayne and Phyllis Calvert. Initially, he mulled producing *The Man from the Sea*, a play he literally dreamed one night and jotted down on the back of an envelope. Unlike many of his dreams, this one presented a detailed narrative, complete with a title. In short, it revolved around a shipwrecked sailor washed ashore on the coast of the Mediterranean. Upon being discovered and resuscitated by villagers, it was revealed they were plagued by a local bandit. According to legend, a 'man from the sea' would come to their rescue. The villagers connected the dots, and the sailor was suddenly burdened with seemingly impossible expectations. Sadly, plans were shelved, and the closest Ken came to the sea was to make an appearance on the BBC's *Desert Island Discs*, a show featuring distinguished personalities discussing eight records that he or she would bring if cast away on a desert island. 'I'm a very adaptable sort of person and I don't get lonely,' he chirped, when asked how he would survive. 'I think I could cope rather well. One of my hobbies is underwater fishing and swimming, so I presume I could cut down a sliver of bamboo and no doubt spear my Sunday dinner under the water.' Filled with genteel reminiscences, the conversation turned to *Genevieve*:

> When my missus was out shopping in New York, she came back with a record one day called 'Music from the Movies' – or 'Music from Hollywood' – I can't quite remember – a selection of tunes, hit tunes, from various Hollywood musicals by Percy Faith and his orchestra and right in the middle was a little thing called the 'Genevieve Waltz' and it said on the blurb on the back, you know, all about things, that they'd put this in because they were so enchanted with the film *Genevieve* and some person – not Larry Adler who did the music in England – had composed this quite new tune and called it the 'Genevieve Waltz', and we think it is absolutely charming.

He spoke of lean times at Byker, and gave insight into life as a new father when choosing Frank Sinatra's 'Young at Heart':

> Now the reason for this is that my nanny – when I say my nanny, the nanny we have to look after our little daughter, Sarah, is an absolute charmer and she regards me, I'm afraid, in much the same light she regards Sarah – rather the wicked small boy, in fact, when Sarah gets scolded, I get scolded just as much. She always finds I'm doing things which influence her beloved charge, but the one thing that we both have in common is the fact that people should not grow old, at least mentally, and we always have this little thing between us about being young in heart, so this one's for nanny and Sarah.

Other song choices came from Doris Day and Ronnie Carroll, and his luxury item, in addition to a family photograph, was an English rock garden to make life slightly more bearable. 'I think I'd find that very comforting to listen to my records in.'

The Admirable Crichton was a spectacular, grandiose picture, which even before filming, racked up £35,000 in expenses. Over the coming months, foreign locations, lavish sets, period costumes, and colour photography saw that figure rise to £221,884. On paper, J. M. Barrie's story – a lightweight Edwardian spree – was simple: it opens with a group of aristocrats getting stranded on a desert island. A talkative lord (Parker), his three snobbish daughters and their boyfriends become hapless castaways along with Crichton, the butler, played by Kenneth, who, it transpires, is the biggest snob of them all.

However, in the battle to survive, the social scales turn. A deft hand at do-it-yourself, Crichton becomes the leader – known as 'Guv' – who is suddenly adored by the daughters, and waited upon by his lordship. Dalrymple had always had an eye for vibrant, quirky humour, and introduced ridiculous touches like a record player created from an old biscuit tin with a seashell as a speaker, and cocktails served in coconut shells. On paper, the shoot looks tight, but conditions were convivial, as Noël Coward's diaries reveal. A resident of Bermuda, Coward found time to take the crew on a tour of the pink-sandy shores and held court at his villa where the cast often dropped in for drinks. He even turned up to watch the rushes and ribbed Ken on his 'strikingly athletic performance' swimming, climbing rocks, and staging stunts. However, there were a few nasty incidents, including the time he nearly drowned during a scene which called for him to swim ashore fully clothed. The sea – stirred up by boats carrying cameras, and fans blasting wind onto the water – created large waves as though a storm was raging. Fortunately, Diane Cilento – the future wife of Sean Connery, playing a maid, dived in to the rescue. 'If it hadn't been for Diane,' Ken exclaimed, 'I would not be alive to talk about it.'

After five weeks under Caribbean skies, the crew returned to film interiors at Shepperton where *Picture Show*'s Edith Nepean turned up to report on the film, but focused on Ken's daughter Sarah who had been present at the studio during her last three visits. 'As I chatted with Kenneth More during the tea break,' she observed, 'a tiny child with fair hair and sparkling blue eyes danced across the ballroom floor like a fairy, smiling at the stars and extras, but quite unperturbed by her audience.' Sarah was one of the few positive parts of Ken's life during what turned out to be a difficult period. He was devastated when Roland Culver's play *A River Breeze* turned into a public humiliation after being skewered by critics as 'a slim little thing'. 'Author Culver gives actor Culver a fine, fat part then leaves the others in the cast to fend for themselves,' was the opinion of the *Daily Herald*'s Anthony Carthew, who reckoned the play couldn't have been saved by the funniest men in England. *The Stage* noted it was 'not a well-contrived or important work'. That debacle was crushing enough, but then Ken received a drubbing with the release of *The Admirable Crichton*. 'I thought the dialogue and the film script were rather trite and poor,' he admitted. 'And the critics thought so too. We didn't get a very good press. On the other hand, it was a great commercial success with the public because the story was so strong.'[1] In fact, audiences were undeterred by poor notices and Ken was named Britain's top film star in 1956 by the *Motion Picture Herald*, the American trade journal. Perhaps his proudest achievement, though, was the rise in his social stock. In fact, he was close enough to dispense with protocol with Queen Elizabeth and her husband, Prince Philip, and prized memories of an evening at the Astors' country home when the Queen kicked off her shoes to prove that in spite of all the walking she did on ceremonial occasions, she had no bunions. 'Ken cherished his friendship with his monarch,' the writer and producer Maurice Sellar said. 'And it is well known that she admired his ability as an actor, having attended many a film premiere in which he appeared.' Along the way, there were frequent encounters with other royals, including Princess Margaret and Lord Mountbatten, both regulars at the swanky

The Film Star

Savoy Grill, or Kettner's. Mostly though, parties revolved around a close circle of friends like Jack Hawkins who entertained with 'tripe dinners', followed by poker, or bridge. Christmas was also spent playing board games with Jack and Doreen Hawkins. 'We always have the same food,' Doreen confessed. 'Round the fire we eat veal and ham pie from our local pub!' In contrast, New Year's parties spent with Noël Coward's chums, Charles, and Ham, at their flat on Greek Street, were riotous affairs. As Coward's secretary Cole Lesley recounted, guests were usually 'fully lubricated' before getting down to the 'serious business' of the evening – The Game – a trickier version of charades where 'you really had to act your heart out in a dumb show, to convey the impossible word or terrible message on your slip of paper'. The star of the show was always Joyce Carey, as Cole later described:

> By general consensus, because they were the best, Noël was always captain of one side at these parties and Kenneth More of the other. It was clearly understood (and dreaded) by all that the phrases on the slips of paper doled out by Kenny would be either of an erudite or of a deeply shocking nature. No one present ever forgot the exquisitely pretty Margaret Lockwood, a Fragonard-like figure, emoting away, viciously kicking from time to time, and Joycie inquiring of her, ever so gently, 'Darling, could it by any chance be "Taking a flying fuck at a galloping mule?"'

The Game was equally popular on the Riviera, and sometimes played at the Hôtel du Cap-Eden-Roc where regulars included Rex Harrison, Somerset Maugham, and screenwriter Jack Davies. Perched on a cliff overlooking miles of ocean, the hotel had attracted Charlie Chaplin and Rudolph Valentino in the 1920s, while the Duke of Windsor and Wallis Simpson sought privacy there after the abdication. In its heyday, guests could step out of their cars, stroll through the courtyard and into a serpentine green tiled pool. Before long, Ken and Bill purchased a two-bedroom flat in Monte Carlo from where he indulged in his passion for underwater swimming, which occasionally involved chartering a large yacht to cruise near Antibes, and Villefranche. Most appealing of all, though, was Monaco – a tiny nation devoted to the service and pleasure of the rich – which became Ken and Bill's playground. They embraced the cabarets and beaches, but the distinctive feature of life was, without a doubt, the casinos, and culinary delights. Food was important to the Mores – both adored the local lobster and Mediterranean bream (unlike Jack Hawkins whose aversion to 'foreign food' saw him import sausages from Britain). As one friend recalled it, Kenny was 'desperate to enjoy everything fame had to offer' and 'fancied himself a part of the Riviera set'.

To pay for the Monaco pad, the riverside house in Lock End in Shiplake had to go, and the couple returned to Kingston House. 'It was too far away,' Ken insisted, saying he had 'got a little bit more important' in his profession. 'I had to see a few producers and they just wouldn't come as far down as Henley, so we've got to come back into circulation.' In fact, he had been having misgivings about the house, which he thought resembled a lavish theatre or movie set, rather than a dwelling. It was, he reasoned, a place to be seen and snapped, but oddly, not relaxing to live in. Worse still, it was proving exceptionally expensive to maintain as gardening bills, and the services of a cook and housemaid, mounted. He found such costs a growing frustration – 'and gradually a focus for discontent'. Thankfully, the property was snapped up by Major Noel Chavasse, ADC to Field Marshal Viscount Montgomery of Alamein.

Ironically, just as Shiplake was sold, Kenny's financial horizon perked up when Danny Angel offered him the prospect of starring in ten films – seven to be made for Rank – the most prestigious British studio – and three for 20th Century Fox. He leapt at the offer and a few weeks later, the Rank part of the deal was secured at 38 South Street where John Davis was acquiring a stable of stars to compete with the likes of Gregory Peck and Marlon Brando. In a rare press conference, he said Dirk Bogarde, Peter Finch, Kay Kendall, Joan Carson, Virginia McKenna, Belinda Lee, Michael Craig, Tony Wright and Maureen Swanson made up the bulk of his talent pool. 'And, of course, there's Kenneth More,' he added. 'I have just signed him to do seven films for me over the next five years. This group has the advantage over the daddies of Hollywood like Clark Gable that they are young. The public don't get any thrill any more from Gable and his generation. They want new faces. And what new faces have they been given by Hollywood since the war?'

To Ken's regret, however, almost immediately, Davis handpicked him to star in *The Enchanted Hour*, later retitled *Next to No Time,* an altogether forgettable comedy produced by Henry Cornelius. 'It is a straightforward human-interest story, intimate and light,' Cornelius explained from the deck of the *Queen Elizabeth,* where the film was shot. Betsy Drake, the virtually unknown wife of Cary Grant, played the love interest, while the principals included Roland Culver (who had recovered from the panning of *A River Breeze*), Harry Green, and Reginald Beckwith. Though the plot had little going for it, Kenny gave an energetic performance as David Webb, a brilliant but timid engineer who finds himself having to tackle a wealthy industrialist on board the *Queen Elizabeth* to secure support for a revolutionary process he has developed. The character was an unusual one for Ken, but unfortunately, *Next to No Time* was not a particularly good picture, made worse by the fact that Cornelius was a sick man. Looking back, cinematographer Freddy Francis called it 'a mess of a film' and said Cornelius was a lovely man but a bit of a muddler. 'It needed stronger direction and unfortunately, one of the problems may have been, by now, Kenny More who I liked very much. But Kenny was a bit of a law unto himself and Corny hadn't done anything for a long time. So, I've an idea that Kenny may have been a bit too strong for Corny.' There was, in fact, never any question about who had the last word, as demonstrated in a revealing entry in the diary of Kenneth Williams, then a jobbing actor: 'To Shepperton for an abortive interview with Henry Cornelius – whole thing ruined by Kenneth More who said I was too young! Fantasy. This actor's work has always struck me as being intrinsically vulgar.'[2] When work on *Next to No Time* came to an end, Cornelius was admitted to hospital and died not long after in a London nursing home. He was just forty-three.

Ken detested *Next to No Time* and was relieved when editing and post-production held up the release. (He eventually acknowledged it was a failure, saying he was in 'the privileged position of being able to blame myself'.)[3] However, his overall frustration was short lived. Almost immediately, he snubbed

The Film Star

the role of a German pilot in *The One That Got Away* (Hardy Krüger took the part), and sank his teeth into a meatier repast by preparing to play Second Officer Charles Lightoller in *A Night to Remember*, an epic account of the *Titanic* sinking, which, in many ways, was the last great Pinewood epic. One of the first things Rank did was to create a large-scale model of the doomed liner nose down in the act of sinking, setting the stage for what they said was their 'biggest ever production' using VistaVision – a high-resolution, widescreen format – to be photographed by Geoffrey Unsworth, who later filmed *2001: A Space Odyssey*, Stanley Kubrick's epic. Most of the interiors, including the ship's dining room, were built at Pinewood and spread over several sound stages. Ken told one reporter shortly after production began, how the sight of the cabins and lounges re-created exactly as they were, 'never failed to raise startled gasps from the survivors of the wreck who visited the set'. Duly, publicists had a field day with the film, and even before shooting began reported that producer Bill MacQuitty had received over 500 letters from survivors and relatives of those lost onboard the doomed vessel. It was fertile turf for MacQuitty who had actually seen the *Titanic* being launched in 1911 and remembered the occasion vividly. He also watched her maiden voyage departure the following year. Armed with personal accounts and recollections, Ken talked with Lightoller's friends and family, including his widow Iowa Sylvania Zillah Hawley-Wilson. As a result, the screenplay accurately depicts the 'unsinkable ship' the night she struck an iceberg from the reaction of the captain down to passengers in steerage – all picked out by Unsworth's camera constantly on the move. It is filled with scenes that rank among the most famous set pieces of cinema history, including the iceberg collision, Bruce Ismay's cowardice in securing a lifeboat seat and the final plunge of the great liner into the depths of the Atlantic. 'Undoubtedly, as far as pure camera illusion is concerned, *A Night to Remember* is by far the most perfect film with which I have ever been associated,' Ken noted in his memoirs. Often when a ship is meant to be sinking in a studio, the effect is reached by raising the level of the water, but director, Roy Baker did it much more convincingly by having it on rails and sliding them down into a vast tank. Always demanding, Baker also arranged a shooting schedule spread over 23 weeks, featuring 160 speaking parts. 'It's a funny thing,' Ken said. 'Directly I get this uniform on, it's as though the years have slipped away and I'm on the deck of the old *Victorious* as it bombarded the Japanese mainland.'[4]

Everyone in the cast gave what many critics considered outstanding performances, including Laurence Naismith playing the small but significant part of Captain Smith, and Michael Goodliffe as the designer who went down with the ship. During production, Baker went 'all out' to create the frozen, icy atmosphere and, like in *Scott of the Antarctic*, he instructed the cast to suck pellets to produce visible breath, and left the main studio unheated. To create the illusion of a freezing ocean, scenes were filmed late at night in the ice-cold waters of the Ruislip lido, where 'five times in one night Mr More changed his clothes to go into the water,' journalist Kenneth Passingham observed. 'And if he looked like drying off, they doused him with buckets full of the stuff.' In fact, the extraordinary physical effort required by the cast taxed the crew's patience, as coughs, splutters and sneezes messed up take after take. Even Ken complained about being

Baby Kenneth with his sister Kate and mother, 1914.

Ken had especially fond memories of his father, Charles Gilbert More, a civil engineer, known as an outgoing and gregarious man.

Kenny said he acquired a new vitality at Byker: 'It was pure magic. A marvellous old Victorian blood-and-thunder theatre.'

During his time at Byker, Ken took an instant shine to Beryl Johnstone, a newcomer from Ellen Compton's repertory company in Cheltenham, lauded by the regional press as an 'artist of considerable promise'.

Above: The HMS *Aurora* took Kenny on many wartime adventures, including the invasion of North Africa and the Allied landings on Crete.

Left: In 1947, Noël Coward offered Kenny a part in his new play, *Peace in Our Time*. The play shows what might have happened had the Nazis occupied Britain in 1940.

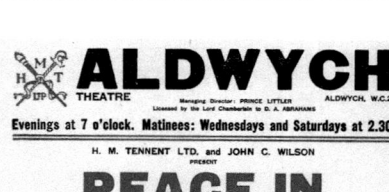

Kenny starred alongside Basil Radford in *Chance of a Lifetime*. (Pilgrim Pictures/ Public Domain)

Above left: Kenny and Kay Kendall appear on the cover of *Picturegoer* in June 1953, a clear sign his star was rising. The two enjoyed a brief affair during the filming of *Genevieve*.

Above right: Mabel ('Bill') and Ken. The two tied the knot on 18 August 1952 and remained together for another decade. (Reginald Davis)

Our Girl Friday turned out to be a leisurely affair, where the crew could often be found romping in the waters off Paguera. 'I wore a bikini and no make-up,' Joan Collins later said. 'It was quite restful and more like a holiday than work.' (Langley Minter Productions)

Group Captain Sir Douglas Bader who Ken portrayed in the 1956 film *Reach for the Sky*. (Norwegian State Archives)

An early autograph card. Whatever the reason, autograph seekers were also something Ken found hard to fathom. 'It gives people happiness to have my autograph, that's fine but I'll just be walking down the street and people come up and shove old envelopes at me ...'

Above: Jack Hawkins, Lord Mountbatten and Kenny at an event to honour the Royal Navy Film Unit. (*The Times of Cyprus*)

Below: Lauren Bacall receiving a kiss on the cheek from Kenny, with Laurence Olivier in the background, 10 November 1958. (Trinity Mirror/Mirrorpix/Alamy Stock Photo)

The Duke of Edinburgh shakes hands with Kenny at the world premiere of *Sink the Bismarck!* at the Odeon, Leicester Square, 1960. Bill is standing to Ken's right. (Keystone Press/Alamy Stock Photo)

Above left: The Rank Organisation's John Davis and Ken came to blows, notably after Ken's behaviour on a goodwill and promotional tour of twenty-one British cities.

Above right: 'Jolyon was the role that marked the end of my being typecast as a one-dimensional ageing juvenile and I thank my lucky stars for it,' Ken recounted, after signing up to make twenty-six episodes of *The Forsyte Saga*. The adaptation of John Galsworthy's trilogy by BBC Television was broadcast in many countries.

Kenny showing a model Spitfire to Prince Bernhard in Holland during promotions for the *Battle of Britain* in 1969 as Angela looks on. (Dutch National Archives)

The wedding reception of Roger Moore and Luisa Mattioli at the Royal Garden Hotel, Kensington, 11 April 1969. The couple are pictured with best man Kenny and Angela Douglas. (Mirrorpix)

In 1972, Lew Grade persuaded Ken to star in G. K. Chesterton's *Father Brown*, saying the role would be lucrative and fun.

Kenny appears at the topping-out ceremony for the Kenneth More Theatre. Next to him (fourth from left) is manager Vivyan Ellacott.

Left: The Kenneth More Theatre, 1975. (Vivyan Ellacott)

Below: Ken enjoys dinner with the cast of *Journey to the Centre of the Earth* in Spain. (Lone Faerch)

The Film Star

dunked in water, and then hauled out for half an hour. 'I lose my sleep. They put our clothes in front of a high-pressure turbo jet drier. Then they rubbed us down till we looked like boiled lobsters ... I tell you, if my wife hadn't been alongside with a bottle of rum every night, I wouldn't have survived.' His physical exhaustion worsened when the unit moved to Scotland to shoot aboard RMS *Asturias*, a liner in the process of being scrapped. Although the port side had been demolished, its starboard remained intact, and was repainted in White Star Line colours. Throughout the difficult location shoot, Baker did his best to spread cheer, and claimed Ken pulled the whole thing together: 'He had the central character, and he was very good at working with all the other actors in the film, he was very much a naval man.' Indeed, the character was heroic – a sleeves-rolled-up, sturdy, gallant sailor, battling to save lives under impossible circumstances. Baker took care to personally oversee several scenes that gave Ken a depth and a dimension he'd never displayed before. One of them shows him finding a dead child and gently placing the corpse in the water. Several critics gave pride of place to his performance, remarking he could have been 'stiff upper lippish' but succeeded in being human. In fact, what emerged was a thrilling and beautiful movie, worthy of the compliments it received. One enterprising bookie even laid ten to one that Ken would win an Oscar. Audiences didn't mind the film's gloomy story and after enjoying unqualified box-office success, it became one of the best-known movies in history, spawning papers, books, documentaries, and websites devoted to extolling and studying the picture. In fact, the production file of memos, meeting transcripts, telegrams, and letters concerning the project is as thick as a phone directory.

Having conquered the British market, Rank assembled a crack publicity team to promote *A Night to Remember* in the United States headed by Geoffrey Martin, a talented adman. A week before the US premiere, he sent out thousands of swizzle sticks – used for mixing cocktails – to critics, journalists, and bartenders. Unusually, the sticks carried a plastic model of the *Titanic*, with the gimmick being to let the stick rest on the ice in the cocktail and slowly sink as the ice melted. Flabbergasted, one well-known journalist returned his 'souvenir' describing it as a 'disgusting stunt'. Angry articles began appearing in the New York press and even *Time*, America's most influential magazine, chipped in. 'If the talents of the movie's producers come close to matching the tastelessness of the promoters, *A Night to Remember* should be a smash hit.'

In an age before spin doctors, Martin giggled that his simple promotion 'had obviously worked' and pointed critics to Bosley Crowther's review in *The New York Times* lauding *A Night to Remember* as a 'brilliant and moving account' that should never be forgotten. It is a 'tense, exciting and supremely awesome drama ... [that] puts the story of the great disaster in simple human terms and yet brings it all into a drama of monumental unity and scope.' However, promotion for the film took an even more bizarre turn when Ken touched down in New York and, after a whirlwind of Broadway theatregoing, took it upon himself to brief the press on his thoughts on the American film industry. It wasn't his finest hour. In a cocktail haze, he lectured a UPI journalist that 'bust size, rather than talent' had become the gauge for an actress's success, and pointed the finger at Marilyn Monroe and Sophia Loren for 'killing off such sophisticated performers as

Lauren Bacall, Rosalind Russell and Barbara Stanwyck'. Monroe, he pondered, was wonderfully effective on the screen but was 'like Lassie – one bark and she steals a scene'. On Loren, he said, 'I don't see much in this woman at all,' and wondered how Ingrid Bergman remained popular in the face of such 'voluptuous competition'.

A Night to Remember was a box-office winner from the outset – and went on to become one of the highest grossing films that Rank ever released. Better still, it won several awards, including a Golden Globe for Best English-Language Foreign Film. However, not long afterward, the British movie industry continued to slide into crisis. Behind the glamour, the sound of a death rattle provoked Rank to sack 300 staff at Pinewood, reduce production, and pare down opening times at suburban cinemas. Fighting the onslaught of television, the company shrank faster than expected, prompting John Davis to threaten more cuts, including axing a remake of Hitchcock's *The 39 Steps*, planned as a vehicle for Kenny. However, if Ken was disappointed, he didn't show it and spent a longer summer vacation exploring shipwrecks with the Club Aquatique near Cannes, the only British-run school for underwater swimmers on the Côte d'Azur, owned by Jack Atkinson. Every summer, members embarked on a specific mission. That year, the goal was to locate an ancient Roman wine galley and, after days of shallow dives, the group discovered the vessel resting 140 feet below the surface, close to a cluster of rocks. The unusually well-preserved earthenware amphora – used to carry wine, oil, water, or grain on long voyages – remained in place, partially obscured by mud. Tragically, seven days later, an unknown diver detonated explosives to salvage mementos from the wreckage, destroying the entire site in the process. 'The French diving clubs were hopping mad,' Ken remembered. 'They regarded the wreck as a national treasure.'

On returning home with a golden tan roughly the tone of a well-cooked chicken, his attention was diverted from work by pleasurable activities, including appearing in *Oranges and Lemons,* a sketch at the *Night of a Hundred Stars,* a charity benefit. Written by Noël Coward, the skit concerned two spinsters whose boudoir was invaded by two men, Rex Harrison, and Jack Hawkins. Laurence Olivier and Kenny played the spinsters, and for the press, they delighted in mincing along the Haymarket in Edwardian skirts and rouge. 'Larry was totally loving the experience of getting every laugh he could wring out of what was a very funny sketch anyway,' Ken remembered. 'Here was this wonderful, powerful Shakespearean actor, who was without doubt the greatest actor in the world, and he was having an absolute ball playing for laughs in drag. The audience went wild. There were hysterics when we all appeared for our curtain call, and Rex presented Larry to the audience, and Larry went into the persona of a ballerina and did a wonderful curtsey to the audience.'[5]

Shortly thereafter, Betty Van Damm persuaded Ken to appear at the Windmill theatre's twenty-fifth birthday concert, where – with the look of a mischievous lad – he opened the show in overalls, sweeping the stage. His one line was: 'You've got to start somewhere.' Sadly, the post-war years had not been kind to the Windmill which almost stopped turning as a new wave of clubs lured customers with racier delights. As the years passed, the atmosphere changed too; a weariness, even a grubbiness, set in. 'I did fear an end to my sentimental journey,' Ken lamented. 'I suspected its imminent demise. Nothing lasts forever.'

With *The 39 Steps* shelved, Danny Angel – by now, one of the savviest producers in Britain – stepped forward with an offer for Ken to play the lead in the western-spoof *The Sheriff of Fractured Jaw*, alongside Jayne Mansfield, the American pin-up star. After much cajoling, he signed to portray Jonathan Tibbs, an impeccably tailored Englishman and heir to an ailing firm of London gunsmiths. Based on a novel by Jacob Hays, the story tells how one morning, after reading an article in *The Times*, Tibbs notes 'a lot of shooting going on' in the American West – and heads there to drum up trade. 'I'm in the gun business,' he announces when arriving in Fractured Jaw, a sleepy Wild West town. A few hours later, he is made sheriff and falls into the arms of Mansfield, portraying an alluring but brassy saloon keeper. Getting the film off the ground had been a long, difficult process. £15,000 alone went on constructing a Wild West town in the Spanish countryside, a much cheaper option than building a set at Pinewood. And amid the gunslingers and bar room brawls, Kenny now embraced the possibility of a career in America – and harboured hopes the film could provide a ticket to Hollywood. However, as Lewis Gilbert observed, the days of British stars making headlines dithering about whether to go to Hollywood, (and garner more publicity when he decided not to) were over. He told *Picturegoer* that local actors were fine for the home market but, 'outside, as I found with *Reach for the Sky*, they mean nothing'. Undeterred, Kenny placed his hopes in director Raoul Walsh – an American known as the curmudgeonly 'one-eyed bandit' – who had over 105 movies under his belt. However, when shooting *The Sheriff of Fractured Jaw* finally got underway in June 1958, Ken was astonished to find his part required an 'exceptional amount' of ad-libbing. 'Raoul Walsh, bless his heart, this one-eyed horse thief as we used to call him, didn't believe in dialogue. Actors who spoke lines were all a load of cissies – dialogue just held up the picture. He wanted horses and pistol fights, and bar drinking scenes and he didn't want to bother with dialogue.' After a few arid months in the Spanish desert, Kenny thought the scope and flavour of the film resembled a classic Hollywood western, complete with thrilling gunslinger scenes and snappy dialogue. Soon, he was talking to the media about the picture 'turning him into a name to be reckoned with in America'. In one interview, he said the film presented Mansfield with the chance to show she was not merely a cut-rate imitation of Marilyn Monroe. 'So far, all she's done in pictures is to display that wonderful wiggle,' he asserted. 'We don't want her to do that in this picture.' And if those words weren't demeaning enough, he added:

> In our film, although you could call her role that of a junior wisecracking Mae West, she's got one of the best roles of her career. And it is a British film that is giving it to her. It could put her back on top again, for let's face it, people say she's been slipping lately. An American director and Jayne should help put the film on the map so far as America's concerned. And that's a good thing for me.

Though perplexed by such astounding condescension – receiving the remarks as malicious – Mansfield delivered a free-spirited performance helping to make it one of the highest-grossing British movies of the year. She later described Ken as 'that bumptious man,' adding she 'never wanted to work with him again'. In his own defence, Ken claimed he gave Mansfield a gold watch when shooting was complete. 'And my wife,' he added, 'had a letter from her saying we were the nicest two people she had ever met.' Moreover, as a parting shot, he claimed Mansfield was simply courting publicity because 'a rift' made good copy.

At the end of the seven-week shoot, Angel was busily pitching *Have Monocle Will Travel,* a yarn based on the adventures of Christopher Powell, an ex-British colonel. He gave Ken a draft script to read during a break at a secluded cabin in Davos, but as bad luck would have it, he was transported home a few days later cemented in a leg plaster after being hit by a boy on skis on the slopes. 'There I was, doing nobody any harm and then, boof, I was flat on my back! Unlike most actors, I am solid from the neck down', he joked at Heathrow, as an ambulance met his plane and, skipping customs formalities, drove him to where his Rolls was parked. Before limping off, he held an impromptu press conference on the tarmac explaining how he would have to stand up most of the time as when he sat down 'this plaster practically cuts my legs off. Fortunately, I haven't another film to make until May.'

Though dozens of scripts continued to come his way, he jumped at an offer from the publisher Robert Hale to write an autobiography and began cobbling together memories and anecdotes. When his leg healed, he steadfastly refused Angel's continued overtures to appear in *Have Monocle Will Travel* (which was never made) and opted for a spot of seclusion at Noël Coward's house in Les Avants-sur-Montreux, a gorgeous property providing stunning views of Lake Geneva, where he sketched out an outline for the book. Back home, a rigorous schedule of promotional appearances for *The Sheriff of Fractured Jaw* set the stage for a series of gushing reviews. Summing up the critical opinion in her *Daily Herald* analysis, June Herbert thought Ken keeping 'Injuns' and bad men at bay with his brolly was hilarious, if a somewhat protracted farce. 'Mr More prevails not only with the wild Westerners but also with the audience as well,' *The Guardian* added. 'He is very funny.'

Even though *The Sheriff of Fractured Jaw* did not exactly set the American box office on fire, it was a personal triumph. During all of this, word circulated that *The 39 Steps*, the picture shelved during Rank's cost-saving measures, was to be resurrected. Duly, Ken met producer Betty Box and supported her decision to recruit the newly divorced Finnish actress Taina Elg (for whom he worked up quite a fancy) for the role of Fisher, the romantic interest. It seems casting the part had been an enormous undertaking. Box first sought Kay Kendall, then approached June Allyson, whose reign as an A-list movie star was waning, before settling on Elg, who was eager. Typically, a supporting cast of players, mostly Rank stalwarts, signed up, including Brenda de Banzie, Reginald Beckwith, and Michael Goodliffe.

Kenny had just turned forty-four when shooting commenced on 21 September 1958. Running at a galloping ninety-five minutes, the film tells how his character, Richard Hannay, finds himself framed for murder and goes on the run to the Scottish Highlands pursued by Scotland Yard and other shadowy enemies. It is not all that difficult to understand what attracted him to this thriller. For one thing, he took pride in doing stunts without the aid of a double, and careered around on a bicycle, leapt from an open window into a passing truck, crawled along the Forth Bridge and jumped from a train.

But despite such heroics, there's a blandness to his performance and critics felt the pace was too leisurely. Some blamed director Ralph Thomas – who'd been endlessly watching Hitchcock's original – for shooting the picture almost frame by frame as Hitchcock had done. However, after five long, busy, and ultimately enjoyable months of filming, *The 39 Steps* opened to lukewarm reviews. The *Liverpool Daily Post* led the chorus of disapproval by scowling that Hannay was a 'bit too comfortable', lacking spontaneity, despite being a wanted man and a hero. 'Hitchcock made a thrilling first-rate film ... which is something we cannot say for the new Rank version.' Even more astounding, *The Guardian*'s critic called it a dreary piece of work and took exception to the inclusion of Elg: 'Considering she was cast as an English games mistress, she talks very foreign.' Their unnamed critic did, however, add that Ken was a pleasure: 'his screen manner has an English modesty and a quality of understated humour'. As a side note, at the time of writing this book, Taina Elg (aged ninety-three) had lost all her memory, which her son, Raoul Björkenheim, told the author was 'a very ironic turn for someone who would have had such cherished memories'. *The 39 Steps*, he said, 'was one of the few serious films that my mother was in (though not without its sense of humour). She always spoke well of it and that she enjoyed working with Mr More.'

The final weeks of filming *The 39 Steps* were marred by a triple dose of tragic news. Firstly, on 18 October, Miriam Warner – the woman instrumental in Kenny's early career – died suddenly. Eleven days later, tragedy of a far greater kind struck when Harry Dubens, the agent that had given so much fatherly care, also passed away, aged sixty-eight after hailing a taxi in Regent Street. As he climbed in from the kerb, he was struck by a fatal heart attack. In his autobiography, Ken praised him as the 'one man who had always expressed his faith in me'. Whenever he pursued advice, be it day or night, Dubens provided wise counsel. Then, in another cruel blow, his old pal Ronnie Squire died after becoming ill at his Great Ormond Street home having just returned from Hollywood. Ironically, two days earlier, he had been due to dine with the Mores – but 'for some reason or other,' Kenny broke the date, to his 'eternal regret'. Clearly upset, he muttered a few words to the Press Association about being a 'great admirer of Mr Squire and learning a lot from him', adding, he never made an enemy and was 'always the perfect gentleman'. During this low point, as friends rallied round, John Mills recommended that Ken's professional affairs be transferred from Dubens' office to Laurie Evans, a businessman regarded as the dean of theatrical agents. Almost immediately, Evans secured an appearance at the *Royal Variety Performance*, alongside Eartha Kitt, Antonio and his dancers and a cast of singers, jugglers, and comedians. Ken relished his spot on the show, which, back then, was considered infinitely more important than it is nowadays. Straight afterwards, he boarded a TWA Starliner for a holiday junket in New York but soon fell sick with jaundice, abdominal pain, vomiting and itchy skin. After a battery of tests, his condition was severe enough to send him home, as Jack Hawkins' wife, Doreen, recounted in a newsy letter to columnist Radie Harris:

The Film Star

'Kenny and Bill are off to France for ten days before he starts work on his film with Betty Bacall. It is nice to have her among us. Kenny is much better. He has to watch his diet still, and of course, no drink.' Funnily enough, mortality never crept into Ken's thoughts, but keeping fit did. Within a week, he rose from his bed like Lazarus from the grave, installed an exercise bike, and cut out booze, late nights and fatty foods. He was excited about the Bacall film – *North West Frontier* – set to begin shooting in Rajasthan, and as his health improved, he attended costume fittings, was jabbed with inoculations, and sent reams of script revisions. At the same time, Bill secretly conspired with ITV to ensure he would be 'thoroughly surprised' when *This is Your Life*'s Eamonn Andrews pounced on him with the 'big red book'. It was a proud day. A surviving tape of the show, broadcast from Lime Grove, has an air of antiquity. It shows Ken's first blush reaction – to feign fainting – when confronted by Andrews at the Gaumont Cinema, Shepherd's Bush. A few minutes later, Nanny Gessing ran onto the set and planted an enormous kiss on his cheek. Then, after being chased around the stage by Kay Kendall, he regaled the tale of his disappointing role as a pilot in *School for Secrets* (Peter Ustinov also appeared on tape to tell the same story). Other tributes came from 'surprise guests' Sally Ann Howes, Frith Banbury, and – for comedy effect – the St Bernard from *Genevieve*. Even Dirk Bogarde rejoiced in telling stories about when they 'lived on beer, bread, and baked beans'. Douglas H. J. Hardy, a cameraman for British Paramount News, spoke about the war years, and the finale came with a patchy 'live link' to Kingston House, where Bill, perched in an armchair with Buster on her lap, and Sarah, sitting beside her, nervously uttered, in an almost regal accent, 'Hello Kenny!' and then instructed Sarah to 'Say goodnight to Daddy, darling!' Considering Bill hated the glare of publicity, it was a brave performance.

In the following weeks, preparations for *North West Frontier* attracted great excitement. The film mixed a blend of genres – adventure, romance, and suspense, circling around ethnic tensions within British India. Promoted as an epic-scale production, it told how Muslim rebels attacked a fortress and killed a Hindu maharajah. To appeal to foreign audiences, the film fell in line with (yet another) new Rank policy of making movies with international stories in 'actual world settings' using well-known names. Brand new cameras – equipped for Eastmancolor and CinemaScope – were flown to India just ahead of Kenny, who was set to play an army sergeant (later changed to officer), who, with the help of Bacall, whisked a young Indian prince to safety during a rebellion. To make this formidable enterprise less severe, director J. Lee Thompson, Ken's chum from *The Yellow Balloon*, slimmed the shooting schedule to six weeks beginning in Bombay, followed by six more in Spain and a fortnight of filming interiors at Pinewood. The ordeal of working in the balmy Asian heat was eased, somewhat, with support from Herbert Lom and Wilfrid Hyde-White, both dependable British players, enjoying plum parts. On arriving in Rajasthan, Bacall remembered locals gawping at her trousers – 'they had never seen a woman in pants' – and she'd certainly never seen peacocks strutting in a hotel garden. Born in 1924, she'd started out as a model before making her screen debut at the age of twenty opposite Humphrey Bogart, her future husband. Then, she captivated audiences in *The Big Sleep* and *Key Largo* and by the time she arrived in India, she

The Film Star

was recovering from a failed romance with crooner Frank Sinatra. Ken's public assessment of his co-star – given her reputation as a 'difficult customer' – was that she was a charming woman: 'If she didn't like anybody, she told them so, for she hates falseness of any kind. That's how life ought to be.' In reality, with his libido remaining sky-high, and Bill in London (ironically, hosting actress Deborah Kerr who had become a chum after Kenny's earlier insults), he dreamt of a clandestine romance with the American beauty, but it is impossible to say if they ever slept together. It is, of course, entirely plausible, but the mercilessly hot temperatures of over 40°C in the shade were hardly ideal conditions for impromptu romantic assignations – worse still, he suffered from 'Delhi belly,' and kept off alcohol because of jaundice and his 'recuperating liver'. Bacall also endured an ordeal – running a raging temperature requiring 'constant rub downs with pieces of ice', and, according to *Picturegoer*, she even took ice to bed. One newspaper cheekily observed that 'every now and then', she was spotted opening a camera case and taking a nip of vodka. Despite all this, Ken said though they inched toward physical intimacy, they did little more than a little harmless flirtation 'enjoying each other's company and holding hands'.

Those attending the premiere of *North West Frontier* witnessed a noisy affair – amplified by the glorious Technicolor showing the sweltering atmosphere of a country in turmoil. Donned in khaki, Ken oozed charm and grit as he rescued the young prince from the jaws of death. Amid explosions and gunshots, they broke out of a besieged fort on an old engine patched up by the Indian driver, I. S. Johar, whose broken English turned out to be one of the films delights. To add even more excitement, Mischa

Spoliansky contributed a powerful score, and Geoffrey Unsworth was back behind the camera making the whole thing look epic on the large screen. On the whole, reviews were good. 'No Western stagecoach ever went through more perils than this lot in their gallant old engine,' the *Sunday Mirror* opined. 'A guarantee of an exciting evening for everyone!' Though Bacall's name alone was enough to sell tickets, Rank lamented the picture would have been more commercially lucrative had its subject matter been familiar to American audiences.

Though Ken's pursuit of Bacall confirms his marriage was revealing signs of strain, Bill remained a loyal and dedicated wife. On his return from Spain, she soothed his mood when plans for him to star alongside Doris Day in *Roar Like a Dove* never got beyond the talking stage (and was eventually abandoned) and she pulled together his 250-page autobiography *Happy Go Lucky*, set to be published by Robert Hale. Though mostly a saccharine account, it proved an ambitious undertaking made easier by Bill's collection of cuttings, reviews, interviews, and photos, a kind of 'Kenny archive' amassed over the past seven years. Though Hale's editors excised anything racy, sexual or inflammatory, the original press release described it as 'the funniest frankest show business autobiography of the year'. Ken's wit struck a chord with critic Mike Gothard who thought it was a thoroughly enjoyable and readable life story, written 'with much relish' and gave the impression that More 'couldn't give a damn. He tells the story of his rise frankly and without evasions.' Ken felt completely gratified when sales exceeded expectations, and donated a proportion of the royalties to the *Kay Kendall Variety Club Fund* for research into leukaemia in children at the Imperial Cancer

The Film Star

Research Fund. Better still, the book had three pressings in late 1959 and was snapped up for serialisation across the regional press, including in the prestigious *Manchester Evening News*. Strangely, the national dailies didn't bother with it.

Around this time, Bryan Forbes and Richard Attenborough approached Kenny with the prospect of some 'real acting' with an offer to play Tom Curtis in *The Angry Silence*, an independent picture bankrolled by the National Film Finance Corporation (NFFC) and the first release through Forbes's *Beaver Films*. It was a gritty, working-class drama – and, like *Chance of a Lifetime* a decade earlier, tackled the issue of unions and workplace strife. Despite its obvious potential, Ken reluctantly agreed but was never happy with his character – a factory worker with a pregnant wife and two kids, under pressure to make ends meet. In the story, Curtis refuses to take part in an unofficial strike and is accused by co-workers of being a scab and given the 'silent treatment'. Luckily, just ten days before the shoot was set to begin, the film found itself in financial straits and the cast was offered far less than their usual fees. As Attenborough remembered it, Ken had been strapped for cash before embarking on the project, then 'with money going out at an alarming rate, a devastated Kenny More rang to say he had to pull out, he'd been offered real money to star in the prestigious Fox film, *Sink the Bismarck!*'.

Though Ken jumped at the opportunity to work with *Bismarck* director Lewis Gilbert, he was disillusioned with the war genre, especially after the release of *Yesterday's Enemy* – a blood and guts Hammer production, starring Stanley Baker and Leo

McKern. 'The kind of brutality you find in some films should never be screened,' he glibly observed. 'I wouldn't appear in such a film. You can put over the horrors by implication far more successfully and harrowingly than by showing it all. People say there should be no censorship in the cinema. After all, this is life, is their argument. I don't agree. You do certain things every day, but you don't make films about them.'

By comparison, *Sink the Bismarck!* was a different proposition altogether, a psychological drama affording Ken a grown-up, emotional role. It was a deal too good to resist. With Gilbert directing the £700,000 epic, 20th Century Fox dubbed it their 'costliest British production', utilising CinemaScope but – for some reason – they decided to film in black and white. The plot tells the true story of a mighty Nazi battleship and how she was hunted, fought – and destroyed. It was a slow-going production, featuring a cast of seasoned character people, among them Laurence Naismith, Geoffrey Keen, Maurice Denham, and Dana Wynter, a tall, dark, Levantine-looking beauty, who excelled in playing both victim and villain. A strong-minded perfectionist, she had moved to Rhodesia from Berlin with her parents in the 1940s and was destined for a career in medicine before being lured by the stage. She found American fame in the science-fiction classic *Invasion of the Body Snatchers*, the tale of a town whose residents were replaced by duplicates grown in pods.

On the floor at Pinewood, Kenny gave a strikingly intense performance as Captain Shepherd of the Royal Navy – a boorish man with a take-charge attitude who helped to sink the *Bismarck* from a poky office below the War Room of London's Admiralty Building. 'It is like a game of chess,' he explained.

'But much more exciting. Almost for the first time, a British war hero isn't a man with a stiff upper lip. He does his job, refuses to become emotionally involved, until he finally breaks down when he hears his son is missing. I don't mind admitting it's a terrific test for me. Picturegoers have never seen me like this on screen. The character is cold, ruthless, dedicated, with no humour.'[6] At one stage, when his character softened and dissolved into tears, Ken had no idea how it would be done. 'Then the director and I worked it out between us,' he explained. 'When the Admiralty chiefs saw it on film, they okayed it.' In some ways, the scene was reminiscent of Jack Hawkins' famous performance in *The Cruel Sea* when he also shed a tear. Curiously, that wonder was nearly spoiled by Ealing's boss Michael Balcon, who – reckoning men didn't cry – wanted it cut but was thankfully overruled by the head of Paramount who demanded, 'The shot with Jack Hawkins crying stays in the picture … It has balls!' Grudgingly, Balcon agreed.

As *Sink the Bismarck!* approached the finish line, the Queen and Duke of Edinburgh brought Prince Charles to the set. The young prince (now King Charles) was captivated by the layout of the German warship and received a personal tour from Ken. That very same day, Carl Foreman offered Ken the role of Sergeant Miller – an explosives expert – in Alistair MacLean's *The Guns of Navarone*, a $6 million epic with worldwide distribution, backed by American money. It tells how a heroic band of men and women attempt to blow up a massive gun on a Nazi-occupied island in the Aegean. It was, Ken later wrote, 'the chance of my lifetime and consolidated all my years of work'. Foreman, writer of *The Bridge on the River Kwai,* was busily assembling a top-line international cast, including Gregory Peck, Anthony Quinn, Anthony Quayle, and Gia Scala. For a while, there was talk of the Greek singer Maria Callas joining the team, and Foreman even flew to Nicosia to discuss with President Makarios using Cyprus as a possible location. After much back and forth, Rank's John Davis gave his approval for Kenny to join the production but as filming was set to begin in Rhodes in early 1960 (Cyprus was by then considered too dangerous), he insisted Kenny first embark on a 'goodwill tour' of twenty-one British cities and towns to say 'thank you' to the millions of people who had made his films so successful (and promote *North West Frontier*).

According to the Rank archives, the tour kicked off on 30 November 1959 and was the most comprehensive provincial expedition ever planned for any artist in the history of the organisation. Not surprisingly, the chance to tour Britain on an all-expenses paid jaunt held great appeal to Ken and to begin with, he was on his very best cheeky, quick-witted form. 'I think it's great at the top,' he beamed on arriving in Leicester, adding the disadvantage of being a star was the difficulty in keeping a private life. 'The more famous you are the greater responsibility you have to those that made you famous,' he explained. 'Of course, there are advantages too, and to me one of the greatest is that I am able to say "no" – "no" when I don't want to take on a film, "no" when I don't want to do something that I believe would imperil the integrity, which an actor, especially if he's well known, must always maintain in his attitude to others.' Continuing, he said, 'Somebody once asked me if it is difficult to keep level-headed when you find you are a big success. My answer is this: I sincerely hope that I don't appear swollen-headed. I should hate people to think that. The man who is conceited because he has become famous doesn't deserve that fame.'

Strangely, by the time he arrived in Birmingham, his behaviour was slightly more spontaneous. One evening, he held court in a hotel lobby discussing his intention to vote Tory in the upcoming general election, saying he wanted things to 'stay as they are'. Given the political realities of the time – the Suez crisis, along with an uprising in Cyprus and the ongoing Cold War – Rank's policy of their stars refraining from political comment took a battering. He was also remarkably frank in a *Birmingham Evening Mail* interview about turning his hand to directing when his 'present long-term acting contract finished'. Then, after a couple of drinks, he complained about British horror movies – most produced by Hammer and distributed by Rank – saying they did the industry 'great harm' by driving away middle-aged filmgoers:

> We've got to make more big pictures that will draw the whole family. It is a fallacy that these cheap horrors are packing them in. They fill cinemas in some situations with a minority audience. People are sick with perversion and sex and horror. These films make a good profit because they cost so little to make. *North West Frontier* cost half-a-million pounds – which you have got to pay to make a film for the world. And it is films like this which are the only hope for the industry. Purely national pictures like *I'm All Right Jack* aren't worth tuppence in the world market.

It is hard to imagine John Davis being impressed by such rhetoric or Ken's further declaration that he would like to work on TV, which by then was drawing 10 million viewers, with the number set to grow. 'Television attracts me,' he waxed. 'But the reason I do not appear on it is that I cannot get the right sort of plays. Those I want to act in, I find cannot be produced on TV for a simple and perhaps ironic reason ... film companies, you see, own the production rights.'[7]

By the end of November, he was well on the way to accumulating a record of quotes that made him the most gaffe-prone star in the Rank stable. His trip around Britain ended on a maudlin note when he spoke at length about Kay Kendall, who had died a month earlier at the age of thirty-two from leukaemia. Remarkably, her condition had been kept secret by her husband Rex Harrison, who convinced her she had an iron deficiency. According to her biography, during her last moments, as she lay on her deathbed, Kendall stared at Harrison and asked, 'You would tell me if I was dying?' To which he answered, 'Don't be stupid, of course I would. You're not dying.' Soon after, she lapsed into a coma. 'How heroically Rex kept that dreadful secret,' Ken said, welling up. 'What an awful situation.'[8] Interestingly, Dirk Bogarde's memoirs reveal that Ken and Bill, along with other close friends, had been growing 'increasingly alarmed' at the changes in Kendall's health during the late 1950s. Despite her youth, she had lived life to the full – in addition to her dalliance with Ken during *Genevieve*, she had enjoyed a long romance with Syd Chaplin, the son of actor Charlie Chaplin. There were also affairs with a Swedish prince, supermarket heir James Sainsbury and reportedly – if the British press is to be believed – a fling with Prince Philip, Duke of Edinburgh, before she found happiness with Rex Harrison. 'Miss Kendall was that stage and screen rarity, a beautiful clown,' *The New York Times* obituary stated. 'The talents of a superb comedienne are so seldom conjoined with statuesque, classic beauty that producers along Miss Kendall's hard road to the top tended to distrust her qualities as mutually exclusive.'

8

A NEW REALITY

John Davis was so angry about Kenny's behaviour throughout the run of his tour – and his statements about politics and film – that he nursed a bundle of grievances. By mid-March 1960, however, things finally came to a head during a BAFTA dinner at the Dorchester hotel. After an evening of lively socialising with the Duke of Edinburgh, who presented statuettes to Peter Sellers and Hayley Mills, a star-studded dinner got underway. 'Kenny had been celebrating rather too much,' Betty Box recounted for a filmed documentary. 'He was certainly pixilated, and he started chi-hiking and haranguing John Davis ... but I could tell that John Davis was desperately upset by this rudery from Kenny More.' Oblivious to the danger, Ken's hectoring continued as Davis's horrified staff – including Earl St John, and F. D. Russell – looked on. When Bill attempted to restrain him, the louder he became. 'After a couple of drinks too many, nobody can stop me,' Ken once confessed. 'And nobody can get a single word in edgeways. Whenever we go to a party, Bill watches for the danger sign. As soon as she hears me declaring what a wonderful party it is, she knows I'm off like a non-stop express train.'[1] However, this night was different. When Davis concluded his speech, the heckling died down and polite conversation resumed. Amid the mutter of small talk, someone asked Ken what film he was planning to do next. Grinning elfishly, he began talking excitedly about the upcoming *Guns of Navarone* shoot. In the middle of all of this, Davis softly cleared his throat, then chipped in, 'Oh, no you're not doing that film,' he said, explaining that given Kenny's links to Danny Angel – who had been selling his films to TV companies against the wishes of Rank – that the *Navarone* deal was off. At first, Ken roared with laughter – thinking Davis was kidding. Then came the heart-stopping moment when he realised this was no joke. He was visibly rattled. 'You're a cold bastard,' he reportedly bellowed, before storming out, gripping Bill for support. It was a personal disgrace played out before an audience of friends, and colleagues. 'I should have controlled myself,' Ken lamented in his memoirs, 'but I was now beyond control.' Lewis Gilbert kept a precise memory of that evening and confirmed Davis was not the sort of person to shrug off humiliation lightly. 'He (Kenny) was the number one box office in England, but I don't think those sorts of things counted with Davis. I think if he had the knife out, it was plunged.' Indeed, the Dorchester episode betrayed the precariousness of every actor on the Rank payroll.

The next morning Ken phoned Davis to apologise, but as no details of the conversation exist, what was said remains in the realm of surmise and speculation. What is certain is that, from this point on, the curtain fell on Kenneth More's career as Rank's leading star. Worse still, his disgrace was sealed when David Niven – the man who had cut his best scenes from *Appointment with Venus* – signed to replace him as Corporal Miller in *The Guns of Navarone*. For a few weeks, Ken did what he had always done when he felt wounded or baffled: he retreated into his armchair at the Garrick, and spent endless hours on the golf course doing his best to seem cheerful. However, from here on, his film career would be mostly a downhill trip as he joined other older talents in the shadows – as younger faces, like Albert Finney, Laurence Harvey, and Tom Courtenay stole the limelight. By this time, Jack Hawkins, a man practically born in a Savile Row suit, and Trevor Howard, pot-marked and balding, already belonged to a fading era and were adapting to life without a studio contract.

For all that, however, Ken always claimed he bore no rancour toward John Davis. That might be true, as not long after the Dorchester fracas, they sat together at the premiere of *Sink the Bismarck!*[2] And when it was all over, the *Sunday People* hailed a new graver and tougher Kenneth More. The film even conquered the United States where the *Washington Star* observed it 'twanged with tension,' and *The Washington Post*'s Richard E. Coe thought Lewis Gilbert's 'canny mastery' made it an absorbing, 'evidently factual record of a historical naval event'. Gilbert described the picture as a milestone of sorts, marking the end of a particular type of bulldog British war movie before a new wave of cinema arrived to dominate the sixties.

Following the incident at the Dorchester, Kenny was still working, even if the opportunities became thinner. Aside from making a few remarks for *The Kenneth More Story* on the BBC Overseas Programme, he found time to fuss over Sarah – then six years old and affectionately known as Titchpot. As for matters monetary, he wasn't poor, nor did he make economies. In fact, he ensured that news about him becoming a Lloyd's underwriter was literally broadcast over the press wires after guaranteeing £75,000 – with unlimited liability – proving he had a huge chunk of 'disposable' cash in the bank. At the same time, his balance was boosted by shares in the Grade Organisation, agents to a galaxy of theatrical talent. Nonetheless, there were, he confessed, occasional financial missteps. One time, fearful about the future of sterling, he ploughed £10,000 into buying a diamond after Hatton Garden experts assured him it would double in value. 'When the scares had subsided a few years later,' he admitted, 'I decided to sell the stone and dropped £2,500 on it!' The same happened with a collection of paintings, 'I buy them for hundreds, and then when I move house and sell them, I lose. It's life, I suppose.'[3] On top of his private dividends, payments from freelancing boosted funds. He was frank about his own desires and capabilities, saying he would only accept parts that interested him. 'I'm not a complicated person and don't want to play Hamlet,' he told a writer. 'The days are over when, for 10 years, Dirk Bogarde and I could pick our roles, when we saw every new script and said "Yes, I'll play this," or "Sorry, I don't fancy that."' He made clear he had no time for period dramas or historical films. 'There are two kinds of actor,' he expounded. 'The one who puts on the wigs and nose putty and is a character in the true sense. Then there is the "contemporary" actor – of which I am one.' He wasn't the 'slightest bit interested' in grotesque characters, profound psychological roles or loud – full volume – Shakespearean theatricals. 'If you are lucky enough to have a personality the public like, then you will be all right.'[4] One project he certainly wasn't interested in was Betty Box's offer to reprise his role in her latest 'doctor spin-off', *Doctor in Love*, a project, ironically, bankrolled by Rank. He loathed the thought of a small part in a 'tired replay' and suggested Leslie Phillips put his own stamp on the character. Phillips did, and found fame after uttering his catchphrase 'Helloooo' for the first time. 'I was forever thankful Kenny refused that job,' he said years later. 'It changed everything.'

With no films of his own in the pipeline, Ken's mood was perked with an offer to star in the *Man in the Moon* – a space satire produced by Michael Relph, who was riding the crest of a wave after striking gold with *The League of Gentlemen,* a picture Carl Foreman had dropped a few years earlier. Produced by Allied Film Makers (AFM), the budget was low – a mere £80,000 – meaning it had to be made in a hurry, filmed in black and white and shot out of sequence. Despite that, the plans were met with enormous enthusiasm and, as a studio press release put it, AFM spent months 'in scientific research' so that 'those scenes in which the space men are trained for their trip to the moon' were credible. 'With the consent of the British Air Ministry, certain top-secret information – including experiments in rocket propulsion, conditions under tests, and the reactions of bodies to extreme pressure – was made available. Additional data came from America and, strangely, even more from Russian sources.'

Owing much to the old Ealing comedies, the plot brims with outrageous gags and sees Kenny's character, William Blood, chosen for a lunar mission due to his strange immunity to wine, weather, women, and worry. In preparation for the mission, he gets frozen in ice, broiled in an oven, hermetically sealed in a gravity device, and catapulted out of a rocket sledge. Ken took filming in his stride from the moment location work began on 14 April 1960 at a cement quarry near Dunstable, where he gave a touch of slapstick by traipsing around in a spacesuit. Again, he was beautifully supported by his old chum Michael Hordern and the velvet-voiced Charles Gray, playing an aspiring astronaut oozing silken arrogance. Shirley Anne Field, a sexy redhead par excellence, played the romantic interest. This voluptuous twenty-four-year-old, with an adorable figure, wiggled on to the set fresh from filming *The Entertainer* with Laurence Olivier. Though Ken was absolutely bowled over by her, they enjoyed a platonic relationship, but the film provided dozens of on-screen opportunities for passionate kisses and embraces. 'Best part of the job, old boy,' Ken joked.

Despite being hampered by a modest budget, *Man in the Moon* shines with humour and justified director Basil Dearden's belief that independent pictures could turn a profit. Indeed, his efforts seemed to pay off, despite lukewarm reviews from the likes of Alexander Walker, who hated to see the man who saved India, squired Jayne Mansfield through the West and sank the *Bismarck* treated to a course of assault and battery: 'If the rocket carrying Kenneth More to the moon goes off course, something goes even more astray – it is the casting of Mr More in a role that almost certainly should have been played by Norman Wisdom.' Likewise, even before the film's big opening, the *Daily Mirror*'s Dick Richards thought it a 'praiseworthy attempt' to return More to his *Genevieve* comedy days but 'misfired on several cylinders'.

On Saturday 3 September 1960, just five weeks before *Man in the Moon* opened at cinemas, Ken began working on *The Greengage Summer*, Rumer Godden's best-selling romantic novel. Though Cary Grant was the original choice for the male lead, producer Lewis Gilbert – after wading through a list of 'possibles' – made overtures to Ken on condition he shed weight, especially from his 'moon face'. So, after embarking on a low-fat diet, he arrived for filming at his fittest in years. Shot at Shepperton and in the Champagne district of France, the film gives a balmy, idyllic look at the joys and pains of becoming a woman seen through the experiences of nineteen-year-old Susannah York, left to her own devices on a holiday when her mother became ill. Growing from a prim schoolgirl into a beautiful woman, she falls too trustingly in love with the mysterious Eliot, a cat burglar-like character, played by Ken.

Jane Asher, who gave a highly praised performance as York's younger sister, Hester, found Kenny an immense joy to work with, saying he was the same in real life as on screen, 'utterly relaxed, charming and kind, with an ever-present twinkle in his eye and a delightful way of talking to children'. 'I realise, of course,' she told the author, 'that there was far more going on behind that lovely persona, but at that age I took him totally at face value.' She admired his technical brilliance and his easy-going relationship with the camera. 'He knew exactly what his audience expected from him and loved about him and in *The Greengage Summer* that's exactly what he gave them, making the character of Eliot – whom we might see nowadays with our more knowing and cynical eyes as a sinister criminal toying with the affection of a young girl while enjoying the convenience and available sex of an adoring older woman – into a lovable and charming rogue.' Interestingly, Asher was also endeared to Bill, who, she remembered, was always around on location in France. 'With hindsight,' she says, 'I wonder now whether she was keeping an eye on him rather than just enjoying being with him ...'

The film finished shooting in December 1960, and was rush-released into theatres the following spring. According to journalist David Lewin, during several publicity junkets, Ken took credit for launching Susannah York's career, despite her previous success with Alec Guinness in *Tunes of Glory*. On one occasion, he reported that when Princess Margaret met Kenny at the *Greengage* premiere, the following conversation took place:

The Princess: And what are you doing now, Mr More?
K.M: I've just finished a film and am launching a new star.
The Princess: That sounds ominous. How do you launch a star – with champagne?
K.M: Almost. The film was made in the champagne country of France and here is the star, Susannah York.[5]

Ironically, York later expressed disapproval of what she called Ken's 'miscasting,' saying she felt that Dirk Bogarde was the right person for the role: 'It needed someone with a touch of dark mystery and Dirk would have been perfect.'

While waiting for publicity on *The Greengage Summer* to begin, Ken held a series of fruitless discussions about playing racing driver Stirling Moss, but the idea never took off. Instead, he abandoned his art and recorded a television advertisement, spawning a lucrative sideline. 'I suppose you could blame me for starting the whole business of celebrity advertising,' he once boasted. 'It was considered frightfully infra dig when I made three commercials. I was paid around £20,000 a go.' Though he insisted he had to be persuaded to record adverts, it was an 'agreeable chore' leading to other offers to plug cigarettes, headache tablets, breakfast cereals, chocolate, sports gear, and automobiles. Creatively, though, with a desire to do 'something worthwhile', he set his sights on a return to the theatre and agreed to direct a stage version of Anthony Kimmins' wartime saga *The Angry Deep*, set at a submarine base in Malta. Believing in the power of a good story, plans were made with impresario Steven Mitchell to land the play in the West End. Carried away, Ken rhapsodised that he had always wanted to direct a play. 'When I saw this one, I realised it was the ideal subject, since I have so much confidence in Kimmins and since, I myself, know very well how vividly he brought to life this chapter of war in the Mediterranean.'

Barry MacGregor was one of the first actors signed up for the production, taking the role of a midshipman. 'There were no women in that play at all, it was a totally misogynistic production,' he recounted. 'However, it was a happy time. Ken was a gentleman of energy of the kind I don't think I've ever met before or since. He just lived life. He was kind, he loved actors, and he enjoyed directing because he was with actors.' Another of the players, Tony Wright, said Ken was strict 'but at the same time he has that wonderful quality of understanding exactly how actors like to work. He gets the best out of them because he is always aware of those difficult moments when a player needs encouragement. It is a great pleasure to be directed by him and I know the rest of the company feels this too.'⁶

In fact, Kenny had made it a long-standing rule that he knew the names of all the cast and crew – more crucial than ever now that he sat in the director's chair. Everyone was greeted by their Christian name; crew members were asked their opinions and evenings were often spent 'as a unit' in the local pub. After three weeks of rehearsals, the play opened at the Royal Brighton in January 1961, and Ken followed performances in Edinburgh, Glasgow, and Newcastle. 'Throughout,' MacGregor recounts, Ken's ideas about what he wanted to do on the stage were ironclad, nothing was done without his say-so, 'there were plenty of teething troubles. He concocted some material, including his strange decision that we would have little piglets in the cast':

> So, we each had a pig under our arm with its arse toward the audience because that is where a swastika was to be painted by the admiral. Unfortunately, the pigs got stage fright and shat green diarrhoea down all of us. We were in whites, which of course didn't help a great deal! It was then decided we should have goats – so we had goats with cloth coverings over their bodies with the swastika to be painted on ... and they were fine, except they tried to eat our shorts! It was bloody chaos! All through the second act all you could hear was the bleat of 'baa, baa'. The goats took over the performance.

While such antics wound up stealing headlines, critics weren't ecstatic. 'The heroics have an air of casualness; we are never really convinced these young men have in fact been risking their lives fathoms below the angry deep,' the *Liverpool Post*'s theatre scribe opined. Another review in the *Echo* praised the acting and the characters but said the play 'failed to come to life and real interest until the third act'. On 10 February 1961, like the rest of the cast, MacGregor learned the play would close at the Royal Court a week later. 'So, it never reached London. There was not one false note in any performance. I think we did it for six weeks,' he told the author. 'We were informed during the last week it wouldn't be making the West End. It was a shame as I thought it was a good little play. Everybody felt miserable. Perhaps the investment was not quite up to snuff.'

In fact, the play was 'officially' taken off for rewriting, after critics complained it was lacking in plot. Kimmins admitted he had written 'too much from personal experience', and had not done good business on tour. Making light of the matter, Ken insisted he was glad to have opportunities elsewhere – but was, in fact, bitterly discouraged by the experience. In an off-the-cuff comment, he claimed to be 'weary of the theatre' and savagely attacked stage audiences as snobs 'whose only enjoyment is to wave a programme in front of their neighbours. To do a show in the West End is suburbia's greatest status achievement.' He was, in fact, beginning to talk about British theatre in the sort of disdainful terms he usually reserved for journalists who had bad things to say about him. In private, his outrage extended to a new generation of working-class writers and intellectuals, dubbed the 'Angry Young Men of British Theatre' who poured scorn on commercial shows and light comedies. Subjects previously unbroached, or alluded to, were enjoying universal critical acclaim on the stages of London. This new breed – including John

Osborne, and Alan Sillitoe – churned out gritty urban dramas featuring working-class males in a leading role with a beef against society, hardly the stuff of Kenneth More.

As it happened, Ken never directed again. Bill thought he had wasted his energy and should concentrate on acting. He agreed. It is possible that stress contributed to his being wheeled into hospital for a kidney stone operation, where his mood further darkened after *The Guns of Navarone* opened to rave reviews in April 1961. It must have been galling to see so many newspapers making special mention of David Niven's triumph playing the explosive expert, Sergeant Miller. 'The film is absolutely superlative of its sort,' was the verdict of the *Sunday Telegraph*, while the *Evening News* thought Niven gave a brilliant performance, and the *New York Herald Tribune* added he was 'superb'.

Unsurprisingly, Kenny's relations with Bill were strained more than ever during these months of illness and disappointment, and even the presence of Sarah couldn't drive the troubles from their relationship. Though they had weathered infidelities, it's worth quoting one comment he gave to a French magazine some years later: 'When I was married to Bill,' he confessed, 'I sometimes saw lovers holding hands and I envied them with all my heart. But I was a good husband for eleven years. But I wasn't happy. And in the end, I will never forget it was at Jack Hawkins' house I was reduced to complaining publicly. I found it unpleasant. It was unseemly.' Presumably, this outburst occurred sometime in the autumn of 1960 or early 1961. Though it isn't clear if Bill was present, it's unlikely.

Remarkably, despite his inner turmoil, the marriage still proved durable and Bill supported his efforts in pushing for a film version of *The White Rabbit* to fulfil a dream of portraying Wing Commander F. E. Yeo-Thomas, a French Resistance leader. Despite warnings that it was a 'non-starter', Ken navigated thickets of copyright issues, before throwing in the towel. 'I've wasted a whole year of my life waiting to make the film,' he complained, claiming it was the best script he'd ever read and could be 'twice as successful' as *Reach for the Sky*. 'Three or four different companies claimed it. I shouldn't think it will ever be made at all now.'[7] Confident that he could eventually see the project through, he found solace when Danny Angel blew in from the cold with an offer to star in some 'trivial nonsense' about a British officer seconded to the US Navy. The production, though, would take time to materialise, so to kill time, Ken accepted a part in *Some People*, a piece of film propaganda for the Duke of Edinburgh's Award Scheme, wrapped up as entertainment. It was a curious choice of project. And, in contrast to the pampering he'd enjoyed as a star, he agreed to appear just for expenses and a room at Bristol's Grand Spa Hotel, overlooking Clifton Bridge. To his way of thinking, the only reason to make the film, apart from helping his friend Prince Philip, was a chance to get away from the prickly situation at home. Set against the bleak landscape of Bristol, he portrays a middle-aged aircraft designer whose hobby is helping a youth club, and encouraging a ragtag group of teenagers to develop 'their type of music' at his club. 'Kenny only arrived the night before shooting,' recalls Anneke Wills, who played his daughter, alongside David Hemmings, Ray Brooks, and Angela Douglas. 'The rest of the cast had been working for a few weeks in Bristol, which was the way director Clive Donner liked to operate. He wanted us to get the Bristolian accents right and get a feel for the place. So, by the time Kenny came we were all very melted together.' The first thing Ken did was buy the cast and crew dinner. 'So, that put us all at ease and we all thought what a jolly good sort he was.' On set, Wills never forgot her first big scene, where Kenny realises his daughter is becoming sexually aware. 'I'm in the bath, which was filled with dry ice – I suddenly looked up into his eyes which were melting with tears of love, and I thought "Crikey, this guy can act!" He was so charming, so generous and so sweet.'

Off set, Anneke and Angela Douglas, a twenty-two-year-old frosty blonde with enormous blue eyes, became close. 'We were in this gorgeous hotel, and it was all being paid for! We'd be using room service, ordering prawn cocktails every night. Anyway, very early on, we were giggling about all the crew and who we would "get it on with". I jokingly said, "I'm going to go for the Duke of Edinburgh, and you better go for Kenny More!"' In the confined life of location shooting, getting to know each other posed no problem, and, in fact, it was Kenny who took the overt first step toward Angela. 'She was just happily flirting away with him,' Anneke remembers. 'We were feisty young girls, we felt invincible. For us, these mature lovely men and mature lovely actors were what we were interested in. We weren't interested in the boys. It made for a wonderful shoot; we were all enjoying ourselves.' Ken and Angela traded flirtatious looks for a few days, and despite the age difference, he was tempted in a way he found hard to resist. Indeed – she was adorable, lively, and full of the fun of a woman embarking on an exciting journey in the theatrical profession. He was struck by a similarity to his own background, she too, had been born at Gerrards Cross and – like him – began acting in her teens. In fact, her career had started a few years earlier in local rep before making her West End debut in 1958. Within a few years, her CV included modelling jobs, a *Crunchie* bar commercial, a scene in *Dixon of Dock Green*, a small role in *No Hiding Place* and work as a 'glorified extra' in Rome on the Elizabeth Taylor epic *Cleopatra*. Speaking to the *Daily Mirror* in 1961, she attributed her growing success partly due to her 'tip-tilted nose' – acquired, the paper reported, by plastic surgery at a cost of £300.

Kenny had had countless liaisons throughout the years, but this one had a tenor of its own. The affair began in room 49 of the Grand Spa Hotel. 'I was 46 and she was 21, which is quite disgusting,' he later joked, when recalling the room had twin beds with a telephone and table between them. Angela ripped the telephone from the wall and pushed the beds together.[8] From that moment, the affair blossomed on the understanding there was no aim of permanence. Anneke was the first to get wind of it, and remembered there were many knowing, curious eyes. However, after Bristol, the dalliance cooled down for eight weeks, as Angela recalled:

When he left Bristol, I began to think about him far too much for just a friend. I was terrified. I hoped it was just a crush. All of a sudden – I was getting over it – working hard and getting lots of lovely plays – I got a phone call at 8.30 a.m. It was Kenny saying, 'I've got to see you' and he named a time and a place. He didn't say anything else, and I didn't ask. I knew. I said OK. Then I went through my wardrobe and threw everything out. I didn't know what to wear. I arrived for our date five minutes early and I told the taxi driver to drive round. I walked into the River Club, Chelsea – and he was there surrounded by show business people. It was like a scene from a film. I saw him and he saw me, and, at that moment, we fell in love. We hadn't had any contact for eight weeks. We fought it for that long. But then we knew that, come hell or high water, we were going to be together. You get a sort of mental block, and you know you're going to ruin people's lives and change your own.[9]

When Kenny confessed his love to Angela, he said he was 'excruciatingly lonely', living only for his work. He claimed to have 'fallen into his marriage with Bill', she'd tidied him up, been a great hostess and mother – but there was no love. From that night the affair flourished, and though still ensconced in the marital home at Kingston House, he was quick to engineer an apartment for Angela at Cross Keys Close, off Marylebone High Street. 'I never forget Angela on the phone saying he's [Kenny] got me a little flat … it was all very exciting,' Anneka Wills explained. 'We kept our friendship going.'

To avoid scandal, they were seldom seen in public together. Ken told Bill he would be late on Sundays after playing golf and had another night out every week 'with the boys' – this time was snatched by his new lover. In a letter to Angela, he confessed to being 'miserable' for being unfair 'to you and Bill' but accepted he couldn't be sensible all the time. For Angela, it was a see-saw of a life filled with stolen moments, brightened by love notes (signed Joe Bloggs), and gifts – including a gold shamrock broach and a diamond encrusted replica of Ken's naval cap badge.

During the spring of 1962 after *Some People* completed post-production, critics shrugged it off as 'more propaganda than plot'. However, one kind review in *Variety* noted Ken handled his part with 'charm' but reckoned the revelation was in the performances of some of the younger cast members. 'Angela Douglas,' it tellingly noted, 'is pretty provocative as a young blonde who can handle a song and a boy with equal assurance.'

For the first time in their years together, Bill didn't attend the premiere. And, interestingly, around this time, Ken got wind that an American tabloid was reporting Cary Grant had signed to play Professor Higgins in a movie version of *My Fair Lady*. The paper, *Inside Story*, also claimed Kenny was offered the Colonel Pickering part, but turned it down with the unsporting comment, 'It's an old-man part and I'm much younger than Cary Grant.'[10] Whether this was tittle-tattle, or a scoop will never be known but in the event, Grant backed out believing he couldn't play a dialectician (to be replaced by Rex Harrison) and Wilfrid Hyde-White – who had featured in *North West Frontier* – delivered a standout performance as Pickering, in what turned out to be a blockbuster. In the event, as the *Inside Story* 'scoop' hit the newsstands, plans were being laid for a new film – *The Longest Day*, a sumptuous adaptation of Cornelius Ryan's D-Day bestseller stuffed with celebrated actors, including John Wayne, Robert Mitchum, and Henry Fonda. Tapped for a small part providing an £8,000 pay packet, Ken played Commodore Maud, the officer in charge of the Juno beach landings in a picture that is brimming with action. Maud, acting as a technical adviser, even provided the walking stick he waved about during the operation. While working in France allowed a pleasant diversion, it was a slow-going production, especially for director Ken Annakin who endured 20th Century Fox boss Darryl Zanuck following him around the coast like a general planning a real military operation. 'For the big scene where Ken More stalks up the beach with his pet bulldog, three thousand troops were being bussed in from all over Brittany,' Annakin recounted. 'It had been a great day, and that night, being Saturday, we piled into the cafes and stuffed ourselves with oysters, shrimps and lobsters.' Having enjoyed himself so much in Ken's company, Annakin had other projects in mind. He vowed to use him for *Crooks Anonymous*, a caper earmarked for Terry-Thomas. However, as he made his plans, a tiny budget forced him to settle with Stanley Baxter and Leslie Phillips. 'Despite all my directorial efforts,' Annakin bemoaned, '*Crooks Anonymous* remained a typical low-budget picture, making a small profit to the very insular producer and British distributors. Once again, I learned you may write the best script in the world, but if it is a comedy depending on a certain type of offbeat characters, unless you cast them with the A-team, it is all a complete waste of time and effort.' Annakin's temper was soothed when *The Longest Day* won high profits and critical praise from *The Washington Post* which lauded 'a tingling, eye-gripping, fantastic picture', while Brendan Gill of *The New Yorker* called it 'a tour de force of audio-visual verisimilitude'.

At the beginning of May 1962, Kenny started work on Danny Angel's *We Joined the Navy*, supported by Lloyd Nolan, John Le Mesurier and Derek Fowlds, a young actor plucked from a local theatre in Worthing (who later found fame playing Bernard in *Yes Minister*). All of Angel's showmanship was poured into the project with no skimping on sets or locations. 'It's one of the funniest scripts I've ever read,' Ken radiantly declared. 'I play a lieutenant commander – a drop in rank after the *Bismarck* – but the complete opposite of the stiff upper lip variety.' From the get-go he felt enthusiastic about the role. The plot revolved, naturally, around Ken as Lieutenant Commander Robert Badger – a naval officer with one major problem: he speaks the truth at the most inopportune times. Known as the 'Artful Bodger', he was posted as an exchange officer to the flagship of the United States Sixth Fleet where his antics set back Anglo-American relations. As Bill joined the location shooting in Villefranche-sur-Mer, Angela secretly kept in touch by letters sent to his French bank and he responded with hastily scrawled notes on deposit slips. After seventeen days of this precarious business, filming moved to Associated British Studios where Kenny struck up an immediate friendship with Roger Moore, a dashing young actor making *The Saint* in an adjoining studio. 'We saw each other all the time, thereafter,' Moore recounted. And, with both enduring marital problems, they made a pact they would be each other's best man if they ever remarried.

Though Kenny was delighted with *We Joined the Navy*, it failed to garner much enthusiasm, in spite of being an enjoyable, undemanding romp stuffed with gags. 'The humour is of the well-tried variety,' one columnist cattily remarked. Regardless, Ken seemed genuinely unperturbed and embarked on a round of socialising. One night, he turned up at a Noël Coward party in high spirits for an evening of drinking and flung 'four-letter words about like confetti' with Vivien Leigh. 'It was all nice dirty fun,' Coward wrote, 'and nobody seemed to mind except me, who wished they would go home.' Though mostly harmless, Ken's 'little outbursts' – usually forthcoming after consulting the drinks cabinet – occasionally seeped onto the airwaves. One afternoon, after a few G&Ts, he caused a flap after catching Eamonn Andrews off-guard during a TV appearance with Jimmy Edwards. 'Kenneth More is not loth to take a swig or two in the hospitality room before the show, although on this occasion we were victims of circumstances,' Edwards later explained.

> Both of us had vowed not to have too much to drink before the show, but there were one or two technical hitches, which meant a late start, so our vow went to the wall. By the time we did get on the air we were both in good form and the show really swung along. Then dear old Kenny really set me up for one which I couldn't resist. It was just after the Profumo Affair and a few days earlier there had been a picture of Mandy Rice-Davies in the papers out hunting. Kenneth, knowing my interest in hunting, suddenly said: 'I say Jim, what did you think of Mandy Rice-Davies going out foxhunting?' Before I could stop myself, I let slip a remark so loaded with double-entendre that viewers poured in complaints and a report had to be made to the Independent Television Authority.

Most shocking of all, though, was when Ken stunned Andrews for a second time when discussing Elvis Presley. 'The giggles More's remarks got from the live studio audience seemed to spur him on to be even more outrageous,' Andrew's biographer Tom Brennand noted. 'First, he [Ken] attempted to mime the gyrating, hip swivelling actions that caused Elvis to be dubbed Elvis the

Pelvis, then he started to conjecture on the cause of the prominent frontal contours of the singer's tight-fitting trousers.' Ironically, though he made very few TV appearances, Ken returned to the same studio a few days later to deliver a speech on behalf of the National Society for the Unmarried Mother and Child. Why they invited him to spearhead the task will never be known: 'What kind of race are we when we put sick dogs before pregnant single mothers?' he asked BBC viewers. 'Yet this is the current situation. The last reported annual income of the RSPCA was £177,004. The charity for unmarried mothers asked for only £8,000 but all they got was £5,000. And this reason is because this country still contains a majority of two-faced snobs.'

Soon after, he dismissed talk about appearing in a West End comedy – and revealed his immediate commitment was learning the part of David Mann, a distrustful interviewer in Terence Rattigan's *Heart to Heart,* a play written for thirteen international TV networks. With television becoming the wonderous cash cow of entertainment, producers could afford to assemble a strong cast including Ralph Richardson, making his first acting role on TV, as the interviewee Sir Stanley Johnson, Peter Sallis as the director and Wendy Craig playing the secretary. 'Ken was a late choice for the part. Richard Burton was supposed to play the role,' director Alvin Rakoff told the author. 'But at the last minute Burton decided he didn't want the part. So, Rattigan, who wrote it, called on his friend Kenny More to take over.' Several contemporary books pay attention to this project. In one, Rattigan's biographer Susan Rusinko described the interviewer and politician as flawed characters, Mann by booze and Sir Stanley by corruption. 'Kenneth More's and Ralph Richardson's powerful performances were equal to Rattigan's compelling characterisations and the brilliant, hard-hitting dialogue. David succeeds in exposing and bringing down Sir Stanley, but in the process he, too, suffers.' In his memoirs, Sallis, too, recounts Ken's character was plagued by alcoholism. 'There was a shot where you saw Kenny and Wendy Craig walking along a passageway together when she said to him, "Why do you drink so much?" and he turned to her and patted her hand and said, "Because I can afford it, darling." I thought that was a good line.' Rakoff's memory and contemporary news items indicate the production was an important forerunner to the type of international TV co-productions seen today. The experience didn't do Ken any harm either, and he absorbed how to work with multiple cameras and new videotaping systems. Funnily enough, it later transpired that John Freeman – then television's most celebrated interviewer – had been desperate to play the David Mann role. 'He was terribly piqued that Kenneth More got to play him, rather better than life, I think,' the *Evening Standard*'s Alexander Walker revealed in 1989. 'I'd wanted Richard Burton, actually. He'd have been perfect. The man's got to be an utter bastard, and Kenny was just too chummy.'

9
COLD SHOULDER

On Friday 1st February 1963, Kenny summoned the courage to tell Bill about his affair with Angela. It's probable she already had suspicions, but kept them to herself. But it couldn't have come as a total surprise. Just a week earlier, like many guests – including John Mills and Diana Dors – she must have noticed her husband sharing amused glances, and tipsily buzzing around Angela at a British Film Producers' dinner at the Savoy. When some guests began exchanging 'private looks', Angela was convinced the 'secret was out'.

The break with Bill would never be clean but was final. 'It is regrettable,' Ken lamented, 'that things worked out this way.' For a short while they remained together at Kingston House for the sake of Sarah, but life under the same roof turned unbearable. As with Beryl, he could not stomach the constant bickering which always descended into a chilly silence. When he could no longer stand it, he quietly packed his bags and moved out. 'Oh gosh, yes. Everybody seemed to know,' says Anneke Wills. 'There were whispers and little sympathy for extramarital romances in those days. Such news travels very fast.' Though painful at the time, Kenny eventually felt a profound remorse at his behaviour. In his 1978 memoirs, he admitted it was a 'terrible time' for Bill and he was 'ashamed of the way' he handled things, adding he should have left the marital home immediately.

In the days and weeks that followed, any apprehensions about his new life were soothed by Angela who became the 'perfect mistress' for her 'widely read and articulate lover'. Perfecting the part, she purchased exotic lingerie from Weiss on Shaftesbury Avenue, along with piles of books ranging from how to cook to the history of the Second World War.

Amid all this, Ken had a full-fledged acting career to maintain, with new deals to cut. Reactions to *Heart to Heart* gave Alvin Rakoff another shot at directing him in *The Comedy Man*, a film about the travails of an ageing repertory actor – plagued by thoughts of unfulfilled dreams – living hand-to-mouth in a bedsitter, making a belated success in TV commercials. To his surprise, Ken was 'profoundly struck' by the script. 'After all,' he mused, 'if I hadn't got my big chance in *Genevieve*, this could so easily have been the story of my own life.' He insisted on having Angela as his co-star and was soon on the phone to British Lion demanding Rakoff be given full creative freedom. 'At the time there was a glass ceiling between making television and making films because the film people thought TV was harming their revenue ... but it was Kenny who insisted I be hired,' Rakoff explained, adding that he knew about the Angela situation: 'A director always knows what's going on with his cast. I know Kenneth was feeling guilty about his relationship with Angela, but he was in love.' There were no demanding locations, but Rakoff beautifully captures the grubby backdrop of London, the false optimism, the small heartaches, and dingy theatreland pubs – all creating the strange little world of life on the fringes of showbiz. 'Ken just loved it,' Rakoff said. 'It was grubby. It was the story of an actor struggling, he loved doing it. He was one of the most affable human beings I have ever met and certainly one of the most easy-going stars. He was comfortable within himself, and it showed in everything he did. He was very secure. He was aware he had limitations as an actor because of his height and looks – but those limitations were minimal.'

Now recognised as a classic of relatively low renown, *The Comedy Man* was released after sixteen months of editorial fiddling and proved an unqualified failure. 'I cut the film, then the Boulting brothers at British Lion recut it,' Rakoff explained. 'And the film was never distributed properly; it was released as a double bill with *Lord of the Flies*. They killed it. That showed how inefficient British Lion had really become to do that.' The most galling thing from Kenny's point of view, though, was the way a risqué bedroom scene with Angela was cut down. He also never forgave critic Felix Barker for warning audiences that they would find the film downbeat and sleazy. 'There's no love story,' Barker mused. 'More picks up the frayed ends of an affair with a former repertory colleague (Billie Whitelaw) and tumbles half-heartedly with a blonde and eager extra (Angela).' Barker thought it a 'merciless and accurate' picture of a brave band of actors living hand to mouth and commuting between the pub and the job centre. 'If the film had featured the old Kenny More, gaily heroic in uniform, it would have been blazoned all over Leicester Square ages ago.'

Worse still, the film had trouble securing a foreign distributor and was only ever seen in a handful of commonwealth territories like Gibraltar and Malta. 'And it was never released in America,' Rakoff lamented. 'Such a pity.' Ken disliked the way British Lion had bungled the project and – probably in way of consolation – he was offered the lead in *The Cyprus Story,* a drama about Cypriot fighters launching a guerrilla campaign against British troops on the island. Set to be produced by Kenneth Shipman, British Lion tapped Harry Andrews, Elsa Martinelli and Herbert Lom for leading roles. The draft screenplay called for Ken to have a film romance with Martinelli, playing the daughter of a freedom fighter sympathiser. Excited, Ken said his character was not a typical stiff upper lip officer but the kind of man who made a nuisance of himself. 'He has a lot to say about the sort of treatment meted out to the Cypriots.' As the project gained steam, writer Jack Pullman was sent to Cyprus to interview Greek Cypriot leaders, British troops, government officials, and people caught in the conflict. 'We have got the cooperation of the army,' Kenny told reporters. 'I am to start work on June 17 or 24. The Cypriot authorities wanted one or two changes in the script. In a few instances they thought we were being a little too kind to them and a little too harsh to ourselves.' However, as Carl Foreman had discovered in the late 1950s while planning *Navarone*, Cyprus continued to endure very real political problems. And when a shaky peace between Greeks and Turks erupted into sporadic clashes and gunfire work on *The Cyprus Story* abruptly folded. Interestingly, it wasn't too dangerous for

Ken to whisk his mistress to Nicosia during June, the one bright spot in an otherwise dismal summer. Probably at British Lion's expense, they checked in to the Dome Hotel on the northern coast, and embarked on three weeks of romantic dinners, exploring in a hire car, and bathing in the warm Mediterranean. His ego was boosted when, even in this remote part of Europe, he failed to escape attention. One afternoon, a reporter from the *Cyprus Mail* – notebook in hand – caught him spending a day in Famagusta to meet an old friend from his Royal Navy days, 'and he called at the Ship Inn and the Acteon Beach Restaurant where he enjoyed a meze'. Explaining the presence of Angela – described by the *Mail* as a 'talented young actress' – Ken said she was 'absorbing the atmosphere of the island' before returning to make a film 'probably later this year'. Much later, Angela revealed that 'Cyprus was the one place that meant more to me than any other. It was there we went for a holiday after we had decided that we should be together all the time.'[1]

Back home, amid his rotation of golf and the Garrick, things were on the up when – after a lapse of eleven years – he returned to the stage in *Out of the Crocodile*, a comedy with Hugh Williams and Celia Johnson, written by Giles Cooper, author of *Evening in the Garden*, and known to TV viewers for his adaptations of the *Maigret* detective novels. In it, Ken played Peter Pounce, a man who discovered an imaginative way of living in luxury without any visible means of support. After three weeks' rehearsal – in which Hugh Williams was diagnosed with throat cancer and replaced by Cyril Raymond – the show opened to mixed reviews, except on a pre-London visit, when it came in for some harsh notices. Though acknowledging the 'very fine acting', the critic of the *Evening Post* thought it a 'sadly unfulfilled piece', and accused Cooper of trying to do stunts on a one-wheel bicycle. 'When the curtain falls, the message we have got is mainly one of frustration ... the play just does not make it.' 'I'm not despondent,' Ken chirped. 'Let's say I don't think it was a play for northern critics.' Behind the scenes, though, he was tetchy. Words were exchanged with producer Michael Codron – mainly about 'meaningless jokes' and a weak second act. Despite the setbacks, the reception at the Phoenix was warmer, opening a three-month run – an impressive feat given stiff competition from Terence Rattigan's *Man and Boy*, and Robert Bolt's *Gentle Jack*.

Meanwhile, after months of whispers and wagging tongues, Kenneth finally shattered his image of the stolid, domesticated actor by publicly revealing that 'everybody knows I have left my wife and I suppose that makes me a swine in some people's eyes'. Though, he claimed, 'his heart ached for Bill', he waxed tearful about being trapped in an unhappy marriage: 'Now, for the very first time, I'm in love. I'm not worried about the difference in our ages.' Typically forthright, he admitted to receiving hate mail and resented the idea – as peddled by some – that he was an old man falling for a beautiful girl. 'I still feel young; I always have.' Bill, he claimed, had made the split more painful by constituting the biggest stumbling block to his marrying Angela: 'I don't see my wife ever divorcing me. I'm not trying to make excuses ... I left my home and my wife and split our marriage. It was my fault.' But above all else, he insisted his daughter, Sarah, was handling the situation well. 'I think children understand better about these things than we know. They accept things much more readily. I think people make too much fuss about how children feel about these things. You can sacrifice your life for them in an unhappy marriage, and when they grow up, they say to you, 'Why on earth did you bother? You must be mad.' For several weeks, the saga was followed avidly by the entertainment press. In a half-page spread, Jack Bentley, a columnist with the *Sunday Mirror*, noted 'Mr More had sacrificed his marriage, risked his career, and lost some of his friends.' In fact, this sentiment seemed overly pessimistic as offers of work continued to flood in, including from the BBC. For them, he played Major Colum Fitzgerald in *The Scapegoat*. 'Kenny seemed very cheerful. It was a smooth production,' says Francis White, an actress cast as a 'big hearted tart', who remembered 'for its day' it was a little bit racy. 'We rehearsed it like a normal theatrical production. Back then, it used to be like putting a stage play on tape. Ken was just like I expected him to be! He was nice to work with and very charming ... he wasn't a disappointment.' In fact, his influence gave the cast access to the BBC restaurant, a place usually reserved for top brass. 'Very unusually, we ate quite a lot in the restaurant which I didn't even know existed,' White explained. 'I had been so used to the canteen but somehow when we were working with Kenneth More, we all ended up going to the restaurant!' Sadly, given the BBC wiped recordings of programmes that had 'exhausted their usefulness', no video survives, but White's private scrapbook contains a cutting describing an exciting plotline:

Who killed Tiberius? When Major Colum Fitzgerald convenes a Court of Enquiry, as regulations demand, it is without much hope of discovering why anyone should slit the throat of the regimental mascot – an inoffensive goat. But as witness after witness is called, what seemed at first a pointless crime begins to take on a more sinister aspect. The circle of involvement widens, and Fitzgerald becomes determined to unearth all the facts despite the protests of his fellow officers of the Court, like Captain Phipps. But for Fitzgerald, the enquiry becomes an intellectual exercise in following and finding out the truth – which brings with it tragic consequences.

Notices weren't wildly complimentary, but they were, generally, positive. Amid all this, Ken and Angela installed themselves at a mews house at Porchester Terrace, off a little cul-de-sac in Westminster. From there, he continued to lament friends and acquaintances distancing themselves. 'I try to treat people well – much better in fact than they treated me, because many were really hideous,' he complained. Though some pals remained warm, he endured a few traumatic experiences. Take, for instance, when he gave an astonishing demonstration of dignity at a soirée for the London premiere of *Out of the Crocodile*. 'He stood waiting in his dressing room, but hardly anyone showed. It was all very uncomfortable. Very unpleasant,' says Alvin Rakoff. 'I never personally saw him being shunned socially. To any casual observer things looked normal. However, I was aware that his star was descending – his lustre had faded – which was inevitable, and he was aware of it.'[2]

Routinely presented in an unflattering light, Angela suffered tattered nerves after receiving letters of protest, some explicit. 'I remember somebody smeared dog poop all over the front door of her mews house,' Anneke Wills told the author. 'It was horrible. She phoned me in a terrible state about it.' At the time,

Angela expressed sympathy for Bill, saying she deplored hurting a fifty-two-year-old woman who, over a period of eleven years of marriage, had watched her husband climb from obscurity into being a great star and then seen him disappear from her life with a girl twenty-five years his junior. For Ken, who had no use for salacious tabloid articles, especially after they had begun to write with irritating regularity about his private life, the intrusion was intolerable. On one occasion, visibly rattled, he handed out an angry warning to a photographer taking pictures at Heathrow: 'The next time you do that I'll poke you right between the eyes,' he said after being snapped kissing Angela goodbye before she left for Manchester.³

During this period, Roger Moore continued to be a shoulder to lean on, and Ken was grateful for it, especially when forced to avoid the wedding of his eldest daughter. 'He had intended to give Susan Jane away,' ex-wife Beryl Johnstone explained. 'Then he thought that if the news got out his presence might cause a shambles and spoil the big day.' By this point, Susan, aged twenty-two, was working as a nurse at Westminster Hospital, while Beryl was enjoying small-screen success playing Kitty Jarvis in *Crossroads*, a low-budget ATV soap opera, often described as a mixture of slice-of-life drama and sublime calamity. Funnily enough, Susan Jane made an appearance in the soap during 1964. 'Jane wanted to have a look around the studios where we do *Crossroads*, but this wasn't allowed,' Beryl recounted. 'I mentioned it to Reg Watson [the producer], and he said, "Well if she wants to come on as a non-speaking extra and get £5 for it, she can." That's how it came about that Kenneth More's daughter made her acting debut.'⁴

In the nightspots of London, Ken and Angela were by now a familiar sight. To help insulate herself against unwanted criticism, she changed her surname by deed poll to More, so they 'didn't get embarrassed' when travelling together. 'We would never go abroad if the name on my passport wasn't the same,' she explained. 'We wouldn't want to be running up and down hotel corridors when we live openly together in London.' On the work front, Ken made his first foray into American filmmaking playing George Paston, the heroine's lover in William Wyler's *The Collector*. In fact, the job landed on his lap during a visit to see Angela in Hollywood where she had a bit part in *John Goldfarb, Please Come Home!* a Shirley MacLaine comedy. There was even a tiny buzz about the project – including a small note in the *LA Times* reporting he was 'to create the character known in the girl's diary as "GP", the philosophical artist with whom she imagines herself in love'.[5] Starring Terence Stamp and Samantha Eggar, the film follows a young Englishman (Stamp) who stalks a beautiful art student (Eggar) before abducting and holding her captive in the basement of his rural farmhouse. In the end, after weeks of work at Columbia Pictures, the project was blighted by perverse luck when thirty-five minutes of material was deleted. 'Some of the finest footage I ever shot wound up on the cutting room floor, including Kenneth's part,' Wyler lamented. Robert Swink, the editor, was in the projection room when 'Willy picked up the phone, no fussing around, and called Kenneth More. He told him what he had to do. Willy didn't have to make that call personally, but he did. He respected the performance and the actor, and he didn't want him to hear the bad news second or third hand.' In contrast, the author of *The Collector*, John Fowles, was delighted with the edits. 'Kenneth More played the artist – an actor I don't like, and I never wanted him to play the part,' he asserted. 'In the cutting room, they suddenly realised they had the thing running for over three hours. How they hadn't worked that out before, I don't know. So, they cut all his scenes with Sam Eggar. I've never seen them. In the version one sees now, I believe there's still one sequence where you see his head.' It's ironic, that the single Hollywood performance Kenny ever made never saw the light of day.

In the aftermath of this, Ken returned to London and the Garrick – one of the sources of comfort that continued to sustain him. It was there that Laurie Evans delivered the cheerful news that European television critics had awarded him the Venice trophy for his role in *Heart to Heart*, which, by this point, had been seen by 20 million viewers in Germany, Italy, France, Spain, and Sweden. 'What a boost that was,' says Alvin Rakoff. 'We were all thrilled. Kenneth was cutting a reputation as a capable television actor.' In fact, always susceptible to the flattery of a gong, Ken told the Italian journalist Fredrico Molinari that if he had to choose between a film award and a television one his 'preferences would go to the small screen, because it is a more modern means of expression, of greater responsibility as it reaches everywhere and therefore more demanding'.[6] TV, he contended, constituted a challenge that he could not resist, 'because it is like working under a microscope as absolutely nothing escapes TV cameras, while film cameras are more benign. With TV, you must learn by starting over and, above all, completely forget what you have learned about acting in a film or on stage.'[7] In another interview, he warned people who had made their names in films to ignore TV at their own peril. 'If you get a good part, it can help enhance one's reputation. But if you flop it doesn't do your box-office image much good. Nowadays in films, you're only as big as your last picture. Yes, the days of having a sure-fire success here – even for the old brigade of Hawkins, Bogarde, Mills and me – are over. It depends on how good the film is – which is really as it should be.'

The mid-1960s were the absolute heyday of BBC and ITV dramas, and as far as the public could tell, Kenny was never off the box. In *Collect Your Hand Baggage,* he portrayed Crispin – a man in his forties, a wrecked marriage behind him, continually chasing excitement. 'I know people exactly like this man,' Ken smirked, 'and I think a lot of others will, too.' Soon after, when filming ITV's *Old Soldiers,* a drama about a retired officer settling into civvy street, he yearned to play Harry Palmer in *The Ipcress File,* a downbeat alternative to the Bond films. 'This agent has no number, no blondes hiding under every bed,' he enthused. 'However, the role has gone, and rightly to Michael Caine. He is nearly 20 years younger, after all. And an actor to watch.' Expounding, he said he'd like to play a villain and stick a knife in someone's back. 'I've played too many goody-goodies, but they have grown up with you, the public is loyal, and you are expected to live up to the code you have set.' And while he was being so honest, he admitted his days as a film star may be over: 'I can't expect to carry films much more and will then be quite happy to do what certain other actors are doing – playing second or even third leads if they're OK. People like my old chum Trevor Howard are doing remarkably well at that. They don't have the top responsibility of carrying the film and therefore don't get much blame if things don't work out at the box office. It would be nice to be certain of one good film a year and to spend three or four of the other months in the South of France.'

During the balmy autumn of 1964, Ken continued to take stock. By now, he had appeared in thirty-four films, six of them since signing with Rank nine years earlier. He still wasn't divorced but passionately wanted to be. And, like Jack Hawkins before him, he celebrated his fiftieth birthday in Paris where he gave a candid interview which appeared under the banner: 'Kenneth More: L'amour a 50 ans (pour une fille de 23 ans)'. 'The fiftieth birthday is a day of reflection in the life of every man,' the opening paragraph declared. 'This is especially true for Kenneth More. What can he see when he looks back over his life? His eleven-year marriage to Mabel More is over. And his career as England's most famous young lead is dead too. He killed his marriage himself when he fell in love with another woman.' In the interview, Kenny spoke candidly about friends taking Bill's side, believing that Angela had broken up a beautiful marriage. 'How dare people take a stand about what happens in a marriage? No one can break up a happy marriage, everyone knows that. Before Angela and I were living together, a whole bunch of people called her and slandered her. It was really awful.' He mentioned Angela's father was only three years his senior but insisted: 'age doesn't matter when you love each other. We have already joked a lot about it.' He concluded by saying he wasn't interested in what people said about him, and revealed he'd given up his press cutting service and abandoned his scrapbook. 'All I know is that I've never been happier.' Strangely enough, as Ken shunned press exposure,

Angela enjoyed a few moments in the limelight and even agreed to a full-page interview with *Titbits* magazine. In it, she sobbed that she didn't think she'd make it professionally: 'I used to think I might, but you have to want success badly. Anyway, I don't have time to work. Now my char has left, I have to do the housework.'[8]

At around this time, with his TV career blossoming, there was talk about Kenneth's next project being a film based on the life of plastic surgeon Archibald McIndoe, the man who treated badly burned RAF aircrew after the war. In truth, he hated everything about the idea, thinking the story was gloomy, dark and miserable, and fretted a picture focusing on disfigured men might fail to attract audiences (just as Korda thought about the Bader story). As it turned out, the job didn't materialise but an offer arrived to repeat his film role in a fluffy stage musical version of *The Admirable Crichton*, retitled *Our Man Crichton*. Producer Bernard Delfont thought Kenny the only star who could do justice to the role and offered a flat fee of £1,000 a week. It was a temptation he couldn't resist. Moreover, any lingering reservations about the project evaporated when Millicent Martin, George Benson, and David Kernan signed on to provide support. The script still roughly followed J. M. Barrie's original story, and at first, Ken was spared the nightmares of singing and dancing – until composer Herbert Kretzmer inserted several speak-sing numbers, including 'Were I As Good' and 'I Never Looked for You'. Glyn Worsnip, an aspiring young actor, remembered Ken 'could not sing for toffee but carried the part with his immensely likeable personality'. Though the production brimmed with outrageous funnies matching the film, after a short run at Manchester's Palace Theatre, it opened at

London's Shaftesbury Theatre to lukewarm reviews. Always one to rock the boat, Noël Coward was typically frank and openly critical. 'Never,' he snapped, 'become involved in such a thing again.' Just as demoralising, B. A. Young of *The New York Times* was not sure what to make of the spectacle, saying Ken revealed a pleasant singing voice, 'though I don't know how it would sound away from the battery of microphones that line the front of the stage'. Young also complained about the flatness of the score, saying it was a pity because the adaptation 'had been done with wit, the lyrics are uncommonly deft and the direction by Clifford Williams, an associate director of the Royal Shakespeare Company, is brisk and stylish'. *Theatre World*'s critic was predictably leery saying a 'stronger singing voice would have been an asset'. However, with £1,000 a week in the bank, Ken took any dissent in his stride; he'd heard it all before, and worse, and knew the show was a success. In fact, by the time it was over, *Our Man Crichton* clocked up 208 performances and led to him crooning three numbers on a soundtrack album under the direction of George Martin, the Beatles producer. Better still, the show prompted publisher Michael Joseph to offer him a book deal, penning a light-hearted tome outlining the hazards of acting, filled with theatrical anecdotes. The blurb for *Kindly Leave the Stage* stated that 'Kenneth More, one of our most experienced and successful actors, has a shrewd but twinkling eye for the pitfalls and absurdities in the profession he loves.' Mercifully, it sold well – and, like *Happy Go Lucky*, was serialised by the regional press.

10

SAVED BY THE SAGA

Throughout 1965, Ken toiled diligently to keep up Jack Hawkins' spirits as his chum showed signs of grave illness. They often shared old stories; a favourite being about when they joined Trevor Howard for a jaunt to Paris for the premiere of Otto Preminger's *St Joan*. It proved so boring that all three 'escaped' the screening halfway through by tiptoeing off to a pub, only to be met with a withering glance from a British journalist. However, by the new year of 1966, Hawkins was an extremely sick man. After endless tests, he was wheeled into surgery to have his voice box removed – the operation left a hole the size of a penny in his throat. At first, the stress of his injury saw him suffer persistent melancholy. 'Of course, I'll never act again,' Hawkins rasped. 'I'm resigned to that. There's no point thinking about the past, in regretting anything. The most I can hope for is to vary the pitch of the sounds. The actual croaking quality, I'm afraid, is here to stay. It's a damned nuisance, but there you are.' Ken considered Hawkins one of his best and most loyal friends and convinced him not to throw in the towel on his career. He didn't, and as time wore on, he resumed his social life at his Kensington apartment, where guests supped 'black velvets' (a mixture of champagne and beer).

Amid all this, Angela was enjoying a run of plum roles in film and TV. After featuring with Ken's old chum John Gregson in *Gideon's Way*, she landed the choice part of Annie Oakley in *Carry On Cowboy*, produced by Peter Rogers, the husband of Betty Box. In it, she had a memorable saloon bar scene, singing 'This is the Night for Love'. Over the next few years, she returned to Pinewood for roles in *Carry On Screaming*, *Follow that Camel* and *Carry On Up the Khyber* (Peter Rogers once told the author that *Khyber* was his 'absolute favourite' in the series of thirty-one films).

At around the time Hawkins underwent surgery, Alfred Shaughnessy, who had scripted *Brandy for the Parson*, sent Ken a specially tailored drama, which also included a juicy role for Angela. 'Kenny and Angie were dead keen to do the play and I told ATV so,' Shaughnessy remembered. 'But suddenly, when the day came for Kenny to commit to it, he became covered in confusion. He had just been offered a very big job by the BBC. It was "a Galsworthy thing" with a nice part and lots of episodes. He couldn't do both and he felt he must go for the money.' The 'Galsworthy thing' – was, in fact, *The Forsyte Saga*, a BBC TV period production based on John Galsworthy's novels, spanning from the 1870s to the 1920s. Destined to unexpectedly provide a renaissance of his career, Kenny signed up to play Jolyon, a member of a well-to-do family who gets by, more or less, by artistic endeavours – mainly sketching and painting. 'Jolyon was the role that marked the end of my being typecast as a one-dimensional ageing juvenile and I thank my lucky stars for it,' Kenny recounted, after signing up to make twenty-six episodes. At first, he objected that Jolyon was a dim character but the 'beauty of the part, because it wasn't a great role, is that Jolyon is the narrator of the story, and he really is Galsworthy. Galsworthy saw himself as young Jolyon.' As the show progressed, the character ages from his mid-thirties to his seventies, giving Ken the 'chance of doing a bit of acting again, which one rather drifts away from in films and one is playing essentially a personality.' After some tweaks on a script extending to 1,500 pages – writer Donald Wilson offered many delicious lines, some of which – given the circumstances – could have been penned by Kenny and directed at Bill and his detractors. For example, in the first episode, Jolyon, who – appropriately enough – was busily conducting an affair with the au pair behind the back of his wife, Frances, tells his lover how he avoided an important family gathering:

My darling, it would have been the easiest thing in the world to go. Sit in the church, rub shoulders with all my friends and relations, kiss the old aunts, drink the champagne, listen politely while my uncles talk about their money. Walk around with Frances, hand in hand, smiles, and small talk, pretending that everything's perfect, that we are the most devoted, loving couple in the whole of London. And who knows what's being said behind our backs? Make no mistake it's got around; I've heard enough to be sure of that. I expect they all think I'm the very devil of a fellow and the ironic thing is ... I'm not. All I want is to live openly, decently, lovingly with one woman.

Strangely enough, the show turned out to be one of the highlights of Ken's late professional life, and a huge advance for the supporting ensemble, including Eric Porter, Susan Hampshire, and Martin Jarvis. 'Kenny's expertise as a natural screen actor was an education for me,' Jarvis told the author, recounting watching him 'like a hawk' during rehearsals and being intrigued to see how, with apparent truth and simplicity, he related every moment of his character's behaviour to the camera. 'I put it down to his immense film experience, having been directed by quite a few masters of the medium.' The production team, he recalls, also seemed thrilled to be working with a genuine star. 'We all blushed with pleasure when he hailed us blithely, remembering all the names. I soon got the feeling that Kenny himself was delighted – even relieved – to have secured the juicy role of Jolyon Forsyte.' Remarkably, even the director seemed happy for Kenny to create his own positions, even though these choices could have influenced a change of camera angle. 'An attempt was made to suggest some alternative moves in one emotional scene that Kenny had to play with me, where my character's storyline was equal in importance to his own,' Jarvis explained. 'Kenny considered the option then shook his head. "No, no, old love," he said, "the punters will want to know what I am thinking. They won't have a clue if I'm over there." He was right of course.'

As Jarvis got to know Ken, he wondered if his 'jaunty manner' might not cloak some insecurity. For example, just after the show's final performance, he remembered Ken being nervous at a publicity party given by the BBC for the *Forsyte* actors to meet the press. 'I wondered if his hand was shaking a little as he cheerfully passed me a glass of white wine, chortling,

"Come on old darling, don't be shy!" His slight vulnerability – if that's what it was – only made him seem more human to me. I have wondered since if that occasional shaking hand was the beginnings of the cruelly debilitating Parkinson's disease that led to his early death.' Like Francis White before him, Jarvis also found Kenny's influence as a bona fide star at the BBC was surprisingly extensive:

> I recall how I (and my battered old car) was always refused entry into the main BBC car park. Vic, the guardian at the gates, was implacable. Until ... after one Sunday night when a particularly strong scene between Kenny and me had enthralled the viewers, things changed. The next day, always optimistic, I drew up outside the entrance. Vic took a look, seemed about to repeat his usual, 'No chance mate, you park down the road.' Then he took another look, actually smiled, and said 'Ere, I saw you on TV last night with Mr More. In you go – you're all right – park next to Kenny's car.' He opened the gates. I had arrived.

After *Forsyte*, Ken landed a part in Hugh Whitemore's BBC TV production *Final Demand*, a quirky yarn about a man set on never paying another bill. After receiving a red letter, his character opts out of society, leaves his job, stops paying bills and retires from the community. The *Daily Mirror*'s Kenneth Eastaugh was deeply moved and found it 'outstandingly pictorial', showing a perceptive regard for what is often underplayed on TV – 'communication by more than words'. Further TV work followed with *Lord Raingo*, a four-part BBC serialisation of the Arnold Bennett play, and straight after, he accepted a 'nothing part' in

Rod Taylor's blood-and-gore film adventure, *The Mercenaries*, telling the story of a band of men battling through war-torn Congo to steal $50 million in uncut diamonds. In later years, Ken was reluctant to talk about this project, but did admit it was 'an appalling miscalculation'. Set in Africa but filmed in the Caribbean, it was the first time he worked on a film and was not leading in it: 'It was an astonishing feeling not to be the first person to get the seat in the helicopter, not to be the person the make-up girl was worrying about,' he said. As the shoot progressed, he despised the fact that everyone's views about shots and angles were sought except his. And yet, he had acted in more movies than the rest of the cast combined. If he had a good line, it was sliced down, and then cut back further, and would ultimately vanish altogether. Worse still, he was dumbfounded by Rod Taylor's overbearing personality and fully loaded ego. In a delightfully catty moment, Ken told writer Michael Munn of the 'unfortunate happenings' during this ego-bruising experience:

Rod Taylor proudly told me: 'I had Johnny Mills in my last film.' Most people would have said: 'I've been filming with Johnny Mills.' I had a feeling he would tell the cast of his next film: 'I had Kenny More in my last film.' He was the star, and I was billed below Yvette Mimieux, and American football player Jim Brown. I just felt I didn't belong with them. If Rod or Jim weren't on the set on time, we would have to wait about until they arrived. Sometimes we didn't get started till 10 o'clock, which is a late start on a film. It was all so undisciplined. They thought they were such big stars, but they just created tension. Taylor had been an amateur boxer and Jim of course was a former American football player and was a big man and he and Taylor kept threatening to settle their disputes with their fists. They appeared to hate each other. If they were only acting, they were better actors than I thought. They all put in their ten pennies' worth about what they thought should be filmed, but nobody asked my opinion, and I'd been in more films than the rest of the cast put together. Director Jack Cardiff cut all my best lines in deference to the Hollywood stars. I'd wake up in the morning, unable to face another day on that film.

Thankfully, Ken's prickly mood was lightened when a journalist phoned from London with news that *The Forsyte Saga* – by then showing on BBC Two – was a phenomenal success. The call had an electrifying effect – for all his experience and sensibility, he burst out crying. In fact, over the coming weeks, the show became so popular that many old acquaintances sought to renew friendships. While some were welcomed, others – after being soberly re-evaluated – were 'left out in the cold where they had put us'. Another clear benefit of *Forsyte*'s success was that it provided a pretext to avoid the promotional campaign for *The Mercenaries*, which critic David Adams called one of the most ghastly, tasteless, and sadistic movies he had ever seen. 'Rarely do films make me physically sick,' he scowled. '*The Mercenaries* nauseated me mentally and physically ... one of the most disgusting and worthless movies to reach the screen.' *The New York Times* was kinder, noting the film was basically low grade, 'there was a lot of carnage that will probably infuriate anyone who scrutinises movies for their politics'. Eventually, *The Mercenaries* became a painful topic with Ken; interviewers who probed too closely at the subject often felt an icy chill.

11

AGEING JUVENILE

The domestic success of *The Forsyte Saga* reinvigorated Kenny spiritually, and financially. While the world awaited the arrival of the show, he gussied himself up for a series of promotional interviews. A shrewd player at the art of publicity, he referred to *Forsyte* as 'Britain's most successful television enterprise' and boasted of receiving sackfuls of letters from Romania, Yugoslavia 'and places which one would never dream of being seen or heard in'. He cooed when it became the first Western-made series to air on Soviet television after being deemed 'acceptable viewing' because it showed the decline of the 'highest echelons of the ruling British bourgeois class'. To overcome the language barrier, the Soviets chose the 'read-over' technique using a single presenter trudging his way through a Russian translation just loud enough to saturate the original soundtrack.

Forsyte laid the foundations for the rest of Ken's career, transforming him from a British star into one of the few actors known throughout the world. It also enabled him to prod the

Ageing Juvenile

BBC to buy the rights to a project he had long wanted to do, a series of *The White Rabbit*. 'I thought the chance had gone forever. I finally had the opportunity to play Commander Yeo-Thomas,' he confessed. 'It will make an enormous impact because it's strong stuff with strong words.' Right from its inception, BBC Two controller David Attenborough spent money on a royal scale – £50,000 – including a generous fee for Ken. And although the story more or less followed the book, it was filmed in four parts and weaves together the various threads of Yeo-Thomas's ordeal. One of the most highly decorated agents in the Second World War, Yeo-Thomas had been a fashion worker in Paris who became a resistance leader using the codename 'White Rabbit'. However, as he tapped out secret messages, the Gestapo was tipped-off about his activities, and tortured him near to death, practically creating a martyr. After some script jiggling, the company worked twelve straight days in rehearsals at the Acton Drill Hall, finishing on the afternoon of 27 July 1967. Then, as shooting progressed, Ken was presented as never seen before – battered, bruised, tortured, and antagonised. Though he was unable to lose enough weight to resemble a skeletal-like concentration camp victim, his hair was shaved and covered with a bald bladder wig. Then, he almost drowned when dragged with ankle shackles through a bath – just like it had almost drowned Yeo-Thomas. The most harrowing scene was when he was placed in solitary confinement in a damp cellar, replete with live rats. It was, Ken said, the hardest job he'd ever had, both emotionally and physically. 'But it was the most rewarding. I would gladly do it all again. It was much tougher than playing Bader – and that was gruelling.' Interestingly, actress Fiona Lewis who played

Jeanne Helbing, told the author all four episodes were transmitted live and recorded for the single repeat: 'I froze in front of the camera – much to everyone (including Kenneth's) horror.' On the credit side, the production had many of the familiar contours of a 1960s' BBC drama – studio based, unhurried dialogue and slower pace – but a quality in writing and acting that audiences had come to expect from the corporation. But on the debit side, the real trouble with the play was that hardly anyone saw it because under the agreement with the rights holder, recordings had to be destroyed within twenty-eight days. 'It's a pity we can't offer this tremendous story of courage to other countries or show it again at a later date,' the BBC acknowledged. 'But we felt we would rather do it on these terms than not at all.'

The year 1967 brought good and bad news in equal measure. In the five years since Ken and Bill parted company, both had carved out new lives – however, they were briefly reunited in grief when Jonathan Barkby, Ken's stepson, was killed in a collision on the M4 at Slough. An inquest revealed he was well over the alcohol limit. Soon after, when re-evaluating her personal priorities, Bill finally agreed to sue Ken for divorce. At the London Divorce Court on 7 July, he offered no defence and Bill (listed as Mabel Edith More of Moore Street, Chelsea on the court papers) was granted a decree nisi because of his adultery with Angela. Solicitor David Jacobs gave evidence in support of Bill's petition and produced statements signed by Ken and Angela. Justice Lloyd-Jones approved arrangements for Kenny to pay his ex-wife a lump sum of £25,000 and £23 a week for the maintenance of Sarah, then thirteen years old. Strangely enough, just before Bill's decision, Angela gave one of her frankest interviews – 'My life with Kenneth More' – insisting she and Ken were not amoral or immoral people. 'We're rather old fashioned. I know this may sound like a joke considering all that's happened, but we're very sort of suburban, Kenny and I. And we believe in marriage.' Talking to Michael Kirsch at the mews house, where, he observed, the walls were studded with 'happy looking pictures of them both together', Angela said 'people often take me for Kenny's daughter. It's awfully embarrassing. He is much older than me but everything's marvellous.' She admitted to being riddled with insecurities, while Ken was so secure. 'Going through what we have either makes or breaks you. Newspapermen crawling up the bathroom drainpipe to get photographs and things. And people staring. I know they would stare at Kenny anyway, but they stare extra hard now there's a bit of scandal about him. You take it extra personally. Then there are phone calls in the middle of the night saying dirty rotten things. Sometimes when you pick up the phone there is nothing – just a click.' Talking about how show business people had reacted to their affair, Angela admitted that 'lots of Kenny's friends are terribly embarrassed. Understandably, I'd be just as embarrassed if a dear friend of mine left his wife. I certainly wouldn't want to know anything about the new partner. His friends thought maybe he would go back to his wife. So, they were giving it time. Now I think they realise I love him. One lives in hope, of course, of a divorce.'[1]

In August 1967, Kenny turned down the lead in *A Girl in My Soup* – 'a dreadful play' – slated to open at Broadway's Music Box Theatre.[2] He had no desire to be in America during the so-called 'summer of love' and pushed ahead with 'long delayed' plans to marry Angela on 16 March the following year. 'Everybody knows about Angela and me,' he noted in a press release, announcing the big day. 'We've been together now for a long time waiting for this day to come. It will be a wonderful day.' It was. The Revd Thomas Caryl Micklem, a Free Church minister, conducted the service at Kensington Congregational Chapel, which by showbiz standards, turned out to be a quiet affair. Photographs captured the moment: a car pulls up to collect the newlyweds. Angela in a snappy dress and hat. She is beaming. Ken is beside her, hand facing the crowd in a wave. They are – thankfully – both overjoyed and relaxed. Afterwards, the newlyweds chatted to a clutch of onlookers and posed for pictures before a reception at the Royal Garden Hotel. A honeymoon in Nice would follow in July, delayed due to Ken signing on to play Group Captain Barker, Station Commander at RAF Duxford, in the mammoth production of the *Battle of Britain,* which not only promised to be one of the year's major releases, but also reunited him with Susannah York and Douglas Bader, who worked as an adviser. Designed as a colossal tribute to the RAF – full of dizzying fast cuts and aerial dog fights – it was pulled together by James Bond producer Harry Saltzman who secured the services of Laurence Olivier, Ralph Richardson, Trevor Howard, Robert Shaw, Harry Andrews, Michael Redgrave, and Michael Caine. The film, which began shooting in April 1968, strived to provide an accurate account of the Battle of Britain, when in 1940, the Royal Air Force exacted a defeat on Hitler's Luftwaffe and ensured the cancellation of Operation Sea Lion, the Nazi plan to invade Britain. Though the film ran virtually non-stop, somewhere or other, during 1969, the dramatic plot and a

£5 million budget failed to produce a single 'stand out' sequence. Gene Siskel, the snippety critic at the *Chicago Tribune*, blasted a '12-thousand-megadollar bomb' featuring 100 vintage planes eating up 40 minutes of screen time. 'The film has absolutely no dramatic interest in the other 93 minutes, and I challenge the notion that it is worth seeing just for the aerial sequences.' It's an odd fact that the movie – now considered a classic – endured dreadful reviews. Even local critics didn't do anything to help it. For example, a notice in the *Kensington News* even went after Kenny personally by complaining it should be renamed: 'How Kenneth More Won the War':

> Any person like myself, who was born after the war, could be forgiven for thinking this was the case. In the many war pictures I have seen, Kenneth More appears to have wiped out the German army single-handed, sunk their entire fleet, and now in the desperately disappointing 'Battle of Britain', he had destroyed their air force with the aid of a few Spitfires. Of course, this is not intended as an attack on Kenneth More's qualities as an actor, but I swear if I see him sink another sub, I shall begin to believe Churchill never existed.

Apparently neither Kenny nor Saltzman were the least bit concerned about the reviews. In fact, no sooner had Ken convinced everyone that he was 'slowing down' for a few months to relax, singer Dorothy Squires popped up from out of the blue threatening legal action after he referred to Luisa Mattioli as Roger Moore's wife during a television show. A bulletin from the Press Association – cleverly labelled 'Moore v More' – hit the wire on Thursday 11 April 1968: 'Singer Dorothy Squires, aged 44, estranged wife of actor Roger Moore, is suing actor Kenneth More for libel over remarks alleged to have been made on television about Moore's marriage status.' The crux of the case concerned comments Ken made at the British Film Academy Awards, shown by Granada Television in March 1968, when, acting as a commentator, he described Mattioli as Moore's wife while Roger was still married to Squires. In reality, though, the Bond star had been dating Mattioli since 1961 and in the upshot, Squires' refusal to divorce him prompted Luisa to change her name to Moore by deed poll. They lived together and even had children, Deborah, aged six, and Geoffrey, two. At first, Ken laughed off Squires' menace, viewing it as a silly and malicious threat. In fact, he thought no more of it before embarking on playing the po-faced Kaiser in *Oh! What a Lovely War*, a musical directed by Richard Attenborough – who was so desperate to make the film that he convinced Paramount Pictures to back it by singing and dancing his way through the entire score for CEO Charlie Blühdorn. Having witnessed Attenborough's resolve, he cut a cheque for $6 million on condition he placed six well-known names in the picture. Attenborough did better, bagging thirteen, including John Mills, Dirk Bogarde, Maggie Smith, Vanessa Redgrave, and Laurence Olivier, who went on to win an Oscar for Best Actor in a Supporting Role. The early notices were fantastic, the papers rhapsodised over every element of the film – Attenborough's direction, Gerry Turpin's evocative colour photography and Don Challis's exquisitely controlled musical score. *Variety* called the film 'dedicated, exhilarating, shrewd, mocking, funny, emotional, witty, poignant and technically brilliant'.

Ageing Juvenile

That summer passed pleasantly. During July, Angela gave some insight into her life for *Woman*, the weekly periodical, by claiming that being Kenny's wife was much more exciting than any career could be. 'The way we live is great fun, yet it is made up of so many ordinary, little things. Kenny is sunny side up. The supreme optimist. He never seems to get depressed or worried, and even if he's feeling ill, he'll still be smiling about it.'[3] In fact, Ken was more relaxed than ever, happily plodding along with the occasional broadcasting job until John Gale turned up with an offer to star in William Douglas Home's *The Secretary Bird*, a comic yarn, alongside Jane Downs, Terence Longdon, and Judith Arthy at the Savoy Theatre. With a sudden urge to return to the stage, he grabbed the role of Hugh Walford, an author past his physical prime who is distraught that his wife (Downs) is leaving him for another man. Shocked into action, his character has a weekend to prove to her that she was making a mistake – but not by threats or arguments, but by being devilishly civil to her sporty boyfriend, played by Longdon. 'In my opinion, it is Willie Home's wittiest play since *The Reluctant Debutante*, and perhaps better than that,' Ken said. 'My wife goes off with another man, and knowing I'm no match for him in youthful appeal, I set about getting her back by relying on my superior intellect.'[4] And to give his wife grounds for divorce, he offered to be caught in bed with his secretary played by Judith Arthy, a young Australian actress who thought Ken was one of the best high-comedy actors in Britain. 'At first, I was nervous about the play, because my part is very hard to carry off well,' she explained. 'But Kenneth has taught me to relax on stage, which gives me more confidence.' Typically, Ken described the play as the 'biggest success of his career,' at a time when the theatre was going through the doldrums, 'in fact,' he added, 'it has broken every single record for a straight play in the history not only of the Savoy, but also the history of the London theatre. It's incredible ... We go to four figures every night, which is most encouraging.' Indeed, critic Arthur Thurwell thought he gave the smoothest, 'most accomplished performance' of light comedy for many a year. 'The play is virtually a one-man show, which enables Mr More to superbly demonstrate the flippant witticisms provided by William Douglas Home.' After seeing the show, even Noël Coward – suitably recovered after his shock at *Our Man Crichton* – confided in his diary that Ken was a lovely, deft comedian in the proper Hawtrey, Du Maurier, Coward tradition. 'In fact, he doesn't apparently make any effort to get his effects and manages to get everyone. No asking for laughs or begging for attention. Very satisfactory.'

The only cloud during this sunny period arrived with news that Beryl Johnstone had been admitted to hospital. Her health had, in fact, been shaky for years. Though she'd continued commuting between Cheltenham and Birmingham for *Crossroads*, she was extremely frail and passed away in January 1969 at the age of fifty-four. Forty years of tobacco smoke cutting into her lungs had worn her down, prompting friends to plead with her to kick the habit. She did try switching from cigarettes to cigarillos when *Crossroads* launched, but she was already thin, almost gaunt. 'I had smoked cigarettes all through my career,' she confessed in October 1964. 'As many as 40 a day. Until a few weeks ago I gave them up completely. But when television rehearsals began, I felt I had to relax with something and so I started smoking these miniature cigars. I get through about five a day – they help me a lot.'[5]

All the little bits of work – *The Forsyte Saga*, *The Secretary Bird* and *Battle of Britain* – prompted the BBC to invite Kenny to appear on *Desert Island Discs*. Thirteen years had passed since his first broadcast, and much had changed. 'I've just bought a lovely house with a lovely garden, in the middle of London, like a sort of vicarage garden,' he told Roy Plomley, referring to Bute House. 'It's the sort of garden which I know I'd like to sit in all next summer and try and write something.' When unveiling his choice of records, he spoke of a 'wife that was very much in love with me and I'm very much in love with her'. (A dog-eared carbon copy of Kenny's script shows that in the original version of the broadcast, the sentence ended with: 'We're both incorrigible romantics,' but the line was crossed out with pencil, presumably by BBC censors.)

Records included Keely Smith's 'I Wish You Love' and Mendelssohn's 'Midsummer Night's Dream', which, he said, reminded him of Grimm's fairy tales and 'all the sort of magic things which play, I'm afraid, still to this day a very great part in my life'. For Angela, he chose Frank Sinatra's 'All the Way', as 'all the memories of our relationship would be incorporated in that record'. (The song includes the line: 'Who knows where the road will lead us, only a fool would say. But if you let me love you, it's for sure I'm gonna love you all the way ...') Discussing work, Plomley asked if Ken would like to reinvent himself by directing or producing. 'I used to think that I wanted to direct like Richard Attenborough,' he replied. 'But having seen how well he did it and also the terrific pressure on his shoulders ... I realised I couldn't cope with it. The directing part I wouldn't mind at all, but I'm afraid it would break me into small pieces.'

Twenty-five days after Ken recorded *Desert Island Discs*, Angela suffered a miscarriage; she'd been three months pregnant. 'It would have been the first child of the marriage which took place 16 months ago,' the *Daily Mirror* observed. Angela was fine, but bitterly disappointed. 'She is all right now and has adjusted herself,' Ken said, adding they refused to give up hope of ever having a child together, and would investigate adoption. Over the next month, as they began to recover, Ken secured his release from *The Secretary Bird,* saying his days as a 'dashing lead' were at an end. Given the situation at home, the run of the play had become an ordeal: 'At my age romantic roles just aren't me. But luckily, I've kept my hair on and my stomach in. And there's an old adage that if you can do that you can go on playing juvenile leads forever. But not me.' To prove the point, he grabbed opportunity to portray a middle-aged secret service agent in *Fräulein Doktor,* a First World War story loosely based on the real life of Elsbeth Schragmüller, a German spy sent to Britain to kill General Kitchener. Paramount's synopsis notes: 'Disguised as a Scottish woman, Fräulein Doktor uses her charm to learn which battleship will take Kitchener to Russia. German mines are dropped at her instruction. Fräulein Doktor watches in patriotic exultation as Kitchener's ship explodes.' For Kenny, the financial incentives were attractive, as was the prospect of filming in Yugoslavia. Tackling the script was Stanley Mann, who had been nominated for an Oscar for his work on *The Collector* (and wrote Ken's never-seen part). Possibly as compensation, Mann afforded Ken many good lines and quality scenes with James

Booth, playing a weaselly German turncoat. The result was a medium-paced drama in the same vein as *The 39 Steps*, perked by Suzy Kendall playing the German spy. For spice, Mann made the good Doktor a morphine addict and added a bit of lesbian action. Now an occasional fringe showing on satellite TV – this Yugoslav-Italian co-production climaxed with a ghoulish anti-war spectacle – a poison gas slaughter in the trenches. *The New York Times* applauded this 'cunning entertainment and a gripping evocation of war as the deadliest of all games'. When it was spliced together and Ennio Morricone's score added, *Fräulein Doktor* turned out to be a respectable feature, but was blighted by poor distribution. In fact, Ken never saw the film – he did, however, enjoy a measure of contentment during the shoot which saw him indulge in boozy nights of plate-smashing in Novi Sad. 'There were no egos on that film,' he remarked, 'but we had a lot of laughs.' When it was all over, he returned to London to inaugurate the Malcolm Sargent Cancer Fund (now Young Lives vs Cancer) with a television appeal. In a carefully crafted speech, he spoke about how in spite of all the advances of research, 15,000 children under the age of fifteen died each year from cancer. 'Doctors and nurses do everything possible to relieve the physical suffering, but a tragic situation remains for the parents and the children,' he explained. 'Now, through this fund, we can help the families to face the last terrible months with the minimum of distress.' It was an incredibly noble cause, and funds eventually paid for nursing facilities to relieve parents of the constant tensions; provided the extras that strained family budgets; and offered money to enable parents to visit their child more frequently in hospital.

Early that spring, Ken honoured his commitment to act as best man when Roger Moore finally made his wedding vows to Luisa Mattioli, before a congregation, including Warren Mitchell, Sid James, and Richard Attenborough. It was a moving service – but when the big moment arrived, Luisa lost her voice and couldn't repeat the last six vital words in her vows to Roger. Then, as a nervous hush fell over London's Caxton Hall, the Registrar Donald Borham prompted Luisa ... 'to be my lawful wedded husband'. She nodded and buried her tear-soaked face in Roger's shoulder. He put his arm around her. 'Please don't worry, we are used to this kind of thing here,' the Registrar assured. 'It happens often.' And they were married. 'There can't be a woman in the room who isn't crying,' Angela said, recalling how Luisa arrived ten minutes late due to traffic and a nervous Roger sent her out onto Caxton Street to look for his bride!

Remarkably – despite the wedding – Dorothy Squires surfaced again with her threat of libel action which went before the High Court in October 1969. It was a time-consuming distraction, climaxing with Squires delivering a tearful performance on the stand, saying she felt maligned. 'It was the first time I had ever seen Luisa,' she explained, breaking into sobs. 'And for the first time in my life I was dumbfounded hearing Kenneth More say she was his [Roger Moore's] wife. I was numb. I felt terribly miserable and went upstairs to lay on the bed for a while. A friend came and gave me a tranquiliser and I went to sleep.' Taking a cue from Squires' performance – and against his lawyer's instructions – Ken delivered his own 'magnificent witness box oration' and stole the show. In the end, Squires lost the case, but was thick-skinned enough to accept defeat. Kenny, ever the gentleman, simply said it had been a very traumatic experience: 'I certainly do not feel elated. I feel extremely gratified, and if anything, rather proud of the law which distinguishes between a completely innocent remark and a premeditated libel because if this case had gone against me, it would have indicated a premeditation that was furthest from my mind.' By the end of the three days in court, he was more than ready to begin work on presenting the story of the Windmill in *If It Moves – It's Rude,* a BBC documentary. In it, he takes a walking tour of Soho, recounting his own career, spliced with memories (and gags) from Jimmy Edwards, Arthur English, Bruce Forsyth, and Stanley Holloway. 'Until the theatre closed,' Ken told viewers, 'I kept in close touch with the Windmill. Even now, after all these years, I still have a feeling for the spirit of the place. A British institution or just another tacky little corner of Soho? Whatever it was, it has a great story – it has about it the stuff of life.'

Not long after, Hubert Gregg, the composer of 'Maybe It's Because I'm a Londoner', had Kenny in mind for the lead in a frothy musical about Charles II and Nell Gwyn, tentatively titled 'His Majesty's Pleasure'. Though hardly contemporary, Ken was interested and reckoned it should be presented at the Theatre Royal Drury Lane, if and when it became free. 'The idea is that I should play Charles II,' he explained, and Pat Kirkwood, Gregg's wife, was slated for the part of Nell Gwyn. 'I hope Pat wants to do it; she'd be absolutely wonderful.' Once Kenny read the script, he approved it. Then, almost as an afterthought, he asked for a revamp making Charles the dominant part – not Nell as planned. 'Hubert went to work again on the script and practically rewrote it,' Kirkwood recounted in her memoirs, *The Time of My Life.*

'I prayed that he would not again be disappointed after all the prodigious energy he had spent on it.' With the rewrite finished, theatrical impresario Bernard Delfont declared an interest and said, 'This show, "Nell" [the original title was changed], is going to be bigger than Oklahoma.' Duly, Kenny was publicly named as the star, and as Kirkwood remembered, 'everything seemed set fair. We waited. And waited.' Then, just before rehearsals began, catastrophe struck when composer Tony Hatch and his wife, singer Jackie Trent, stunned everyone by opening a touring production titled 'Nell' with Lonnie Donegan as Charles II and Trent as Nell Gwyn. Aghast, Kirkwood never forgot what happened next:

> There was a newspaper article that quoted Jackie Trent as saying, 'I am Nell Gwyn – a busty red-head!' The show was to be a spoof on the history of Charles and Nell. There was nothing we could do, even though they were using our title and benefiting from the publicity that Bernie Delfont had given our Nell, saying it would be 'the greatest musical since Oklahoma'. Then Prince Littler rang to say that all his backers had withdrawn because of this disgraceful coup. The spoof pop version played a few weeks on tour and was a disaster, gaining terrible reviews – no help to us in our shock and misery.[6]

According to Tony Hatch, his version was written by Philip Mackie and Johnny Worth. 'The show was produced by Richmond Theatre. Jackie's co-stars were Stuart Damon playing Charles II (replacing Donegan) and Hermione Baddeley playing her mother,' Hatch told the author in an interview for this book.

'After its Richmond Theatre run the show toured nationally for four weeks playing Leeds and Oxford and two more theatres. Unfortunately, the show failed to find a West End home.'[7] Even so, the damage to Kenny's production had already been done. Ensuing discussions between angry investors Gregg and Delfont about *His Majesty's Pleasure* infected the already sagging morale of everyone involved. Beside himself, Gregg shelved his own script, and retreated with Kirkwood to the Algarve.

12

A NEW DECADE

By 1970, Ken's face had filled out, his hair, once beautifully groomed, took on a fuller, metallic grey appearance, he sported longer sideburns, bushier eyebrows, and a thicker waist. And while he still wore custom-made suits and shirts, they were typical of the fashions at the time – bigger lapels, buffalo horn buttons, garish cloth, and louder ties. He even owned a sheepskin overcoat with full fur collar and cuffs. His wider girth perfectly suited his casting as the affably bewhiskered Ghost of Christmas Present, in *Scrooge* – a big-budget musical directed by Ronald Neame, shot over a gruelling ninety-day schedule at the start of 1970. Filming was a complicated process, made worse by a string of setbacks in casting. At the very last minute, Albert Finney inherited the title role originally earmarked for Richard Harris, then Rex Harrison. Ken took third billing after eighty-two-year-old Edith Evans. The strong supporting cast gathered at Shepperton included Alec Guinness, Michael Medwin, and Anton Rodgers, who would give an inspired performance as Tom Jenkins, remembered for his musical finale 'Thank You Very Much'. Stunning sets, costumes, and breathtaking camerawork gave the picture a lush Hollywood style as did the score, composed by Leslie Bricusse – one of Kenny's Riviera neighbours – who tasked him to sing 'I Like Life' as he thrust Scrooge through the skies over London. 'It was more of a duet with Albie,' Ken told journalists, dressed in a green velvet gown with fur collar and cuffs, and gold pendant. While he threw himself enthusiastically into the part, shooting was no picnic – make-up took two hours, and several scenes required him to dangle from a high-tension wire. However, *Scrooge* was a surprise hit for Cinema Center Films when it opened, earning over £1 million in its first release. Even better, it took $3 million in rentals in the United States and Canada. By the time the film was finished, Bricusse was already being touted for an Oscar nomination for Best Original Song Score. 'It's the kind of film I thought they didn't make any more,' one critic opined. 'Kenneth More wreathed in a holly crown in mink and enthroned on such a pile of deluxe groceries, pedigree poultry and vintage wines that he looks less like the Ghost of Christmas Present than the reigning spirit of Fortnum and Mason.' As far as Ken was concerned, the movie sat among his best career choices and even eclipsed his joy at being appointed a CBE in the New Year's Honours. However, to celebrate this 'official acknowledgement' of his achievements and talent, he threw a lavish party at the newly renovated Bute House, followed by another bash at the Garrick where Donald Sinden, remembered everyone knew Kenny was in the club when 'gales of laughter' came from the bar: 'He was one of the finest comedians we've ever had.'

Kenneth More: The Making of a Movie Legend

It is not at all difficult to understand why Kenny's antenna shot up when invited on the BBC's prestigious *Omnibus* series to talk about his career with Michael Flanders, a rare honour, made sweeter by a BBC 'Kenneth More Season' featuring his most popular films. Such priceless exposure wasn't lost on impresario Binkie Beaumont who made overtures to Ken to return to the theatre in a revival of *The Winslow Boy*, alongside Laurence Naismith, Megs Jenkins, Christopher Cazenove and Annette Crosby at the New Theatre. So, soon enough, he was busily learning the part of Sir Robert Morton in a story about a famous trial involving a fourteen-year-old boy accused of stealing a postal order. The play was already twenty-five years old when it opened in November 1970, but audiences were gratified to see it had stood the test of time. 'This,' gushed critic R. B. Marriott, 'is a study of depth and imagination to be remembered.' Better still, he praised Ken's mastery of the stage, extolling his 'outstanding performance' as the steely Sir Robert, who bent from 'his high position towards the innocence of the boy'. Behind the scenes, though, Ken was a nervous man. A member of the company, who wished to remain nameless, remembered he could be 'very odd with people' and took an instant dislike to Christopher Cazenove, a dashing young talent and known ladies' man. 'Chris was having an affair with Coral Browne during the play,' she explains. 'He was incredibly charming and good looking; he always had a different lady with him. Kenneth More hated him being near his wife, he was almost obsessed. He never liked Cazenove and avoided him for that reason in case he went off with his wife! That was the rumour that went round to everyone.'

Ken's assessment of Cazenove wasn't the only unusual bit of fallout from that production. It seems he also quietly took out his frustration on David Wilkinson, a promising young actor plucked from obscurity in Leeds to play Ronnie Winslow. Binkie Beaumont, who specialised in prestige projects, had made a speciality of scouting fresh talent and packed off Wilkinson for elocution lessons to mask his Yorkshire accent, before an intense period of rehearsals. Beaumont was, if nothing else, an old-school impresario, and Wilkinson was flattered by his confidence. 'Beaumont had taken me out of my background and introduced me to this wonderful life,' he explained in an interview for this book. What followed, however, was unsettling. After good reviews and flawless performances, he was suddenly, inexplicably replaced: 'The producer said my voice was breaking. I never ever believed that. It all seemed so contrived, and I just assumed for most of my life it was because they thought I was a bad actor,' he said. 'I just couldn't get that out of my mind.' Remarkably, three decades later, the truth of this unhappy episode finally emerged when, quite by chance, he discovered a letter in the loft of his parents' house:

> Now when my father died in 1999, I was an executor of his estate, and I went through all his papers and there was a letter from Madge Godwin [an assistant to the producer] stating that Kenneth More had insisted I be removed because I was working class ... It was all down to him believing I was working class. Frith Banbury and Binkie Beaumont had argued with him [Ken] that I should at least play one week in the West End. And they both felt, according to Madge, that it should be done and Kenneth More just put his

foot down. I had always suspected he was behind it, but I didn't think it at the time.

Backstage, the atmosphere remained all back-patting and bonhomie. And by the time the affair blew over, Ken was absorbed in a campaign to save provincial theatres from bulldozers after being appointed patron of Liverpool's Save the Royal Court movement. Ensconced in a suite at the Adelphi Hotel, he gave interviews and arranged for the London opening of *The Winslow Boy* to be put back so he could give Liverpool a bit of support. 'A lot of my colleagues, who will remain nameless, will not bother to tour,' he explained. 'There can be business here if the public get stage personalities, they can associate themselves with. Your problem is how to keep the theatre going with good productions without personalities. I haven't come here just to make money.' As he'd anticipated, the results were extremely positive and even now – over five decades later – the Royal Court remains open and thriving.

Occasionally, he dashed down the M6 to visit Angela who continued her role of hostess, lover, hausfrau, and struggling actress. In fact, by this point, she was complaining that her career had ground to a halt. 'The scripts used to come tumbling in and I got terribly choosy and gave my agent a dreadful time, saying I wouldn't do this, and I would do that,' she confessed in 1971. 'Being out of work has been a real kick in the pants, and very good for me. The cockiness has gone. Lots of my girlfriends are working in coffee bars and shops because this year has been so bad for work, so I just think how lucky I am to have a husband that pays the rent and to have one or two jobs.'[1] She said she'd work 'at anything, anytime,' if only she'd get offered the jobs.² 'I don't work away, though, and I don't do theatre. That was the only condition he made when we were married. If I did theatre, he said, that would spoil the running of our home – i.e. dinner would not be ready for him.'³ For his part, Ken always asserted that Angela was not ambitious. 'I can't stand ambitious actresses,' he told *Titbits*. 'She just wants me.' Notably, he believed it was 'important to have at least two good meals a day and Angela, bless her heart, always has a meal ready for me when I get home.' Years later, Angela repeated that part of the deal with Ken was that if she was allowed to work, it was secondary to him. He was 'very controlling of me' and 'very caring', she said, but his career took priority. 'I wasn't encouraged to work. No younger woman today would've bought that condition, but I did.'⁴

Interestingly, the *Titbits* article reveals a carefully curated home life in which neither party 'inflicted their friends' on each other, but rather enjoyed 'areas of individuality'. For example, Ken said, 'She can go to supper with her friends. I prefer lunch – when I'm working. I go to my club two or three times a week. I also represent financial security. She's always amazed at how much I can afford. She isn't sophisticated in that sense and can't quite grasp how anyone can earn so much money.' At the same time, he admitted that Angela had been an enormous influence on his life and career. 'She's always telling me to stretch myself as an actor. I have on occasions, but not as much as she'd like me to. And she stops me doing silly things I still might do even now. You see I'm a very naive person in many ways. I trust everybody and love everybody and that can be very dangerous. Angela is an Irish girl and has more spirit than I have. She doesn't trust people until they've proved themselves. But I, she says, go into everything thinking everybody's lovely from the start then make a fool of myself.'[5] One thing they both absolutely agreed upon was the need to fill the empty nursery. After being denied the possibility of adoption due to Ken's age (he was fifty-seven), they were so desperate that Angela continued to visit doctors in the hope of conceiving a child. As all this was taking place, Kenny was, predictably, delighted when invited to be the patron of a new theatre to be built in Essex, to be known as the Kenneth More Theatre – a rare honour he gladly accepted. Equally exciting was a £20,000 pay packet to record commercials for Mellow Birds coffee, along with a further £10,000 payday for a series of Heinz 'voiceovers'.

At the same time, he accepted a small BBC fee to play Simon Crawford, QC, in *Queen's Counsel,* an eight-part radio drama supported by Ewan Roberts and Jean Harvey. 'Television isn't getting much better, and radio is on the increase,' he reasoned. 'I sometimes sit here watching the box and I blush, and I squirm, and it makes me ashamed to be an actor.' But with the radio, he explained, 'I'm painting in the background, using my imagination. That's what it's all about.' Funnily enough, it was while doing some last-minute retakes for the radio series that Alan Bennett appeared on the scene with an offer to star in *Getting On*, his tale about the private life of a socialist politician. Though first earmarked for Alan Bates, and turned down by half a dozen other actors, Ken needed no persuasion. Inside of a week, he was joking that 'living the roles as I do offstage, I'll probably be the biggest socialist around'. But despite several jolly press outings with fellow cast members Gemma Jones, Mona Washbourne and rising young talent, Brian Cox, rehearsals floundered when Ken took exception to some of the lines and refused to utter the word 'fuck' – resulting in dialogue being rewritten. Soon, his charmed relationship with Bennett soured, firstly, over the script and then over his simply ignoring instruction. To begin with, Bennett had felt the part could rejuvenate Kenneth's stage career in the same way that Laurence Olivier enjoyed a late revival portraying Archie Rice in *The Entertainer*, a decade earlier. However, looking back, he lamented Ken had 'no intention' of remaking himself as an actor. 'Why should he? His public liked him the way he was. It would be much simpler to remake the play, and this is what he did.' During a weekday performance, he discovered Ken putting a pencil through more lines and playing the story for laughs. 'Nothing in his debonair and easy-going exterior prepared one for the vulnerable actor he became,' Bennett said. But the worst was yet to come. Ken's relationship with the author reached a nadir when he ordered his 'uneasy presence' be barred from the theatre, leaving Bennett – according to his biographer, Alexander Games – like 'a mother whose baby had been taken away at birth'. Not even Britain's greatest actor, John Gielgud could ignore the gossip and deigned to make the trip across London to see what all the noise was about. In his private correspondence, he confided that the play bored him 'considerably', adding, 'there were hideous rows at rehearsals and during the try-out, and Alan won't come near the theatre'.[6]

Though the script didn't bear Kenny's name, his fingerprints were all over it, prompting Bennett to pen a programme foreword dissociating himself from the amended version. And when the play won an award, he accepted the gong by saying, 'It was like entering a marrow for the show and being given the cucumber prize.' Typically, Kenneth didn't allude to any of this in his memoirs, but chose instead to accuse Bennett of upsetting Mona Washbourne while admitting he 'did not hit it off' with the author. A few years later, Bennett spoke of the astonishing gap between the public Kenneth More and his feelings toward the man himself. Ken wasn't, he opined, the straightforward, good-natured chap he played. 'He was more complicated than that. But because he wanted so much to be liked he left a large tract of his character undeveloped.'[7] Strangely enough, for years after, Ken became prone to lose his calm with anyone who mentioned Bennett. 'Kenneth loathed him,' remembers Vivyan Ellacott, who eventually became the manager of the Kenneth More Theatre in Ilford. In fact, after learning a Bennett play was set to be staged at the venue in the late 1970s, 'Ken went into a long tirade calling him an awful man – terrible and talentless ... there was a lingering bitterness.' The irony of *Getting On* was that the critics liked it and it ran for nine months. As one writer remarked, 'Mr More breezed through the storms and stresses of family and public life on a tide of non-stop talk.'

Soon enough, Ken was back on the market negotiating to be part of the BBC's £4 million drama line-up. After some hard bargaining, he was signed to star in the *Six Faces of Man* – the sort of piece he could do effortlessly, even though it included several nude scenes. 'As soon as I read the scripts, I knew it was right,' Ken said during an interview at the Villa d'Este hotel in Italy, where the show was filmed. The six fifty-minute plays examined the life of a business executive and the different faces he presented. 'I play a wealthy property dealer, very successful, arid, sexy, and these nude scenes really are different and necessary,' he explained. 'One is with Zena Walker, as my wife and the other with Kika Markham, as my mistress.' The idea for the project came when, during a dinner in the West End, producer Stella Richman overheard a chat at a table nearby where two people were discussing someone they mutually knew and having a field day with his reputation. 'Then it dawned on me,' she said, 'that I knew the person they were tearing to shreds. Yet to me, he was quite a different person. That was the beginning of the series which explores a character as he appears to his wife, his mistress, his boss. We all present so many faces.'

While in Milan, Roger Moore called Kenny to ask if he would be prepared to step into Bernard Lee's role of 'M' for the upcoming James Bond film *Live and Let Die*. Lee – who Ken had known since *Peace in Our Time* – was in hospital after a house fire. 'Kenneth agreed that he could be available on condition his fee be sent to Bernie,' Moore recalled. Thankfully, the starting date for *Live and Let Die* kept getting pushed back and Lee was able to appear in the film. When Ken finally got back home, other offers were starting to pile up. One of them came when Laurence Evans put the idea to him of starring as Lord Seacroft in a new London Weekend Television sitcom titled *The Upper Crusts*, about an aristocratic family forced to live in a council flat. By all accounts, he despised ITV comedy – headlined by *On the Buses* and *Love Thy Neighbour* – and saturated by canned laughter 'where guffaws abounded'. 'They'll probably find someone much funnier,' he remarked after turning down the offer. They never did. In the end, Charles Grey took the lead, supported by Margaret Leighton. *The Spectator* called it a 'drivelling, witless comedy' and congratulated Kenny 'who cannily declined the offer ... now we have all seen the thing we can properly appreciate his decision'. The series was cancelled after just six episodes and never repeated.

Despite being a time of widespread gloom in the entertainment industry – worsened by labour disruptions and an energy crisis – Ken returned to the stage in Jeremy Kingston's slender comedy *Signs of the Times* at the Vaudeville. Ridiculous in some ways, the play made fun of journalists in general, and those on *The Times* in particular. The story tells how when the paper needed a circulation boost, the editor hit on the idea of running a daily horoscope. The job of writing was given to Andrew Perry (Ken), a cynical hack who didn't know his Capricorn from his Aries. At first, Perry wanted nothing to do with the task until he realised it could help his complex love affairs. The women in his life, both devoted readers of the horoscope, were unaware that the sly Perry was shaping their future for his own good. Kenny was supported by a decent cast, particularly Sandra Duncan, Norman Beaton, and Dennis Ramsden, who played the features editor as a well-bred scatterbrain. To begin with it was a cheerful show, modestly produced, sprinkled with endless horoscope gags. However, just as the provincial tour began, Ken was rushed to hospital after waking up in the night convulsed in pains under his ribs. He was diagnosed with – yet another – kidney stone, and his doctors were concerned about his digestion. When the tour finally rolled into the Vaudeville Theatre two months later than planned, the press had a ball with it. Many reviews praised the dialogue as witty and perceptive, 'and Mr More's casual style of acting fits the main character perfectly'. And amid all this, even during his own health battles, he undertook countless charity events including opening a Women's Institute and presenting an appeal on Radio Four for ex-Servicemen. He also lent his voice to the Gurkha Welfare Trust in helping old comrades living without pensions and spoke movingly of the Gurkhas' 'glorious record of 150 years' service alongside the British soldier'. In July, he grew visibly upset describing his feelings of loss when Jack Hawkins died following an attempt to fit an artificial voice box. He was just sixty-two years old. 'Jack lost a gallant fight to recapture an actor's most precious gift (his voice),' Ken said at the funeral. 'He stands as an example to us all. And he earned the unstinted admiration of the world. The man who gave … he was always ready to help, listen, sympathise, advise and he always picked up the chips. He was popular and loved by the British public, and he earned and held their respect.'

Even during these difficult times, Kenny was never the sort of chap to sit at home and mope, life still offered many lighter moments. One of them arrived that autumn at the topping-out ceremony for the new Kenneth More Theatre, when he was presented with updated plans showing a beautiful structure with seats for 365 people, a studio, dressing rooms, and coffee bar. It was indeed a project to be proud of and officially opened a year later with a production of *The Beggar's Opera*. However, it took five more years before Kenny made his debut with an evening of prose titled *Kenneth More Requests the Pleasure of Your Company*. However, as Barbara Hills, a board member, recalled, he became a frequent visitor and 'wanted to be as helpful as he could and came along quite a bit to see how we were':

> One time, we were quite busy. I said I had to attend to the bar, and he came too. The fairly primitive bar included a fridge which contained ice cubes. Kenny said, 'I will get those out,' and then there were ice cubes all over the counter and floor. Kenneth even served visitors, with one man exclaiming: 'Oh my God,' at the sight of him. However, he wasn't a natural, as he smashed two glasses and a bottle. He only did one night in the bar. He didn't last long!

In 1974 – a year marked by the three-day week, two general elections, a state of emergency in Northern Ireland and extensive IRA bombing of the British mainland – Kenneth More was focused on becoming a family man. So much so, that when a Harley Street specialist established his sperm was sterile, he embarked on 'cold-water treatment', a fertility procedure involving squatting over an ice-filled bidet. 'It's not very nice to dangle your testicles in cold water every day,' he confessed. In addition to 'icing the balls', he stopped wearing jockey pants as part of the treatment. And, because he'd had two daughters by previous marriages, it was assumed, he said, 'it was Angela who was wrong'. In several headline-grabbing interviews, he vowed to 'carry on dangling' given his curiosity about the outcome. 'Seriously, though, we'd both like a baby very much even though, myself, I'm not a great family man. But I know Angela would be thrilled. If Angela has a baby, I shall be the happiest man in the country.'[8]

Meanwhile, word had been circulating for some time that ITV was trying to sign Ken to a series deal – a rumour confirmed when Lew Grade offered him the star part in G. K. Chesterton's *Father Brown*, saying the role would be lucrative and fun. The two men already knew each other, having first met during the 1950s when ATV flirted with the idea of Ken hosting a Sunday show. Over brandy and small talk at Grade's office, a relaxed Kenny agreed to learn scripts for thirteen episodes playing a Catholic sleuth solving mysteries by 'humanity rather than by magnifying glass'.[9] 'When Sir Lew Grade told me at a party, he'd bought the rights and wanted me to play the priest-detective, I didn't believe him,' Ken remembered. 'It wasn't me. Mind you, my wife thought it was. So did Sir Lew. You know, every time we saw each other he'd address me as Father. When next I saw Sir Lew, I greeted him with "God bless you, my son."'[10] And so, as informally as the offer was made it was accepted. Like Hercule Poirot, the Brown character often embarrassed the police with his investigations and saw Ken smother his own cheeky persona and play a likeable, lumpy little priest. 'Father Brown is the sort of man I'd like to be,' he said. 'He has all the qualities of basic humanity. He is tolerant, has a sense of humour, likes his pipe and a drink, and is aware of the fleshpots.' Having signed Kenny, the rest of the casting went smoothly, and Graham Crowden, James Hayter, Bill Maynard, Charles Dance and Ronald Pickup were hired for supporting roles. Producer Ian Fordyce went out of his way to make the Brown character look frumpish, adorning him with a pipe, Windsor glasses, and cassock, presenting an incarnation of an endearing village priest. 'I'm not a Catholic,' Ken clarified for a curious reporter. 'If anything, I used to be Church of England, which could be called one of the best social clubs in the world. But my religion or, you might say, lack of it, does not come into it, although I am certainly not opposed to the principles of Catholicism. No one has ever convinced me that there is no God. I don't think that anyone who has seen active service, as I have, and who has been near to death, as I have, can entirely disbelieve.'[11]

Though it was an enormous undertaking, shooting at Elstree hummed along better than anyone had hoped – for once, even the notoriously finicky Grade had no complaints. In one episode, Angela teamed up with Ken for the first time in twelve years to play a 1920s' flapper. 'This is the first time we've been on TV together,' she said. 'I had to audition for the role like any other actress.'[12] In fact, the part called for her to pilot a biplane of the period, prompting Ken to call Joan Hughes, the woman who taught him to fly and was with him when the wheel fell off his plane during *Reach for the Sky*. Ken was enormously pleased with his work in *Father Brown* and when the show was released to critical and commercial success, he dashed off to the Cannes TV market to try and impress overseas buyers. He did. From its first transmission in September 1974, the show, like *The Forsyte Saga* before it, found many fans in Europe and behind the Iron Curtain. However, 'thirteen episodes was enough', Ken said when the project ended. 'It was time to move on to new things.' In fact, there were other reasons for not continuing. He genuinely feared he was in danger of being permanently typecast as a frumpy middle-aged man, 'consigned to TV dramas'. So, as soon as his publicity obligations for *Father Brown* were completed, he embarked on narrating a twenty-six-part radio series, *Ragtime to Rock 'n' Roll*, which, according to musician Benny Green, came about when a BBC radio producer had the 'wild idea of getting

More to narrate a history of popular music'. So, Green and the BBC man traipsed out to Elstree Studios to try and persuade him. Unimpressed, Ken reckoned they were daft to ask. 'What did he know about popular music?' Green assured him he wouldn't have to know anything about it. All he would have to do was read the scripts.

'Is he writing them?' enquired Ken, looking at Green.
'Yes,' said the producer.
'Do you know what you're doing?' Ken asked Green.
'No,' he said.
'Thank Christ for that,' he said. 'As long as you're not a know-all.'

From those unassuming beginnings, the series turned out to be a tour-de-force, with Ken rattling his way through hours of scripts, enjoying every second of it. In fact, according to Green, 'he rattled so fast, he was recording the shows quicker than I could write them'. Publicity photos show Kenny perched in a swivel chair at Broadcasting House, spinning discs and telling listeners about developing a musical taste at school that was jingoist and romantic. 'I love Kipling and the Empire that was,' he explained, 'and romantic composers like Tchaikovsky and Brahms rather than classical Bach and Mozart.' The project proved a huge success, and the series was repeated twice by the BBC and transmitted all over the globe on the World Service. By the time it was finished, he accepted an invitation to appear on *Stars on Sunday*, a religious request programme produced by ITV. What is remarkable about these broadcasts, besides the overly spiritual tones, is the undeniable ease at which

Ken – seated in a leather armchair – was able to adapt to any subject. He enjoyed the experience so much that his agent called Yorkshire Television to ask if he might return. They said yes, and it was during a rehearsal that news arrived of John Gregson's sudden death from a heart attack. He was just fifty-five when he collapsed while walking with his wife during a holiday. Rehearsals were postponed and, with a tear in his eye, Ken stood on the steps outside Yorkshire Television and described Gregson a man 'so full of life and energy' when they got their break together making *Genevieve*. 'I can only think of him with affection, he was a quiet gentleman with the Irish gift of the gab.'

One morning while Kenny was sunning himself in the garden of Bute House, Bryan Forbes phoned to offer a 'substantial part' in *The Slipper and the Rose*, a £2.2 million film musical, financed under David Frost's Paradine Productions. It would be, Forbes gushed, a 'typical Sherman Brothers piece,' sugared by a waltz-like score, featuring Gemma Craven as the heroine, and Richard Chamberlain as the prince. As nothing Laurence Evans offered promised to be any better, Kenny gratefully accepted the role of the Lord High Chamberlain and departed for Austria along with Michael Hordern, Edith Evans, and Annette Crosbie, who also took supporting parts. And again, like in *Scrooge*, he rose to the occasion by crooning 'Protocoligorically Correct', alongside Hordern. During the shoot, Forbes transported the cast to Schloss Anif, near Salzburg, Southwark Cathedral in London (the first time it had been used as a film set) and finally to Pinewood Studios, where Kenny flirted outrageously with eighty-eight-year-old Edith Evans, much to her enjoyment. During breaks, Forbes recounted, Ken told the 'most preposterous and scandalous stories without offence', and succeeded in making Dame Edith chuckle. 'I have the feeling, though that even Kenny would have been put in his place if Edith hadn't respected him as an actor.' Actually, there was never a cross word between them, and the shoot turned out to be an utter joy but the notices, sadly, were mixed. On the upside, *Variety* called it 'an intelligent and happy blend of entertainment' and at the Royal Film Performance, the Queen Mother even told the songwriters the waltz they wrote for the ballroom scene was the most beautiful song she'd ever heard.

The rest of 1974 saw Ken dip into a flurry of little projects, topped off by a Variety Club luncheon celebrating his forty years in show business. It was a glittering occasion, and in his speech to peers, he pondered the past by confessing he'd been 'ostracised and shunned' by friends and the entertainment industry because of his domestic life in the 1960s. 'I was dead, buried and forgotten,' he said, but bore no rancour toward those that had cast him into a 'social wilderness'. Not long after, his 'full rehabilitation' was complete when Sir Peter Hall, the most important figure in British theatre, suggested he play Claudius to Albert Finney's *Hamlet* at the National Theatre. Though flattered, he gracefully declined the offer, saying one part of him would have liked to, but the other part said there were so many great Shakespearean actors who could do a better job. 'I stick to the roles I can play better than them.' Interestingly, five years earlier, he confessed on *Desert Island Discs* that classical theatre gave him 'cold feet'. While he loved to listen to and watch Shakespeare – 'the greatest prose of all time' – he wouldn't like to do it. 'I don't think I could manage it. I get bored silly by all those awful old Restoration pieces. I can't stand all that nonsense; they bore me to tears. I'd rather go and watch somebody else having a go at the classics; I'll pay my money and watch.'

13

FINAL YEARS

Though Kenny's union with Angela was considerably more satisfying than his first two marriages, by the mid-seventies cracks were becoming apparent. Angela was and always would be his soulmate, but something had changed, a wedge had emerged between them. He admitted to becoming 'smug and self-confident' and treating his wife with indifference: 'I more or less told her I didn't need her any more and perhaps it would be better if we went our own ways.' With this impasse, Angela abandoned her promise not to do theatre work by signing up for a six-month tour with *The First Mrs Frazer*, a comedy starring Anna Neagle. And, as the wedge widened, she admitted some women could 'go on being Mrs Somebody' forever and be perfectly happy, but that wasn't her. 'I had to do something about it. I think Kenny thought I'd go back to acting more seriously sometime. I think he was expecting it. He's a pretty wise old bird.'[1]

Perhaps genuinely worried by the turmoil in his private life, Ken's geniality occasionally failed. There were 'two sides to the man,' Vivyan Ellacott explained. There was the public side when he was 'on show' and there were occasional little 'off moments' where a slightly different personality seeped through. Around this time, Ken displayed an 'off moment' when he 'took a little gang of us out to a restaurant; he was charming and absolutely lovely,' Ellacott said. 'We had a nice meal and at the end of it the waiter came and presented him with the bill and Kenneth pulled out a cheque book. Then the waiter asked for a cheque card – where you put your number on the back to guarantee the cheque. And Ken basically became very annoyed and really berated this waiter and demanded to speak to the manager. There was that kind of element to him.'

His private life wasn't all a horror show, of course, and he found solace from his worries by splashing out on a trip to the Amazon – from where he wrote detailed letters of his adventures, huge bugs, the exotic cuisine, and its effects on his stomach. After carefully mapping an itinerary, he flew into Rio during the carnival, with a stop in Manaus, 1,000 miles from the ocean known as Amazonia. Brightest among his memories were the people, the food, and breathtaking landscapes. With the freedom to explore, he wrote about the unbearable humidity, huge cockroaches, and torrential storms. 'But it was truly magnificent, the realisation of a boyhood dream,' he gushed, after tramping through a jungle, where alligators roamed free.

Back home, a brief reunion with Angela in Edinburgh proved tepid, prompting *The People*'s Mervyn Pamment to claim the situation had unleashed a 'barrage of speculation' about the state of their marriage. For most observers, it became painfully obvious they'd split, but Ken brushed off rumours, including chatter of infidelities, exclaiming, 'it's all nonsense'.[2] In fact, by this point, Bute House had been sold and they were living permanently apart. 'Physically apart, yes,' he reluctantly admitted. 'But not emotionally.' In fact, Angela had already set up home at Rumbold Road in Fulham, while Ken installed himself at a flat on the King's Road, close to many old chums – past and present – who had homes in the neighbourhood, including Carol Reed and Peter Ustinov. His little pad – plastered in flux-wallpaper and furnished with low sofas and memorabilia – contained a small study for writing. If he had to suffer bachelorhood, at least he did so in unaffected splendour. Characteristically, even at the age of sixty-two, he quickly adapted to a new lifestyle. 'He flirted around furiously,' one chum recounted, 'then embarked on an overheated affair with a middle-aged acquaintance from Essex, along with various other dalliances.' He gave up exercise and lost interest in golf when actor Jeremy Hawk, his partner over many a course, emigrated to South Africa. With plenty of money in the Kenneth More coffers – topped up by a series of lucrative TV commercials for Du Maurier cigarettes – he splashed out on a flashy MG sports car (and was fined for speeding), indulged himself at the Beefsteak Club on Irving Street, and continued to frequent the Garrick for simple dishes like grilled beef, lamb, grouse, salmon – peas, carrots, and drowned in thick gravy. 'Oh, Lord, he took me there on one occasion,' Vivyan Ellacott sighed. 'It was full of elderly, extremely boring men all doing caricatures of English gentlemen from the thirties. Everybody was addressed as "old boy". It was dated. A different generation thing I suppose.'

Strangely enough, boozy late nights never took a toll and Kenny continued to work almost entirely on television. One plum job came playing the lead in *In Praise of Love*; a Terence Rattigan play for Anglia with Claire Bloom, directed by his old chum Alvin Rakoff. 'It was a straightforward part for Kenny,' Rakoff told the author. 'Ken played the husband, Bloom played his wife, a woman dying from leukaemia.' The characters, he added, were loosely based on Rex Harrison and his fatally ill wife Kay Kendall. 'There was no shtick in it, there was nothing brassy,' he said. 'I'm very proud of it and I think Kenny was very proud of it too.' After filming wrapped, Rakoff ran a recording for Terence Rattigan and a few other production staff at Anglia's studios in Norwich. At the end, the small gathering sat wiping away tears, unable to speak. 'The one with most tears running down his face was Rattigan himself,' according to Rattigan's biographer, Michael Darlow, who added, Kenny 'perhaps gave the best performance of his career in a part that might have been written for him'. Even the more reserved reviewers gave it faint praise, including Clive James, an Australian critic known for his caustic comments and negative disposition. 'It is sob-stuff of the highest grade,' he mused. 'But Miss Bloom was touchingly beautiful as always and Kenneth More was the best that he has ever been on television – he only said "Ha-ha!" once.' Kenny was evidently nervous about his next part playing the Duke of Bristol, alongside Geraldine McEwan in a limited run of Frederick Lonsdale's *On Approval* in Toronto. Though he fretted that there was only a short spell of planning, the play turned out to be rewarding from the start date to the conclusion three weeks later. 'It was enormous fun,' he remembered. 'We did this little play, a four hander, in front of an audience of three thousand.' By a strange quirk of fate, Angela arrived in Toronto to appear in *The Scenario* at the Royal Alexandra Theatre, but there was no reconciliation.

Back home, among the letters awaiting his attention, was an offer from Thames Television to play the part of Inspector Maigret, Georges Simenon's fictional detective in a seventy-five-minute film, followed by thirteen episodes. However, weary of lumping himself with another series, plans ran into the sand. Instead, he accepted Hodder & Stoughton's offer to pen a second autobiography, a deal secured with a promise to print 100,000 copies in hardback at £5.95 a time, followed six months later by a paperback. 'The publishers made me a marvellous deal. The money is fantastic,' he gushed. The title – *More or Less* – he added, 'came to me in a flash'.[3] Spilling his life story into a Dictaphone, he took care to avoid malice: 'you mustn't hurt anybody and yet you must be truthful and it's very difficult to balance the two. You'll always hurt somebody, and you'll always make somebody very happy.'[4] However, the final manuscript – chock-a-block with warmed-over anecdotes from his 1959 memoirs and whirred together in 233 pages – presented a chatty, revealing, and funny work. 'It's not a well-written book,' he admitted. 'It's really a lot of rubbish, but it's rubbish of the most amusing sort.' His language was British and blunt, quintessentially his own voice, and an engaging one. Incapable of taint, he revealed that some people said he should have been more brutal, 'but I couldn't be like that. I can easily forgive and forget. I just don't have the mentality to do otherwise.'[5] Yet, there was some self-excavation. In one passage, he wrote that faithfulness in marriage, 'for a man at least, is like a handmade silk shirt, it can wear thin'. Later asked about this on TV, he backtracked. 'I think

I was being a bit too clever because I do believe that faithlessness in marriage doesn't really work,' he clarified. 'I was just a bit carried away I suppose: a bold thing to say ... I'm a terrible flirt, always have been all my life. But I love women, I adore them. But marriage must really rely on faithfulness.' In the original publicity blurb, Hodder described Kenneth as 'Britain's best-loved actor' and critics were generally kind. 'Mr More doesn't write artistically,' one noted, 'he writes as if he were chatting to you at the north end of the bar at the Garrick Club, and his characters come out sharper for it.' Another critic sensed he came over as a cheerful extrovert, a stoic optimist, 'and the man that emerges was an immensely likeable one'. 'More has undoubtedly succeeded,' reviewer Adele Freedman surmised. 'He has compared bunions with the Queen and gone to the theatre with Noël Coward. In his own view, he saw the best of two worlds, the pre-war and post-war. As for the war, like most Englishmen, he adored it. The spirit was so wonderful, there were no class distinctions, it was a superb time.'

Ken was thrilled at the chance to promote the book and give a string of interviews, and edit a serialisation for the *Sunday Express*. Typically, he enjoyed being an author, addressing literary lunches and being accosted by fellow writers. 'It is a lovely sort of feeling,' he said on hearing sales had topped 100,000. 'When people come up to you in the street and say, "Thank you for all the pleasure you've given us in your lifetime" it is rather gratifying.'[6] Amid all this excitement, Dirk Bogarde, was bubbling with fury. As it transpired, his own memoirs, *Snakes and Ladders* had been released on the very same day as *More or Less*. And, true to form, he cattily remarked to a friend that Ken 'secretly came out with his book' and only 'a handful of people' turned up to one of his signings at Selfridges. 'In publishing,' Bogarde bemoaned, 'it is a heinous crime and as daft as opening a couple of movies on the same subject with many of the same players on the same night in adjoining cinemas.'

During the promotion of the book, Benny Green – the man who had written the successful BBC radio series a few years earlier – bumped into Ken as he was leaving Broadcasting House. 'He was coming in, and I happened to say that I had just re-read a book which seemed as though it had been written with him in mind.' In fact, all the time he was reading it, Green recounted, he could see Ken in the leading role. 'The book was that classic thriller of pre-World War I espionage, *The Riddle of the Sands*. That very morning, I went out and bought a copy, sending it straight round to him.' A while later, Ken wrote back to Green explaining that while he thought the book was marvellous, 'he felt, and this was what stunned me, he was too old for the part! He may well have been right.'[7] In fact, at this point, he'd already signed up to a 'middle-aged part' by reprising Ronnie Squire's film role in *The Rocking Horse Winner*, a short, rather bleak version of the story about a boy whose affinity with his rocking horse led him to guess the winners of real races. 'It was a faultless shoot,' director Peter Medak explained in an interview for this book. 'It had a small budget, and I think it was completed in just a few weeks. Kenneth was a dream for a director like me, he never argued, knew his lines and was always on time.' In fact, on set, Ken was beaming to reporters about there being 'more good character parts for a man of my age than for the youngsters' and his fortune at being kept busy. Almost immediately after shooting concluded, he returned to Birmingham for a Jubilee presentation revival of *On Approval*, again, playing Lord Bristol, alongside Patricia Routledge and Carolyn Seymour. Around this time, theatrical agent Michael Whitehall took over Ken's business affairs from Laurence Evans, who retired. There were several notable actors under his aegis at the time, including David Hemmings who had enjoyed a meteoric rise to fame after playing alongside Kenny in *Some People*. Though the pressure for work had eased a little, Ken signed to yet another plum role, playing Sam Turner, a middle-aged hotel owner with a weakness for women – especially the sad ones – in ITV's *Two Stars*. The idea came after Francis Essex, the director of productions at ATV, took Ken out to lunch and asked him to suggest a suitable play. 'I longed to say *Two Stars for Comfort*,' he explained. 'The idea was so precious that I couldn't bear to have it refused, so I didn't even dare to mention my dream. We decided on *The Secretary Bird*, as I had previously had some success with this play.' However, as it happened, Francis phoned a few days later to ask if they could produce *Two Stars* instead. 'I was delighted! There's a lot of Sam in me,' he admitted. 'I too, adore women. I have a compassion for anyone who is helpless, unhappy, or lonely. But I don't necessarily go along with Sam's idea that the only way to rescue a lady in distress is to whisk her off to bed!'[8]

Even before *Two Stars* had completed editing, Ken accepted the role of Peter Ingram in *An Englishman's Castle*, a three-part BBC alternative history thriller written by Philip Mackie. Ken had known Mackie since the early 1960s, when he was a jobbing writer churning out scripts for the long-running *Edgar Wallace* B-movies. However, by the 1970s, Mackie hit the jackpot penning

Napoleon and Love, starring Ian Holm, and following it up by adapting Quentin Crisp's autobiography *The Naked Civil Servant*. For *An Englishman's Castle*, producer Innes Lloyd (a frequent collaborator with Alan Bennett) assembled a superb cast including Kathleen Byron, Anthony Bate and Isla Blair. The plot, in some ways, vaguely resembled Coward's *Peace in Our Time*, but was set in England in 1978, assuming Germany had won the war. In this strange world, Ingram – a man of quiet determination and reliability – worked as a successful author of a long-running soap opera, but after years of complying with the Nazis, he became involved with the resistance. Ingram's soap – described by *The People* as a sort of *Coronation Strasse* – was produced by a state-run British television station set up by the Germans after they overran the UK. For propaganda, it had a strong sub-plot about the characters coming to terms with defeat. Ingram stuffed it with lines, actions, or conversations intended to distort history and put the Germans in a favourable light. 'Here is England that lost the war 30 years ago, it is now like the rest of Europe, a German satellite,' Ken explained. 'The soap opera is specially designed to lull people into quiet acceptance of the political status quo.' The important thing, he said, was 'survival, simply survival'.[9]

Like all good serials, *An Englishman's Castle* left viewers hanging on the edge. The last scene, shot at the BBC Television Centre, shows Ingram giving the signal for a national uprising. Although Anthony Bate nearly succeeded in stealing the show, it was one of Ken's better, if largely unheralded, late-career performances. 'His playing is controlled and well-paced, leaving room for later development,' critic Jennifer Lovelace noted. 'Despite his character's current lack of spirit, he does not allow him to become dull.' A reader of the *Sunday People*, S. Sharp in Stockport, wrote to say Ken used his 'mobile face and expressive eyes' to 'flawlessly out-act everyone' else in *An Englishman's Castle*. 'His improving performances surely deserve something better than the CBE he got a few years ago.'

Two projects followed in quick succession, both for foreign companies. Firstly, *Leopard in the Snow*, a romantic made-for-TV effort designed to exploit *Mills and Boon* paperbacks, featuring Keir Dullea, Billie Whitelaw, and twenty-eight-year-old Susan Penhaligon. The story tells how a young beauty stumbled across a former racing driver living as a recluse, after a bad accident. Ken ran his eye over the script without enthusiasm. He was cast as Sir Philip James, father of the young beauty, and pops into the story every now and again. 'I was aware of how experienced Kenny was in front of the camera,' Susan Penhaligon told the author, recalling his humour during some long scenes together. 'He was a screen actor who knew his stuff. A real professional as well as being charming – a perfect gentleman and a little twinkly and flirty ... I was also a bit star-struck and couldn't believe I was talking to him having been brought up on all the old movies he made.'

In theory, Kenny didn't need to consider the second offer, but accepted the lead in a low-budget Spanish adaptation of Jules Verne's *Journey to the Centre of the Earth* (which doesn't entirely follow the source material) playing Professor Otto Lidenbrock. 'We shot outside Madrid,' recalls Lone Faerch, a Danish actress who played Molly in the film. Working on a shoestring, Juan Piquer Simón was able to direct Kenny on a subterranean expedition, confronting giant lizards, turtles, and a huge gorilla.

It was done with absolute seriousness and took the cast to locations in the natural volcanic settings of Lanzarote and the caves of Valporquero in northwest Spain. Within the financial and technical limitations of Spanish cinema of its time, the film is credible, if one overlooks some ropy dialogue. 'Actually, it was a very difficult movie to shoot,' Lone explains. 'A lot of the special effects were also produced by Piquer who had a studio in the cellar of his house. It was incredible what he did there. He had a swimming pool where he filmed a lot of the scenes in miniature. He was great at doing these special effects.' In fact, using the most basic materials, he managed to create a pseudo-prehistoric world. 'I think Kenneth enjoyed doing the film,' she told the author. 'I had a couple of dinners with him during the shoot and he was always in good humour, also quiet and of course, very professional. We talked about life and movies … normal talk.' During filming, as word of Ken's presence spread throughout Spain, he learned that *Father Brown* was running on TVE, the national television network, and was proving to be a considerable hit. In fact, when filming high above the clouds on a mountain, he was left astounded when an old local woman spotted him, limbered over, arms waving, and began babbling in a local dialect:

> I was dressed in this Victorian garb, you see, and I guess I looked a bit like *Father Brown*. Well, when we finally got a translator, it turned out she was asking me to hear her confession. She had very bad rheumatism, she said, and she couldn't make it down to the village church. So, I very politely told the translator to explain to her that I wasn't Father Brown or even a priest, that was only a role. And furthermore, I was a Protestant. Well, after that was

translated, she started talking very fiercely, and what she said, it turned out, was that none of this mattered. She was too old to go down to the village, she said again, and she had committed a terrible sin and wanted to get it off her chest. Would I hear her confession?

As he did after most projects, Ken repaired to London to recover and catch up on his social life. Some months later, he readily stepped up to the challenge of playing the regent in *The Spaceman and King Arthur,* a Disney feature set to be filmed on location in Northumberland, featuring his old chums John Le Mesurier and Jim Dale. As well as a good pay day, the trip north would allow him a pleasant diversion. Based on Mark Twain's novel *A Connecticut Yankee in King Arthur's Court*, Dennis Dugan – a virtual unknown outside the US – was slated to play a NASA employee who was accidentally thrust back in time with his look-alike android, Hermes. The story tells how they used twentieth-century technology to foil a plot by the evil Sir Mordred to oust King Arthur from his throne. For the duration of the shoot, the cast were accommodated at Newcastle's Holiday Inn but – as John Le Mesurier's wife, Joan, recollected – after a few days, John and Ken tired of the drive to and from the location and found lodgings at The White Swan, a little hotel near Alnwick Castle. Sadly, peeling wallpaper, mossy green carpets, worn furniture and dreadful food did little to broaden its appeal. 'Brown Windsor soup, roast meat and trifle were offered constantly with a "speciality of the day" causing hilarity by its monotonous awfulness,' Joan recounted. On location, the pair shared a caravan, and, at John's request, Joan personally delivered a few joints (reefers) to keep her husband happy. 'Kenneth was a big treat, and it was nice to see how he and John kept each other company,' she said. 'I have a photo somewhere of Kenny and me taken by John. Kenny is standing behind me and we are both laughing because he had just said to John, "For God's sake stop fumbling about with the camera and take the picture, Johnny, I'm getting a hard on."'[10]

It was a joyous shoot, and with his hair a swirl of silver and robed in a medieval cape, Kenny spent hours with visiting journalists at Alnwick Castle chatting idly about ageing and the attitude of younger actors: 'In my day we all had to speak perfectly and be gentlemen,' he griped during one session with the press. 'Great stars of the old days were very star conscious. Nowadays, the young actors and actresses are much more honest.' Ken was pleasantly shocked when *The Spaceman and King Arthur* turned out to be a reasonably involving kids' flick, punctuated by clever special effects. On the whole, he loved the experience but found concentration difficult. Nevertheless, he had kept remarkably fit in past years, and except for the two sharp bouts of kidney problems and a spell in hospital seven years earlier, he had rarely had more than a few days' sick. Then things changed.

14

FADE OUT

A few weeks after the *Spaceman* shoot, as Kenny returned to the bar from the gents' toilets at the Garrick, an old friend remarked that his 'walk was funny'. Not long after, a red flag fluttered when he noticed his 'balance was a little off' when crossing a road. 'I went to the doctor for a check-up, he made various tests and came to the conclusion I had Parkinson's disease,' a brain disorder that causes uncontrollable movements, such as shaking and stiffness. Though shattering news, the doctor said it was mild, but Ken knew very little about the condition, 'except there is seldom a cure'. Worse still, his optimism evaporated when an eminent specialist fiddled with his pencil, 'with not a word of encouragement or what I could expect to achieve for the rest of my life'. The most evident change at this point, he recounted, was increased fatigue and listlessness, caused as the steam leaked slowly from his energy reserves. Thankfully, comfort arrived after a rekindling of relations with Angela. 'When he was taken ill, she reappeared in his life,' Vivyan Ellacott recalls. 'I think that was fortunate.'

Fade Out

In due course, Ken began settling his affairs, packed up some of his belongings from the King's Road flat and moved into Angela's house on Rumbold Road, where he planned to live out the rest of his days. To everyone's relief, a long-time doctor friend repeated the Parkinson's prognosis but also added his condition was mild. There was no shaking, one of the main symptoms, but he was told he would have remission periods and instructed to avoid stress, anxiety, and trauma. 'Afternoon rests would be essential and on no account was I to give way to it,' Ken said, as he continued to visit a dwindling number of friends at the Garrick and other old haunts, with the aid of a walking stick. Sadly, attempts to avoid stress were thwarted when, firstly, proceedings began in the High Court over a £1,600 bill an electrical contractor claimed for work on the Fulham house. And then, ten days later, £3,000 of valuables were stolen during a raid on his Chelsea flat, including an inscribed Victorian gold watch. 'I gave Kenneth the watch on the first night of his most successful play, *The Secretary Bird*,' Angela said. 'I had it inscribed "To the secretary from his bird". The watch was not really a great deal of good to anyone except us.' Desperate to get it back, she spent days traipsing round antiques shops and the markets to see if a dealer had acquired it. Ken was, predictably, infuriated at the break-in but soothed with an offer of the lead in *The Pump*, a television drama by James Cameron. Despite the obvious discomforts, he gave an outstanding performance playing John Carter, a hard-bitten British reporter working in India in the outbreak of war in what is now Bangladesh. The story tells how as millions of despairing refugees flee the country in relentless monsoon rains, Carter hitches a lift across the border in the opposite direction only to become the sole survivor of a head-on crash with a lorry. In a critical state, he is repatriated to Britain. The story then shows him laying somewhere between life and death – swathed in bandages with tubes attached to his body – recalling events leading up to the operation. In a brief interview, Ken claimed to have 'got really worked up' over the role after witnessing a major heart operation at Leeds Infirmary. 'I later saw the patient in the intensive care unit, and he was convinced he would not live,' he said. 'Two weeks later he seemed as fit as a fiddle – really miraculous.' Appropriately enough, Angela was cast as the nurse tending him. 'When I first read the play,' he said, 'I thought it would be nice if Angela could play the nurse. I was frightfully pleased when the producer suggested she did.' There was a lot of importance based on getting the facts of the story right, says Erin Geraghty, who also played a nurse in the production. 'Because it is, of course, a true story. It was an ambitious undertaking; it was a happy experience. We filmed all the external stuff in St James's Hospital in Leeds, and I remember vividly we used an outpatient lounge as a sort of "green room", it was off the main building. And Kenneth More used to tell the most amazing stories, it was just hilarious. If you'd lit a match the whole place would have gone up, it was just incredible. More than once, an assistant director had to come and tell us to keep the noise down because even though we were far away, they could hear the hilarious laughing.'

Back in London, Ken had nothing in the pipeline, until receiving an offer from the BBC to record a forty-five-minute radio drama *Chicken on the Road*, featuring Michael Kitchen. One of the people most pleased with him being cast was author

Bob Wilson. 'It was my first radio play. I was given some suggestions for the cast,' he says. 'John Gielgud and Kenneth More were put forward, and because it was just a weekend job, actors found it quite an attractive proposition because they didn't have to travel anywhere. In the end, I was delighted to have Kenneth More, he was the right person for the part.' Recorded during October 1979 in the basement of the BBC's Broadcasting House, the play tells the story of a young hitchhiker (Kitchen) getting a lift from an older businessman (Ken). As the journey progresses, the hitchhiker reveals a sinister knowledge of the driver's life, his family, and his mistress. But there seems to be no question of blackmail. 'As we went through the script,' Wilson remembered, 'the first thing Kenneth said to me was "How tall is my character?" With this being radio, I thought that odd, Then, I realised he wanted to know how tall he was in relation to Michael Kitchen, it was a subtlety of acting.'

While giving an engaging performance, Ken was clearly tired. And though he was playing a 'world weary character', his voice genuinely sounded old, devoid of its old distinct quality, strong projection, and resonance. 'I was aware he was ill. Kenneth was quite shaky, and going to the toilet quite often,' says Wilson. It was his last radio appearance. Not long after, his attention was temporarily diverted from health matters by Danny Angel, his old chum, who sued him for libel after 'taking exception' to his description in his memoirs of his part in the 1960 kerfuffle with John Davis. In *More or Less*, Kenny had reheated the story by claiming that Davis had said of Angel, 'He's broken the code,' referring to an agreement made by producers not to sell their work to television. Angel claimed those words were libellous.

Once the lawsuit was filed, the case utterly consumed Ken. Despite months of legal letters and attempts to resolve the situation, he appeared in the witness box and he admitted he'd retired from live theatre (but made no reference to the nature of his illness). However, he told Mr Justice O'Connor and a jury a reason why he might 'slur his words' – 'I am not in perfect health at the moment and have just retired.' After the court rose, he said, 'My health has broken down. You have to be fit and have stamina for this work, and I am just not up to it. Until today only my doctor and a few close friends have known of my retirement.'[1] His counsel, Antony Hoolahan QC, told the jury that the action, was an 'unhappy case ... You might say each made the other famous in the film *Reach for the Sky*. Yet here they are on opposite sides of the court, Major Angel suing his star of yesterday over four words.'[2]

In the end, the judge found for Angel but awarded paltry damages of £209. It was a strange sort of triumph for Ken as Angel was saddled with £10,000 costs having refused an earlier out-of-court settlement. 'Danny was an old and very good friend,' Kenny told reporters as he mopped his face. 'I didn't mean any malice at all in my book. I was amazed the case came on. It was all so unnecessary. There is no chance of making it up with Danny now. We didn't even look at each other in court.'[3] In fact, Ken was devastated by the action which harmed his health and led to the verge of a nervous breakdown. On 2 May, in a short clear statement sent through the Press Association, he announced his retirement but noted 'he may consider taking other TV and film roles in the future'. Angela remembered from this point, he 'began to go downhill' as more 'wretched symptoms' emerged.

Fade Out

As the disintegration of his health – a gradual and uncomfortable process – worsened, he spent the spring of 1980 behind the walled garden of Angela's Fulham home, quietly pottering around the house, sheltered from the world. It was, he thought, 'the prettiest little house in London' and though his stamina flagged, he managed a weekend away in Cumberland to visit daughter Susan. However, as a litany of ailments ensued, cherished Garrick lunches stopped, he could no longer drive, bladder problems worsened, and his bones stiffened. The only consolation, as he saw it, was that he could still walk, albeit slowly. Remarkably, he mustered up enough energy to present the first annual 'Kenny Awards' at the Kenneth More Theatre. Vivyan Ellacott – who organised the event – remembered him talking of his great pride in having such a successful theatre named after him, and of the uniqueness of having his name on a series of awards – just like the Oscars. But he was alarmed at Ken's failing health, which he hid only with difficulty. 'He told us how worried he was that he might miss a step on the stage and the audience might think he was pissed because his speech was slurring, and he had a slight swagger. He didn't want it generally known, so it was something he spoke to us about – I think he regarded us as good friends, people he could trust. So, he could tell us, but we weren't to tell the rest of the company and it was to be kept quiet because it could have stopped him working. He was slightly trembling; you could see a slight shake in the hand and body. Then he walked onto the stage, and you would never have known – he was full of sparkle, huge roars of laughter with the audience. Then when he came off, he walked into my office and was sort of a little mini crumple ... an actor to the end, I suppose.'

Despite feeling increasingly out of tune with the world, Kenny granted an extensive interview to journalist Kenneth Passingham. In this as-told-to inside story, he lied about his illness, saying it was kidney related, but repeated he no longer had the 'stamina needed for acting'. It ran three pages, with half a dozen photos and saw him in sombre and reflective mood. He bared some of his soul, stating he was 'something of a father figure' for Angela. 'It's something I like; Angela needs a pair of strong arms around her, and I feel I give her the security she seeks. Love has developed, you see.' And while he was being so honest, he said what was once all sex had become lasting affection. 'One advantage she's always had from our relationship is that I've been able to give her an older man's experience. She values my advice and always has done. But when it comes to assessing people's character, she's as quick as a whip. Fortunately, we share a sense of humour, and can tune in on the same wavelength.' Apart from mutual friends, they had their own. Ken's, as you might expect, still tended to be much older than hers. 'And they're beginning to die off. I suppose my mode of life is a disadvantage for Angela in some respects. For instance, she's a wonderful dancer. One of the best I've seen. She adores dancing and pop music, but we don't go to discos because I don't like them. I don't want to go dancing at my age. When she was younger, she had a fetish about pop, and I put up with anything she wanted to play. She's out of it now, thank goodness. Now she loves Mahler. In fact, she has a passionate interest in everything, but I don't share her enthusiasms.' He gave no hint of his precarious health, but confessed his idea of relaxation was a good seat at the cinema, a holiday in the sun, and taking friends out to a restaurant. 'I don't want yachts, Bentleys, and villas in the South of France.'

Fade Out

There were no more print interviews, and the next few months were not easy. As they both watched for more signs of his progressing illness, there were horrible, sleepless nights, and occasional falls, leaving bruised legs. The days could be long, made easier when friends made a fuss, rounded off by lazy evenings watching television. During this period, Angela embarked on a memoir, providing a 'diversion from despair'. Reams of scribbled notes became the basis for *Swings and Roundabouts*, which, although ostensibly an account of her life, gives a detailed narration of Ken's ordeal. Slowly, but willingly, he read the drafts and provided encouragement. Then, remarkably, amid this health crisis, he signed on to feature in a major American made-for-TV version of *A Tale of Two Cities*, the Dickens classic set in Paris during the French Revolution, starring Chris Sarandon, Dame Flora Robson, and Peter Cushing. The film insurance company, it seems, never got wind of his condition and the effect on his mental health was remarkable. 'I began to feel strong and more confident,' he remembered. 'It was a strain, I admit, but it felt marvellous to be working again.' Arriving on location at Senlis on the outskirts of Paris, he looked much older, with a grey furrowed brow and wrinkled face, a thin neck sticking out of a loose shirt collar. Worse still, his balance, or lack of it, often forced him to lean on a walking stick or use furniture to steady himself. The star of the picture, Chris Sarandon, never had a sense of something being wrong. 'I watched the film recently and couldn't tell any impairment on Kenneth's part. He was like butter to work with – very smooth, very easy. There was no drama and there was always just total professionalism. Of course, I was familiar with Ken. He often played the stolid sort of chap. The dependable Brit – he was the personification of that.'

Angela was inevitably, but willingly, caught up in the project and acted as nursemaid but, by her own account, Ken enjoyed the experience, despite his speech being hesitant; and his hand trembling from time to time. 'It was one of the great experiences of my professional career,' Chris Sarandon told the author. 'The total shoot was about eight weeks, and with Ken around six. He seemed to have a very gentle spirit and was immediate to me in his reaction as an actor. Actors are always looking for partners – some actors don't work in partnership – but Ken worked in partnership on screen. And he was an off-screen partner in the sense that he was comfortable in his own skin. He was interesting. His choices were always spot on. It was a great joy.' The film was more than a pleasant escape. For Kenneth More, it provided a truly extraordinary Indian summer – a late-life embrace from the film industry, and a fitting way to close the book on his career. With justifiable pride, he could claim that for someone who started with a 'blink-and-you-miss-it' performance in a Gracie Fields' flick, he had created an impressive gallery of characters ranging from sea dogs, and academics, to reporters, aviators, and inventors.

As time went on, Ken gently disappeared from view. He complained that the simplest outing became a huge challenge. 'I have to hold Angela's arm to support me most days ... I have to admit I feel like hell and in a way, I find it so difficult to describe. I have a lot of time with my thoughts these days and sometimes they hurt so much I can hardly bear it. However, my friends always associate me with the song "When You're Smiling". It isn't always easy, but I'm trying to live up to it.'[4]

Fade Out

Over time, the slurring of his speech worsened, making talking on the phone difficult. 'He is being so courageous,' Angela said during that period. 'Today we went for a walk in the park – and that was a good day. But it isn't easy for us. People think: "Oh, yes, Parkinson's disease", but they don't know the half of it.'[5] At home, Ken spent a lot of time striving to 'remember the ups rather than the downs' and pondered 'with envy' the energy of colleagues like John Mills, Rex Harrison, and David Niven, 'all older than me and still working'. Coupled with this, he felt a terrible sense of guilt that Angela should be saddled with 'this awful burden'. During the freezing winter of 1981, a few days after the Iran hostage crisis ended, he returned to hospital for a three-week stay after feeling intensely ill. Once installed in a room on the twelfth floor of St Thomas', opposite Parliament, doctors noted a bladder infection, coupled with a damaged sphincter. The ailments caused him unbearable spasms and, to make matters worse, doctors diagnosed a neurological disorder – atrophy of the cerebellum – causing his brain tissue to shrink. As his health declined, he tired easily, endured endless sweats, and described a 'living death'. Bladder problems persisted and required a doctor's help to draw-off the urine – prompting countless late-night trips to the emergency room. On one occasion, medics released a litre of urine. During this period, Angela told a reporter, 'Our marriage has never been better, our life was never worse.' In all, Ken spent five months in hospital during 1981. Visibly weak, he was readmitted with a chest infection in March 1982. By this point, he was in no condition to appear on Douglas Bader's *This is Your Life*. Instead, Angela made the journey to the Royalty Theatre from where the show was filmed and delivered a moving message from Kenny: 'Your inspiration and courage is, quite rightly, a legend. It was with me all through the film and is with me still.'

Ken's health deteriorated markedly during April, May, and June. Having grown reconciled to his fate, conversations could occasionally be morbid. In the last months of his life, he expressed the desire to be cremated and his ashes be kept at home. Then, on Monday 12 July 1982, his ordeal was over. It was a hot, sunny day and he was keen to watch a special programme on the Falklands conflict that evening – but by the time it was on the screen, he was dead. He passed at 10.30 p.m. at Rumbold Road. His last words to Angela were 'Don't grieve little one ... have a long holiday ... I'll be waiting for you.' With her head resting on his chest, she heard his last heartbeat. For someone who had dramatised so many deaths on stage, his own at the age of sixty-seven, preceded by the slow breakdown of his bodily functions, had been a tragic, painful ordeal. In contemplating his passage to eternity, Ken once said his blessings were his memories. 'Life is a sort of daisy chain, if it is not too much of a flight of fancy to put it like that. What I mean is that one incident or one meeting links up with the next. There are bits of good luck, runs of bad luck, even – now and again – runs of fabulous luck coming just at the time when things look about as bad as they can be.'

As word of his passing flashed around the world, tributes paying homage to the little boy from Gerrards Cross began filling the airwaves. Sir Douglas Bader said, 'Kenneth's far happier now. I was in touch with Angela a number of times and Angela was simply marvellous because she spent the whole of her time looking after him, bathing him, shaving him, taking him to the hospital as necessary and trying to work at the same time.'

Fade Out

Within hours of the news, a film tribute, *Doctor in the House,* was scheduled to play on BBC One, while obituaries and deeply felt tributes were being prepared in Fleet Street. William Marshall's in the *Daily Mirror* was among the more notable ones: 'If Kenneth More had made a serious attempt to play a villain, he would have been booed offstage. For what we saw in Kenneth More was what we got – the romantic version of the true-blue Englishman.' Attorney General Sir Michael Havers, who served with Kenny in the Royal Navy, said he was renowned for being completely fearless: 'He'd wander around the deck under fire cracking jokes ... tremendous fun ... tremendously gregarious, a bit of a showman but never pompous. I think that was why he was such a good actor.' Almost every obituary showed photographs from either *Reach for the Sky* or *Genevieve,* barely acknowledging his other movies. Emlyn Williams, who appeared with him in the film version of *The Deep Blue Sea,* remarked, 'He turned up on time, he knew his part, and he did extremely well. It isn't newsworthy, is it, I'm afraid?' Leslie Phillips heard the news while in a recording with Terry-Thomas, who was himself enduring the early signs of Parkinson's. 'Ken was a super actor, as warm and friendly as his public persona but a lot more wild-tongued and fond of women, right to the end, more than his fans may have realised.' In a moving tribute on ITV, Dinah Sheridan said Ken was a man for whom a huge spectrum of people felt tangible affinity:

The word unique – like many other words in the English language these days is used rather glibly, but in Kenny's case, it's used correctly. In *Genevieve,* so many years ago, or so it seems now, there were four of us. We were all totally different, but Kenny was unique. The first unfortunately to go was the youngest, Kay Kendall, a marvellous, wonderful – and in the nicest way 'dotty' person. And then, John Gregson. Dear John, who couldn't drive but drove Genevieve for three months with me sitting beside him, absolutely terrified. And sometime after his death, I was here – probably in this very studio – doing a programme with Kenneth More of *Looks Familiar*. And Kenny came up to me and he slapped me on the back as he would, and said: 'Well old girl, it's a case of two down and two to go.' That's my memory of Kenny. Great courage because he was already ill. And now I feel very lost, very much a lone survivor. But I'm not because out in Australia, there is Genevieve herself, and she will survive us all. She's still being driven up and down the Australian coast and she will be our epitaph. But tonight, we will remember the unique Kenneth More.

Ken's body was cremated at Putney Vale Crematorium and on 20 September 1982, famous faces joined family and friends to pay tribute at St Martin-in-the-Fields where poems and addresses were read by Virginia McKenna, Richard Briers, and Frank Finlay. Among those paying tribute were Sir John Gielgud, Lauren Bacall, Edward Fox, Sir Robin Day, Tony Britten, David Jacobs, Lord Longford, and Julia McKenzie. Lady Bader was also among the congregation, attending just a week after her husband Douglas passed away. 'Coming here today I was reminded of the chicken and the egg situation,' Bryan Forbes remarked. 'Did Sir Douglas exist for Kenneth to play him, or did Kenneth exist in order to play Sir Douglas? Kenny's own tin legs were his tenacity and sense of humour. He was irreverent, often outrageous but never

Fade Out

malicious. He lived for acting, one could see him come alive – his face lit up when he arrived on a film set.'

At his death, Kenneth More was estimated to be worth approximately £186,918. By the time he died, Angela once noted, she had grown up – mentally, she and Kenny were the same age. 'Our last four years were incredibly painful but unbelievably joyous,' she expounded. 'When Kenny died, we were very much in love and that keeps me warm.'

In 1970, during the BBC *Omnibus* interview, Michael Flanders remarked to Kenny, 'I can't imagine the time ever coming when we shall say: "I wonder what happened to Kenneth More?"' 'I wonder what the verdict of my own profession will be.' Ken responded. 'I would like to hazard a guess: same actor, different clothes.'

Though he left us in 1982, Kenneth More never vanished from the public consciousness and still provides a little calmness in today's hyperventilating world. And, though the chorus of praise for his work has grown a little fainter, for all his old chums and associates have long passed, a blue plaque now sits above the entrance to Rumbold Road, the scene of his last big battle. It reads: 'Kenneth More CBE, 1914–1982, Actor, lived and died here.' His face was also placed on a postage stamp, first class, of course. He would have like that.

ENDNOTES

1. Overture
1. Saturday 26 September 1914.
2. *Reveille*, 11 October 1956.
3. Transcript *Desert Island Discs*, 1969, BBC.
4. Mavis Nicholson interview, 1978, ITV (Thames).
5. Transcript *Desert Island Discs*, 1969, BBC.
6. *Torbay Express and South Devon Echo*, 8 October 1956.
7. Transcript *Desert Island Discs*, 1956, BBC.
8. Transcript *Desert Island Discs*, 1956, BBC.
9. Mavis Nicholson interview, 1978, ITV (Thames).
10. The *Globe and Mail*, 8 April 1957.
11. *TV Times* 1974.
12. Ibid.
13. *Birmingham Daily Gazette*, 9 January 1933.
14. *Liverpool Daily Post*, 26 February 1957.
15. *The Straits Times*, 27 March 1955.
16. *Nottingham Guardian*, 17 June 1970.

17. *Reveille*, 15 November 1955.
18. *Liverpool Daily Post*, 26 February 1957.
19. *The Straits Times*, 27 March 1955.
20. *Liverpool Echo*, 8 October 1959

2. The Call of the Stage

1. *The Straits Times*, 27 March 1955.
2. *TV Times* 1974.
3. *Evening Chronicle*, 28 June 1938.
4. *The Straits Times*, 27 March 1955.
5. Dennis, Les, *Must the Show Go On?*, p. 286.
6. *Manchester Evening News*, 28 April 1939.
7. *Birmingham Daily Post*, 25 April 1939.

3. Kenny Goes to War

1. *The Straits Times*, 27 March 1955.
2. *Manchester Evening News*, 26 October 1955.
3. *The Straits Times*, 27 March 1955.
4. Ibid.
5. Munn, Michael, *Stars at War*, Robson, 1995, p. 65.
6. Munn, Michael, *Stars at War*, Robson, 1995, p. 65.
7. RNVR Lists, (National Archives, London) p. 657.
8. Munn, Michael, *Stars at War*, Robson, 1995, p. 126.
9. *Evening Times*, 28 November 1964.
10. World Naval Ships, Operation Reservist, *Allied Disaster at Oran*. See: https://www.worldnavalships.com/forums/thread.php?threadid=13480 (Accessed 18 April, 2024).
11. IWM Archives: 18629.
12. *Omnibus*, BBC, 19 April 1970.

13. *A World Elsewhere: The Autobiography of Sir Michael Hordern*, Michael O'Mara, 1993, p. 79.
14. *Liverpool Echo*, 15 October 1959.
15. Imperial War Museums: 11294.
16. *Birmingham Daily Post*, 10 March 1973.

4. Breakthrough

1. Australian TV, 14 August 1976.
2. *Sunday Mirror*, 13 April 1947.
3. *The Straits Times*, 27 March 1955.
4. *Birmingham Daily Post*, 4 February 1954 and *The Australian Women's Weekly*, 1 June 1955.
5. *Omnibus*, BBC, 18 April 1970.
6. Braden, Bernard, *The Kindness of Strangers*, p. 179.
7. *Birmingham Planet*, 25 March 1965.
8. Ibid.
9. Braden, Bernard, *The Kindness of Strangers*, p. 179.
10. Ibid.

5. The Emerging Star

1. Anneke Wills' conversation with Nathan Morley. Wills was married to Gough between 1965 and 1979.
2. *Bradford Observer*, 17 November 1942.
3. On 17 and 21 January.
4. More, Kenneth, *Happy Go Lucky*, Hale, 1959, p. 127.
5. Ibid.
6. McFarlane, Brian, *An Autobiography of British Cinema*, Methuen Publishing, p. 538.
7. Douglas, Angela, *Swings and Roundabouts*, Corgi, 1985, p. 183.

8. *The People*, 21 December 1969.
9. Wood, Alan, *Mr Rank: A Study of J. Arthur Rank*, 1952.
10. McNab, Geoffrey, *J. Arthur Rank and the British Film Industry*, Canon, 1994.

6. *Celebrity Fulfilled*
1. More, Kenneth, *Happy Go Lucky*, Hale, 1959, p. 144.
2. *TV Mirror*, August 1958.
3. *Omnibus*, BBC, 18 April 1970.
4. *Desert Island Discs*, BBC, 1969.
5. Leader, Zachary, *The Letters of Kingsley Amis*, Hyperion, 2001, p. 382.
6. Wheeler, Dixon, Collected interviews: *Voices from Twentieth-century Cinema*, Southern Illinois University Press, p. 181.
7. In June 1954, the BBC lost its monopoly when the new commercial ITV station was born serving London and the Midlands.
8. Leader, Zachary, *The Letters of Kingsley Amis*, Hyperion, 2001, p. 383.
9. Fairclough, Robert, *This Charming Man: The Life of Ian Carmichael*, Aurum, 2011, p. 97.
10. *Reveille*, 11 October 1956.
11. *Picturegoer*, August 1956.
12. More, Kenneth, *Happy Go Lucky*, Hale, 1959, p. 161.

7. *The Film Star*
1. *Omnibus*, BBC, 18 April 1970.
2. *The Kenneth Williams Diaries*, Thursday 4 July 1957, p. 134.
3. *Birmingham Evening Mail*, 9 December 1959.

4. *Dalkeith Advertiser*, 20 February 1958.
5. Munn, Michael, *Lord Larry: The Secret Life of Laurence Olivier: A Personal and Intimate Portrait*, Robson, 2007, p. 202.
6. *Picturegoer*, February 1960.
7. By this point, Britain was truly in the grip of the small screen. All the most popular programmes like *Emergency Ward 10*, *Take Your Pick* and *Sunday Night at the Palladium* were made by ITV. On the 'other side,' the BBC churned out *Sooty*, *Grandstand*, *What's My Line?* and its biggest ratings earner was *Juke Box Jury*, a music show, hosted by the DJ David Jacobs. (Ken would eventually appear on the show in 1962, alongside the American pop star Bobby Vee.)
8. *The People*, 21 December 1969.

8. A New Reality

1. *Reveille*, 11 October 1956.
2. 11 February 1960.
3. *Liverpool Echo*, 7 October 1970.
4. *Sunday Mail* (Glasgow), 27 September 1964.
5. *The Straits Times*, 2 April 1961.
6. *The Journal*, 21 January 1961.
7. *Nottingham Evening Post*, 25 January 1962.
8. *Western Daily Press*, 31 October 1978.
9. *Weekend Magazine*, Australia. April 1967.
10. *Inside Story*, November 1962.

9. Cold Shoulder

1. *Woman*, 13 July 1968.
2. Interview with Nathan Morley, March 2023.
3. *Daily Record*, 13 November 1963.

4. *Birmingham Planet*, 25 March 1965.
5. 22 April 1964.
6. In the 23–29 August 1964 edition of Italian *Settimana Radio TV* magazine.
7. Ibid.
8. *Titbits*, 21 November 1964.

11. Ageing Juvenile

1. *Weekend* magazine, 27 April 1967.
2. *Bangor Daily News* 12 January 1971.
3. *Woman*, 13 July 1968.
4. *Manchester Evening News*, 7 September 1968.
5. *TV Times*, 29 October 1964.
6. Kirkwood, Pat, *The Time of My Life*, 1999, Hale, p. 362.
7. Email from Tony Hatch to Nathan Morley. 24 June 2024.

12. A New Decade

1. *Liverpool Echo*, 14 August 1971.
2. Ibid.
3. Ibid.
4. *Carry On* films: 'Angela Douglas loved every minute on comedy classics', *Daily Express*, 6 November 2018.
5. *Titbits*, 3 April 1974.
6. *Sir John Gielgud: A Life in Letters*, Arcade, 2011, p. 372.
7. Published in the *London Review of Books*.
8. *Daily Mirror*, 29 March 1974.
9. *Titbits*, 28 March 1974.
10. *Wolverhampton Express and Star*, 9 September 1974.
11. *Sunday Mirror*, 17 March 1974.
12. *Daily Mirror*, 12 December 1974.

13. Final Years

1. *Coventry Evening Telegraph*, 28 July 1976.
2. *The People*, 24 October 1976.
3. *Daily Record*, 14 November 1978.
4. Mavis Nicholson interview, 1978, ITV.
5. *Leicester Daily Mercury*, 4 October 1978.
6. Mavis Nicholson interview, ITV, 1978.
7. *Daily Mirror*, 17 July 1982.
8. *Leicester Chronicle*, 3 June 1977.
9. *Radio Times*, 3 June 1978.
10. Le Mesurier, Joan, *Dear John*, Sidgwick & Jackson Ltd, 2001, p. 227.

14. Fade Out

1. *The Glasgow Herald*, 2 May 1980.
2. Ibid.
3. *The Glasgow Herald*, 7 May 1980.
4. *Liverpool Echo*, 13 July 1982.
5. *Wolverhampton Express & Star*, 17 September 1981.

BIBLIOGRAPHY

Anger, Kenneth, *Hollywood Babylon I & II*, Arrow, 1986
Annakin, Ken, *So You Wanna Be a Director?*, Tomahawk Press, 2001
Armes, Roy, *A Critical History of British Cinema*, Secker and Warburg, 1978
Bacall, Lauren, *By Myself*, Jonathan Cape, 1979
Banks, Leslie, *The Elstree Story: Twenty-one Years of Film Making*, Clarke and Cockeran, 1949
Betts, Ernest, *The Film Business*, Pitman, 1973
Bragg, Melvyn, *Rich: The Life of Richard Burton*, Hodder & Stoughton, 1988
Collins, Joan, *Second Act*, Boxtree, 1996
Donovan, Paul, *Roger Moore*, W. H. Allen, 1983
Douglas, Angela, *Swings and Roundabouts*, Corgi, 1985
Eames, John Douglas, *The MGM Story*, Octopus, 1979
East, John, *Max Miller: The Cheeky Chappie*, W. H. Allen, 1977
Edwards, Anne, *Vivien Leigh*, Pocket Books, 1977

Field, Shirley Anne, *A Time for Love*, Bantam Press, 1991
Gough-Yates, Kevin, *Michael Powell*, London: British Film Institute, 1971
Harrison, Rex, *Rex*, Macmillan, 1974
Hawkins, Jack, *Anything for a Quiet Life*, Elm Tree, 1973
Kulik, Karol, *Alexander Korda: The Man Who Could Work Miracles*, W. H. Allen, 1975
Mills, John, *Up in the Clouds, Gentlemen Please*, Weidenfeld & Nicolson, 1980
More, Kenneth, *Happy Go Lucky*, Robert Hale, 1959
More, Kenneth, *More or Less*, Hodder & Stoughton, 1978
Morley, Nathan, *Disney's British Gentleman: The Life and Career of David Tomlinson*, The History Press, 2021
Morley, Nathan, *Jack Hawkins: A Biography*, Fonthill, 2024
Niven, David, *Bring on the Empty Horses*, Putnam, 1975
Norman, Barry, *The Film Greats*, Hodder & Stoughton/BBC, 1985
Norman, Barry, *The Hollywood Greats*, Hodder & Stoughton, 1979
Robyns, Gwen, *Vivien Leigh: Light of a Star*, A. S. Barnes, 1974
Spoto, Donald, *The Art of Alfred Hitchcock*, Hopkinson and Blake, 1976
Wood, Alan, *Mr Rank: A Study of J. Arthur Rank and British Films*, Hodder & Stoughton, 1952
Woodward, Ian, *Audrey Hepburn*, W. H. Allen, 1984